WRITING
FIRE

WRITING FIRE

AN ANTHOLOGY CELEBRATING THE POWER OF WOMEN'S WORDS

EDITED BY
JENNIFER BROWDY   JANA LAIZ   SAHRA BATESON BRUBECK

GREEN FIRE PRESS   HOUSATONIC, MASSACHUSETTS

Cover design by Adam M Rothberg
Page design by Anna Myers Sabatini

The Library of Congress has cataloged the earlier edition (ISBN 978-0-9861980-0-7) as follows:
Library of Congress Control Number: 2015903059

2017 edition ISBN: 978-0-9861980-7-6
Green Fire Press
PO Box 377 Housatonic MA 01236

Table of Contents

Part One: Hearts Wide Open

Part Two: Questions for Our Mothers

continues

Part Three: Looking for Love

Part Four: Falling Into Family

Part Five: Courage, Resilience and Strength

The Power of Women's Voices and Visions

Part Six: Strong Shoulders

The Loves and Labors of Women

Introduction: Lighting the Sparks

The Editors

Writing Fire. When we called for submissions to this collection, we editors were sometimes asked why we chose "Fire" as emblematic of the kind of writing we were looking for. "I don't feel like my writing is very fiery," some women told us. "I wish it were...."

The truth is that the energy of all four elements is represented within these pages. There are women who write of their fiery passions—for people and places, and for their sense of purpose in life. There are women who write their own trails of tears, sharing stories of grief, wounding and resilience. Some write of their childhoods, of the foundation of their being, and the adults—some wise, some eccentric, some feckless—who influenced them in those early years. In some cases, our contributors share stories of abuse, mental illness, and death, which could be triggering to readers who have experienced similar trauma. In each case, these brave women write from a desire to share their voices and experiences with the world, each one unique, but all infused with the conviction that their perspective matters.

Put together, these women's words represent a potent, combustible cauldron of deeply rooted feminine power. In her famous essay "Poetry Is Not A Luxury," Audre Lorde writes of poetry as "the distillation of experience" that "births thought as dream births concept, as feeling births idea, as knowledge births (precedes) understanding." Particularly for women, Lorde believed, poetry (and we include prose) coming from our deep, often untapped reservoirs of wisdom and creativity—is not a luxury. "It is a vital necessity of our existence. It forms the quality of light within which we predicate our hopes and dreams towards survival and change, first made into language, then into idea, then into more tangible action. Poetry is the way we help give a name to the nameless so it can be thought. The farthest horizons of our hopes and fears are cobbled by our poems, carved from the rock experiences of our daily lives" (37).

At least since human beings made the shift from oral to written cultures, women's voices and visions have been pushed into the background. Even now, in the 21st century, as the VIDA Count and the Women's Media Center[1] remind us annually, men's voices still dominate every form of media, from books, film and TV to newspapers and broadcast networks to news wires and social media news outlets.

There are many reasons why we are less likely to hear from women in the public sphere, but experts like Carol Gilligan, Mary Pipher, and Deborah Tannen point to a tendency for women of all ages to be more cautious in expressing their ideas in a classroom or professional setting, and thus to have less experience speaking up in public.

Over time, this cautiousness translates into a society where it's so normal for male voices to predominate that we accept it as the norm. Once we realize it, it becomes imperative to do something about it—human civilization requires the richness and diversity of all our voices. We can no longer afford to do without the perspectives of 51% of our population.

In many ways, we live in the best of times for taking the initiative to get our ideas into the world. These days it can seem like almost everyone is either writing a book, posting to a blog, or holding lively conversations on social media. The old gates and their keepers, who used to tightly control access to the public sphere, have been stormed by the technological wonders that make the creation and distribution of all forms of media accessible to anyone with a computer and a little know-how.

But still, it can be hard to convince people—especially women— that their stories are valuable and important to share with others. That's where the Berkshire Festival of Women Writers came in. Founded in

---

1 The VIDA Count is a gender analysis of 39 of the most respected English-language media outlets and literary magazines. See http://www.vidaweb.org. The Women's Media Center, founded by Jane Fonda, Robin Morgan, and Gloria Steinem, also conducts an annual review of women in the media, with the goal of enhancing women's visibility and social power. See http://www.womensmediacenter.com.

2011 by Jennifer Browdy and continuing annually through 2017, the Festival inspired, nourished and strengthened the creative voices of women of all ages and from many walks of life. *Writing Fire* would not have been possible without the collaborative spirit nurtured by the hundreds of Festival workshops, readings, and performances designed to encourage women and girls to overcome their habit of hesitancy, step into the spotlight, and begin engaging authentically with one another and with the larger community around them.

As one participant in the 2014 Festival wrote, "It was very inspiring to see so many women gathered together in such unity and purpose. I felt the amazing energy, excitement, joy, and support for each other that is so much a part of the Festival!"

Sparks fly when women get together to speak our truths, and you will feel an electric current running throughout this collection. We thoroughly enjoyed getting to know the lives and stories of the women represented here. They moved us and made us laugh and cry and feel deeply as they brought us along on their creative journeys. It is the hope of all of us, editors and writers alike, that the honesty and emotional intensity of these stories will provide enough of a charge to set off a chain reaction, inspiring more women and girls to take the risk of speaking their truths.

Brilliant woman writer and cultural anthropologist Margaret Mead once wrote: "Never doubt that a small group of thoughtful, committed citizens can change the world; indeed, it's the only thing that ever has." *Writing Fire* adds gender to Mead's formulation, convening "a small group of thoughtful, committed women" out to change the world by widening the conversation to include the full range of human emotions and perspectives. We invite you, our readers, to join our circle, lighting your own fires from the sparks we let fly. Let's see what we can accomplish when we put our hearts and minds together to our task of making a better world.

Jennifer Browdy

Jana Laiz

Sahra Bateson Brubeck

PROLOGUE
Woman Reading with Stubborn Tongue

Lee Schwartz

…I don't know what I was thinking,
I shouldn't be up here,
I'm not ready to read,
I'm an imposter, a bedbug,
I don't think this is what you want,
I apologize for these words —
I'm just a pile of bones
you can make soup out of,
it's not really a poem,
just scattered seeds, a dragonfly's eye,
my messy bed, leftovers in Tupperware,
maybe I'll just fold like a patchwork quilt,
into the firmament of a women's life,
the kitchen, the laundry, the kids.

The podium is for men.
Me, I don't have anything to say, my nervous giggle
an offering, a selfie of creamy breasts,
exposed in synapses of awkwardness,
forgive me,
I'm just a woman, Goddess — *can you hear me in the back,*
I don't mean to take up space or time.
My words expire in the air and crawl under a rock,
I'm nothing but shame and longing
taking notes on the journey we all set out on,
with wings too heavy and a beak pecking at my heart.

So don't put me on a podium, or a stage,
I'll climb up on the table, I'll stand on a mountain top,
to see women everywhere,
digging in the garden, at the potter's wheel,
counseling, teaching, in the food pantry,
women raising children, canning fruit in the cellar,
raising trouble, women opening their mouths
asking for a piece of the pie, equal pay, a voice in the mix,
as thick as meadow grass and as honest as a fried egg,
asking not to be invisible, discarded, nameless, weak.
We are the poem, the change-artists, the blood dancers,
when we rise, take note, hush the hall, from our flimsy bodies
hear the trumpets call, the stained glass light, the words that
will march the earth to less suffering and more singing,
throw all chairs to the side, level all podiums and stages,
I'm giving up excuses, eyes glued to the floor,
The shaky voice, the rounded back,
I'm looking straight out at you,
I have something to say like a loaded gun,
I'm going to set you on fire
with my bee sting, my snake bite,
I know how to braid culture and build community,
under my finger nails the smell of earth from planting,
asking for no ribbons,
I have the words, the powdery silver of truth,
I am ready to speak, to share this mound of dirt,
it is my turn to compost this decay into a ray of hope,
here I come, heels clicking, lips shining, my poem.

PART ONE:

HEARTS
WIDE OPEN

Strange Fancies

Lara Tupper

Herman Melville, the story goes, called his modest, yellow house in Pittsfield "Arrowhead" after unearthing Native American artifacts from his pasture. He composed *Moby Dick* there, peering out at Mount Greylock, which looked like a whale to him.

I know there's more to this story, so at Mobydick.org I sign up for a writing workshop sponsored by the Berkshire Festival of Women Writers called "Inspired by Melville: Writing About Place." We ramble through the house, led by a young guide. I try to write it all down and then we settle ourselves in Herman's study, where the escort asks us to keep our chairs still, so as not to mar the old boards beneath. We'd just been told that Melville might have been bipolar, that he would lock himself in for hours and refuse to come out. His wife had to pound on the door.

It's hard to know if this is crazy behavior or writer behavior or both. There are fourteen other women in the room, no men.

"I had goose bumps the first time I came here," says our workshop leader, the Writer in Residence at Arrowhead. She holds fanned slips of paper that are writing prompts, random lines from Melville's books.

My prompt is from "The Piazza," Herman's short story about wanting a porch at Arrowhead, which he eventually built. A spot where he could sit and consider Mount Greylock. The bit of paper says, "Yours are strange fancies." We have ten minutes to write. I can't quite see the mountain, but I don't want to move my chair. I can see a sturdy birch tree. I don't have anything to say about the tree. I do have something to say about the wife, Lizzie.

I write:

Your children knock at the study door for you. What strange medicine, the quill and ink, numbing your mind to small voices. I knock too, as you instructed. Knock hard, 'til I come out. *But I can't stay. There is bile I can't speak through. I long to turn the key on you and spit.*

At those times I think to take the road to Hawthorne in Stock-bridge, somewhere beyond Arrowhead where I might be heard. Though he would find me just as foolish, interrupting his own work hours to complain about my husband's. Come see us, I could ask. Your bed is ready—in the smallest room, but adjoining Herman's study. You could be adrift together.

I turn to Fanny because she is youngest. I collect her dollhouse implements and arrange them on the floor for her to touch. Tiny shovel, tiny rake, tiny pot for cooking. When you grow up, you'll do this for a man. You'll find reserves in the taut metal of your heart. You'll have your own children and your need for them will harden your desire to flee.

I could hide my husband's book, the pages that will become the book. I could place the papers somewhere dark, like the bread bin. I could burn them. See the ink boil down, the scraps flitter up the mouth of our monster chimney.

I stroke my daughter's hair, small curls in my fingers. Her doll-house pieces—tossed back out and placed back in.

To have daughters. To have sons, but the sons will leave. The girls may stay. They see already that husbands are stormy.

In their father's chest is the crashing of water; the Marquesas winds that made his cheeks flush with adventure, with purpose. He has to drown the thoughts to make sense of them. He has to deafen everything to get the water on the page where it can seep and swirl into chapters and bound volumes to be sold into future Berkshire winters when the cold won't seep in.

"Time," says our teacher.

At home I can't stop thinking about the dollhouse, the bread bin, the chimney—all true artifacts, like the arrowhead.

Lizzie is the story. Everybody wants a view of the mountain, even the wife.

Variations:
Two Poems on Aging

Signe Eklund Schaefer

Elder Flowering

Spaciousness
I feel it growing
around me and within me
After years of busy fullness
I am quieter now
watching more and waiting
against worn habits of direction
This is an opening I cherish
an inner space
to see what comes
to listen into layers
to let what is reveal itself
bird, tree, new idea
or old friend come again
Even familiar hurts
have room to heal

Today I choose to call
this spacious possibility
elder flowering
Gratefully I gather white blooms
and taste sweet tonic

Elderflower Cordial

I am making a sweet drink
this warm July day
The flowers soaking in water
with sugar and lemon
intensifying over time
the particular taste
of this special summer treat
have called to mind
another greater sweetness
the well-seasoned cordiality
of gracious elder flowering

While sorting the white blossoms
I heard myself say
"to make this cordial
you have to deal
with the bugs and the slugs"
and so that other meaning
kept growing too
highlighting the need to recognize
and sift life's many offerings
attend to crawling creeping
beasties from the past
and ancient hits that hurt

The drink takes days
to reach its tonic best
a tasty premonition
of the culmination of years
that might bloom forth at last
as the hearty offering
of a well-aged life

My Paradox in Port-au-Prince

Jennifer J. Holey

I was deployed in Haiti. During my first week in Port-au-Prince, I met many people. One of the Military Police (MP) officers found out that I was a new nurse in the Emergency Room. One morning he graciously offered to take me out in a United Nations truck around Port-au-Prince to see the "sights." He also wanted to show me the Children's Hospital that was to be one of our other missions in Haiti. I was excited to get out there and do some real Army work. I received the clearance to go from the higher ups. I grabbed one of my best friends, Lt. Bates, and we were off.

Before we left, the MP Officer gave us a quick briefing, telling us about the Haitian "tap-taps." He explained that Haitian taxis were generally overflowing with people. Haitian driving, he added, brought a whole new meaning to the term "defensive driving." He gave us a raw scenario of what we were going to see once we were off the base and out in the real Haiti: death, despair, and deplorable conditions. We both nodded our heads and climbed into the truck.

The minute we left the safety of our wired, fenced compound, I knew that we were no longer in "Kansas." The sights in those first few blocks completely blew my mind.

I saw a water source. It was not really a lake, but a big pool of muddied water in the middle of the city. It was the place where masses of people were simultaneously washing their bodies and their clothes while gathering water for their drinking and cooking. The animals were also using this same water for their needs. I saw children wearing only small pieces of thin-strapped leather for shoes and little shreds of cloth as shorts. No shirts covered their massively distended bellies. As we moved on, I saw several unmoving bodies on the ground. It was then that I understood the reason for the prominent smell of death in the air. I saw tap-taps and cars everywhere, chaotically moving as fast as they could. I heard constant honking and screeching, and though I did not speak French, there was no mistaking the drivers yelling, "Get the hell out of my way!"

I saw women with food baskets perfectly balanced on their heads, carrying wares to sell miles down the road in markets where they would receive pennies for their efforts. These weary women walked with the baskets above their heads as well as their babies strapped to their bodies. These were only a fraction of the eye-opening things I noticed in those first few moments in the real Haiti.

We made it to the Children's Hospital, and the officer quickly ushered us into the building, where we introduced ourselves to one of the administrators and were given a quick, impromptu tour. The nurses and aides were kind, but we couldn't communicate well. Not only were they extremely busy; they also only spoke French Creole. As we walked around the hospital, I was ashamed by my critical attitude towards my experience in nursing, and all that I had to "endure" at home. I couldn't believe what these people were dealing with: masses of sick children, from the newborn babies to the tiny teenagers, being treated in small, cramped spaces. I smelled the disease. I saw the debilitation. I sensed the death.

We came to a hallway in the center of the hospital, and our guide pointed to a wall. He said that we would be painting the walls to help brighten up the spirit of the hospital. Painting one freaking wall! He explained that due to politics, pride, and what the pictures could positively show all of the folks back home, painting a wall would be the only way we could help the Haitian people. Painting a freaking wall in a lousy corridor! No one wanted to be accused of mission creep. Oh, how pretty that wall would look in a magazine to show how compassionate we Americans were in helping these poor Haitians. Speechless, I looked at my friend.

We quickly climbed back into the truck and the MP said, "Don't think about it all too much. It will only drive you crazy." Never have truer words been spoken to this "over- analyzer." Trying to make our way "home" in the same direction we had come, we were quickly cut off by a growing crowd of people. It was amazing how fast the streets became impassable. I noticed the furrowed look on the MP's face.

Luckily, we had one more soldier in the back with Lt. Bates and me. The soldier in the back put his hand on his 9MM and said, "Be ready for anything."

The Haitians were quickly forming a mob. In the middle of the mob, we saw a woman with a huge, bleeding gash on her forehead stumbling towards the truck. In an initial briefing for the medical staff, we were told not to administer medical treatment to the Haitians unless we had injured them ourselves. We were primarily in Haiti to take care of the United Nations soldiers.

The Haitians had multiple medical problems including HIV, intestinal parasites, cholera, malaria, and the wounds that they would inflict on each other. Many Haitians practiced voodoo, and they also believed in an "eye for an eye" type of corporal punishment. They often used machetes to enact this immediate, violent retribution and vigilante justice.

We had no idea what had happened to the woman who was bleeding profusely in the street, or what diseases she had oozing out of that gash. We were not just soldiers in that moment, though. We were fellow human beings. We knew that we could find ourselves in serious trouble for stopping, but in that moment, it didn't matter.

I believe that these are the moments in life that determine what kind of person you really are. The woman definitely needed assistance, and we knew that we could give her the aid she needed. The soldier who was with us in the back of that truck grabbed his first aid kit. He said, "Let's get out as a unit, bandage her head, and then get back inside the truck."

He instructed us to double glove and stick together. The driver/officer would have his 9MM drawn, and we would form a circle around the girl to quickly dress her wound. Adrenaline was pumping when the soldier opened the door. The officer who had been driving jumped out and was instantly around our side of the truck with his weapon drawn. Lt. Bates and I, gloved and ready, rushed out side by side and worked quickly as a team to wrap the bandage around her head. It is very tricky to dress a head wound, and we couldn't make it work at first. Suddenly, the officer was shouting, "Get back in the truck now! Get back in the truck now!"

As we were finishing the dressing in haste, blood flew from her wounded head and landed on Lt. Bates' arm. We had our Battle Dress Uniforms on with our American flag proudly displayed on the shoulder, but they were folded Army regulation style into short sleeves, which exposed part of our arms in order to make the heat tolerable.

Two things happened simultaneously in the next moment. I saw Lt. Bates' face turn pale as he saw the blood (highly likely to be HIV-infected) land directly on his exposed arm. I also heard and felt the breath and the bodies of the Haitians as they surrounded us. The best way to describe that moment is to think of ants or bees swarming to sugar. We were the sugar. However, one of the "sweet" things standing there in that street was not like the others. We were all soldiers, yes. We were all in Army green, yes. We all had white skin, yes. However, only one of us was a woman, and those Haitians were swarming and mobbing around me.

I had seen bad-asses before on television. I still love Batman, Superman, Spiderman, Aquaman, and of course Wonder Woman. I had only seen superheroes on television or in the movies, though. That day, I saw an actual superhero in real life. The Military Police officer moved so fast and so furiously, I can honestly say that he seemed faster than a speeding bullet. He would have used one of his speeding bullets too, if he had been forced to do so. He was instantly in front of me, screaming for everyone to get back and waving his 9MM with such authority that even I stepped back. Thanks to his courageous efforts, we were back in the truck within 20 seconds. He was in the driver's seat, aggressively driving us out of there before I could even process what had just happened.

I am forever grateful to that officer, and even to this day I try not to think about what would have happened had he not done what he did. Thankfully, Lt. Bates was fine too, and did not test positive for HIV. We were two naïve nursing officers forever changed by that unbelievable first visit into the real Haiti.

The Earth is Our Mothers

Wendy A. Rabinowitz

I begin by invoking my matrilineal line of ancestors, giving them voice and presence here among us, as I chant their names in Hebrew and English:

Ani Ru'a'chi (I am Wendy, wind, spirit)
Bat Riv'kah (from my Mother Geraldine/Rebekah)
Bat Sa'rah (from my Grandmother/Bubbe Sarah/Sadie)
Bat Mir'i'am (from my Great-Grandmother Minnie)

City gal, born and raised, I come from the South Side of Chicago, where early on I was a wanderer and scavenger. From ages ten through fifteen, I awoke every morning before dawn and crept out of my apartment where the siren call of the sea beckoned to me. I walked and sang the ten city blocks in all kinds of weather to join the sand, wind, rocks, water, birds, clouds, and other living things that abounded at Lake Michigan's shore. There I sat in the cleft of the sheltering rocks to witness the miracle of the sun's rising, its beauty and power captivated me in awe again and again. It was only later that I recognized, as Rabbi Abraham Joshua Heschel wrote in *"God In Search of Man,"* that I was experiencing what he calls *"the pathway to God through awe and Nature."* I always brought home with me some token of my adventure —seaweed, branch, grass (which I finger-wove into little mats), rock or fossil, to add to my growing collection. It is part of what I still do today as a mixed-media artist, incorporating Nature's bounty into my artwork.

Every morning, quietly watching in wonder and amazement, I would be jolted by my father's rough and angry voice: *"Whadayah think yer doing? Get the hell in the car, now!!"* Ah, my frustrated and bewildered parents: to have such a wild, intractable child who did such unaccountable things! It was only later, much later, that they were proud of my singular, stubborn, sensitive, artistic and spiritually-seeking self.

I never set out to be a weaver, just as I never set out to be a committed Jew. Both came from my personal journey of curiosity, discovery and wholeness. My love of weaving began years ago after seeing a loom with a friend of mine at the Chicago Historical Society. I didn't know what it was and had an immediate "*eureka*" moment upon encountering it. I asked my friend about it and she informed me that it was used to make cloth. I told her that couldn't be true, you bought cloth in stores! When she offered to build me a simple loom, I eagerly accepted; she built one out of wood and nails and showed me how to use it. That was the beginning of my walk on the Weaver's Path.

The next summer I took a class in weaving at The Art Institute of Chicago. All the other students were weaving placemats and shawls, but I was using this huge, old MacComber loom and incorporating my grasses, seaweed and found objects with the hand-spun yarns, making a wall hanging while creating quite a scene. The teacher seemed baffled but left me to my own devices. I think she was terrified of me!

One afternoon, in walked a very beautiful, colorful, artistic looking woman who stopped at my loom and questioned me about my work and process. On the spot she asked if I could assist her in her studio on a project she was doing. That woman was Nell Zamerowski, a world-re-nowned weaver. I learned from her that the craft of weaving could be an art, and I became determined to own a "real" loom of my own one day.

Soon after, I took the subway to the one weaving store in Chicago. I opened the door to a dazzling, light-filled place of beauty: so many brilliant colors, yarns, looms and tools! But I froze. I could not go in. Overwhelmed by choices and ignorance, I turned around and fled down the street. As I wandered, dazed and disappointed, I came upon a junk shop, stopped, and looked in the window. Like a homing pigeon I was drawn to go inside. I explored aimlessly until I came across a pile of huge, hand-hewn wooden beams, a beater, a reed, and harnesses, all on the floor. What!? Could this be parts of a loom? I rummaged through the pile and I knew the answer. When I inquired about it, the owner had no idea what it was. I told him I thought it was a loom and I immediately offered him $50 for it, which he eagerly took.

Two days later I came with a car to retrieve it. At home I found on one of the loom's beams a round, metal piece that had someone's Scandina-vian-sounding name, the town of Northbrook, Illinois, and the date 1906 embossed upon it. I called directory assistance and, surprisingly, received a phone number to go with the name. I called it. An elderly-sounding man answered, and I explained what I had come across. He told me that I had one of three Danish counter-balanced looms that his father had made by hand for him and his two sisters. I had one of his sister's looms! He had no idea how it had come to be in the junk shop, but was glad I was going to use it. With this information, I went down to the stacks at the University of Chicago Library and lo and behold I found an old book on Danish looms that even had the blueprints for this very loom.

Of course, I had not a clue what to do with them. One week later, around midnight on a cold rainy night, I heard a loud knock on the door. There stood my former theater director, master carpenter, and friend, Sid, absolutely plastered. He had been kicked out of his house by his wife and wanted to stay at our place.

"Yes, Sid," I said, "you can stay here as long as you help me put my loom together."

"But of course, anything for you," he slurred.

I let him in and the next morning he made me a deal. "I'll help you fix the loom and put it together," he said, "but only by teaching you the techniques. You have to do everything yourself; sanding ("as smooth as a baby's bottom"), staining, varnishing, making new parts for it, learning to use a saw, and putting all its 36 parts together. That way, when you're done, you'll know your loom and it will know you and will do anything you want it to." Sid was right and my loom and I have been happily creating to this day.

Only much later did I learn that my matrilineal ancestors had been weavers in the small town of Bielsk, Poland. I wove my growing love of Judaism and my love of the loom into one path. In my childhood, my Bubbe Sadie lived with us and shared my bedroom for many years. Every Friday night she would bring out the brass Shabbat candlesticks from Poland, put a crocheted "tchotchke" on her head, let me light the two white candles, raise her hands with her palms toward her eyes, and bending slightly over the candles, rock back and forth, and mumble a blessing. Curious, I asked her to tell me what she said over the lights, but Bubbe Sadie always said: "Shah, shah, later, later, when you are older, when you are older."

This continued until I was an adult. When my Bubbe lay on her deathbed at the age of 97, I asked again. "Please Bubbe, please, before you go, tell me the blessing that you say over the candles!" She opened her glazed eyes, tears running down them, and said as she clutched my hand:

"I don't know the blessing. You, you, darlink, go and learn."
And so I did and continue to learn every day of my life.

THE WANDERER'S RETURN

Awakened from my present to my past,
I blithely grab the plumb-line of my soul,
And shimmy down to hallowed desert sand,
and hear the ancient, wailing call:
"SHEMA YISR'EL (LISTEN/HEAR ALL OF US WHO STRUGGLE)
And landing, tumble back upon myself,
The parched and wandering Jew,
Weaving black letters upon white sacred cloth,
Standing silently renewed:
ADONAI YAH SHECHINAH ELOHEINU
(GOD, SPIRIT, FEMALE INDWELLING PRESENCE—
GOD, OUR GOD)
Then robed, in time's remembrance shawl,
I scale the golden cord, hand over hand,
And heave my singing body toward the light,
To wear the holy garment, loosely bound:
ADONAI YAH SHECHINAH ELHAD
(GOD OUR GOD IS ONE).

My art exhibit "The Earth is Our Mothers" combines my on-going dedication to bringing forth women's unique stories, and in my commitment to advocate for sustaining and maintaining this, our sacred planet Earth. This art is expressed in visual and written form using a diversity of materials and techniques: weaving, wrapping, layering, molding, embellishment, calligraphy, etc., as well as a variety of forms and materials from the earth. As I work daily in my Living Threads Judaica studio in the beautiful Berkshires, my intention (Hebrew "kavannah"), is to co-create with "THE-SOURCE-OF-ALL" to provide gateways of connection, healing, renewal, as well as a call to action: *The Earth Is Our Mothers,* we must take care of her, The Earth is our Mothers, we must take care of her. Hei noni, hoo noni, hei non, non. The Earth is our Mothers, we must take care of her.

The Meadow

Mary-Ellen Beattie

She quietly asks, "Do you find yourself beautiful?"
Sunlight slips over our sheathed eyelids.
Ants scaled my calves, a puff of milkweed
floated across my blue soccer t-shirt and
grass suffocated beneath my back.
I wait, knowing my answer affects her.

Slowly, the grass grew strong and rose beneath my skin,
the milkweed sprouted on my shirt with a green shoot.
The ants marched the precise route of my veins,
tunneling a colony on my kneecap.
I wished to ask why…. why we whisper in open air?

I waited longer, the sunlight slipping over
my bones decomposing to dirt:
and caterpillars inched along the milkweed shoot,
clumps of grass peaked through the loose nutrients
and ants piled the decomposed matter of me—
a heap. Presented before my unknown queen.
Bowing my head, "Yes, very beautiful," I said.

Birthed in the Berkshires

Suzi Banks Baum

I am eating an apple I just picked off a tree in my yard. This apple would not win any beauty awards for unblemished skin, but it is delicious. A Greening apple grown on a tree I 'won' in a Silent Auction seven or eight years ago. I planted it in my backyard.

Rose petals flutter in the breeze dropping from a bloom stuck in a yellow Fiesta pitcher crowded with fragrant phlox and constellations of Joe Pye Weed. It is a William Shakespeare Rose plucked off a bush I planted in honor of my friend Annie, an actress, when she died a few years ago. A luscious pink pile of soft velvet petals rests here on my table.

Before me a box of Concord Grapes, cut from the trellised vines that grow along my garage, planted between locust posts felled near here by a friend and put in place by another friend. I cut them free from their spiraled grasp on the wires and vines clustered over the south-facing wall of our yellow stucco garage, while Jonathan stands by with the basket which gains weight with each lusty bunch.

Somewhere in town, my daughter, 15, conceived in Hillsdale, NY, born in Sharon CT, and maturing in this green valley along the Housatonic, gathers with her friends sipping iced something at the coffee shop. She would win a beauty contest if the judges were interested in a real person winning such a thing. She is all that the apples, rose petals, grapes are and more, locally grown and flourishing in the late August humidity. Her curly hair responds well to all this moisture.

I am here on my back porch writing. I can hear David Grover and his band serenading a throng of children around the gazebo behind Town Hall in Great Barrington. I am just up the hill from the grassy spot where this band sings and sings and sings every single Saturday in the high months of summer. The backdrop of "You Are My Sunshine" on this cloudy overcast day works its magic. Yes, there is sunshine down deep in my heart.

The words I write have been birthed in my motherhood, which has been birthed in the Berkshires. One child, my older son, was born in New York City, but that is only because we did not listen to our midwife. If we'd waited two more hours on a steamy summer night in 1994, Ben would have been born in Hillsdale on our futon. I thought I was in false labor so I did not concern myself with getting back to New York. Until, my panting roused fear in the husband that he could not, with his mother, birth our child alone there on a country road in July. We sped south. For all other purposes, Ben is local. He has become a young man in these hills.

My writing has become what it is today because of mothering and because of the Berkshires. I have every reason to thank Town Hall and W.E.B. DuBois, and the Fire Department, and the Prudential Committee, the League of Women Voters, and the Lake Mansfield Alliance, the Parent Association at the Waldorf School, and the Co-op for everything these organizations have done to support and nurture my writing. Fairview Hospital, Otis Ridge Ski Hill, the Children's Health Program, and Marvin's Bagels all pitched in to make this life, this writing motherhood life possible. The Green River, the Lake, every single waterfall I have found, every rain drop that has wet the wash on the line or divided into a rainbow, has made it possible on a cellular level for me to pluck the grapes of my experience and turn them into stories here.

Art made in a place evokes the place itself. Can you smell the roses? If I tell you about a walk we took at Tyringham Cobble, can you see the golden light of late afternoon reverberating in the lush green of that valley, pocked with farms and magical in its remote remove from Main Street, Great Barrington?

Maybe none of this comes clear to you as you read my words, but, as surely as the grapes beckon me to heat them until they relinquish their plump juices, which I will pour in to a glass jar that will be opened for the next Winter Solstice, I am called to distill the sweetness of our life in the Berkshires and write.

It has not always been this way for me. I operated on the outskirts of accepted expression for most of my life. I began as an actress and spent most of my career in new plays in small theatres on the edge of Manhattan. Then I turned to using my sewing skills to pay my rent and made one-of-a-kind clothing for *other* artists.

It was not until I was married and a mother with two young children living here in the bounteous hills of the Berkshires that I discovered, or really, where I heard and grew to value my own voice. The pang to express this tumultuous adventure of mothering in a small town along a river, the demands on my time that motherhood made, provided all the tension and ache I needed to pry open the oyster of my authentic voice. My writing voice, my artistic voice, has been cured in the winter air over Lake Mansfield as I ice skate over black glassy ice with my children. It has been enriched by helping run the People's Food Pantry, dusting off canned goods and organizing donations of produce from local farmers. I learned I had something worthwhile to say, and I do it all just a few blocks up the hill from where William Stanley created the dynamo that generated alternating current to Main Street, Great Barrington; just a few blocks from where he invented the Stanley thermos bottle.

I have opened my heart in the Berkshires.

Achingly beautiful moments have run through my fingers. Tears of laughter have spilt over my cheeks. Gut-wrenching fear has shivered my bones and tightened my sinews. Belly scouring grief has scraped open new space in my heart, forcing me to expand where I might have contracted, simply and only because I live in a place with a family that supports me making art of my daily life, in an ordinary way, that does not place me in fancy galleries or on elite book lists, but does keep me tethered to a group of people who consider my time worth spending on this work.

I have to thank the Berkshire Festival of Women Writers for making room for me and for scores of other women who are mothers and artists and burgeoning writers and seasoned professionals to write from inside motherhood. I have found my voice in the Berkshires and am dedicated to supporting other women in finding theirs.

However you fill your heart, whatever perfume washes through your senses so that you are in a phlox-induced orgy of pink on a late summer day, where, you, like me, stop to write instead of washing off my sticky skin made slick in Zumba class pulsing above the Farmer's Market, I urge you to fill it. Fill your heart. Notice what is in there, notice where you come from, who makes you light up and what causes tension—like the sand penetrating the inner workings of an oyster causing pearl to happen. Do let your prickles and heartbreaks open new territory of understanding among your people by telling your stories.

Let the Housatonic inspire you. Yes, it is tainted by GE up in Pittsfield. We will likely never get to swim in that 'golden river.' But still, as tainted by life as that river, polluted by pain and disappointment, stinking with loss and terror, we can still make our way through the valleys and hills of our lives and be beautiful in our burbles, gushing over waterfalls and under wooden bridges. That river, so sad and yet so incredibly beautiful, lives as I want to live, making beauty wherever it finds itself.

I was born in to my writing life here in the Berkshires.
I have plenty to say.
And so much to be thankful for.

Misunderstood

Michele Gara

Like the wave that appears calm and then unexpectedly pulls you
   under its wrath,
I, too, am an unlikely twist of fate.
My heart and intentions are good; yet my actions often defy them.
How can I be wholesome and pure of heart while deep within I
   am naughty and unclean?
It's extremely challenging to keep my real self from escaping from
   its home.
Try as I may I cannot deny my true North; my internal compass
   points to passion.
Destiny wins out again and again, as I am fatefully misunderstood.

Winged Victory

Mary Kate Jordan

It wasn't an upstart gallery; this was the Louvre. Nevertheless I scanned the treasures just as I do in any museum: deliberate, intent, focused, moving swiftly most of the time, stopping only when an image, a name, a juxtaposition of colors, some slant of light, or, as now, some numinous presence commands it.

I never knew how much of the afternoon swept past me with the crowds. I only know I rounded a corner, stepped through a doorway, glanced up a short flight of stairs and there she stood.

I stood, too, still as marble at the base of the stairs, slack-jawed, staring. At least my eyes stared, while I felt those wings lift the real me up, or out, stretched impossibly beyond myself, tumbling along some kind of birth canal until I was only heart, only power, only victory.

Even when I felt my tired tourist feet beneath me again, the new identity hovered. Even when I shook my head, looked around at the inexplicably solid building and felt the jostling stream of other visitors, all of us in these small fleshy containers, the union with her stayed. Even later, when I remembered I'd been born into this body in a place called Our Lady of Victory Infant Home, and that the theme for my BFA thesis and sculpture show had been Birds, Flight and Wing Symbolism, the whole of the truth was still too big to take in. Now, though I still sometimes forget, I recognize the hospital, my thesis, my sculpture as a preview of sorts: a time-warped trailer for a film of my life that only acquired its theme and its title with my birth in the Louvre: *Winged Victory*.

Blood and Gold

Deirdre McKenna

I can see you.
Even in the dark.
My black glass eyes hold secrets you will never know.

I am sad.
I am tender.
I am misunderstood.

You have become afraid of me.
I must bear this burden.
Do you think you could ever endure this kind of loneliness?

I hold my forehead to my child's, gazing into her eyes.
Our fur entwines, a shimmering constellation of golden stars.

The steam of my child's playful nuzzle hangs, chilled in the night air.
Your cowardly arrow has suddenly pierced my heart.

The pungent aroma of my own blood ignites all my black rage,
all my helpless shame. Like an estranged lover, I am finally
returning to the dance of violence.

I find you and taste your blood.
I slide my tongue over my teeth,
your hot metallic heartbeat finally pulsing in my mouth.

How could I survive without this knowledge?

I am sad.
I am tender.
I am misunderstood.

Fiona, Nellie, Lt. Cable and Me

Nancy Salz

We loved musicals, my nanny and I. Passionately. Luckily, we lived during the Golden Age of the Broadway musical and together we saw *Brigadoon, South Pacific, Finian's Rainbow, Call Me Madam, The King and I*, and many more. Sometimes, my friends had their birthday parties at shows, and we all attended together. But mostly I went alone with my nanny, Miss Hanna.

My parents generously bought all the tickets I wanted. The shows meant more to me than anyone knew, even Miss Hanna. They were the happiest times of my childhood. I listened to the albums incessantly.

The moment I heard the first three notes of the South Pacific overture—da-de-daaah, Ba-li-Ha'i—the music took over inside of me. And it still does. The orchestra repeats the three notes six times—first punctuated by the timpani, then the brass, incessantly louder and faster until on the seventh repeat the glorious melody bursts forth—"Bali Ha'i may call you, any night any day"! The music drew me onto an island in the South Pacific in the early 1940s. I'm told that the reason the notes are so haunting is that the third note is chromatic; it doesn't belong in the scale, and so it is jarring. It tells us something is wrong. What was wrong was World War II.

The music in the musicals opened me to feelings that I hadn't seen or felt in the real world: get-out-there-and-dance happiness, longing, romance, and love. I wanted to live in those shows. Not just to be an actress; I wanted to be the characters, be their friends, breathe the air in their fictitious towns.

When Tommy left his life in New York City forever for the once-in-a-hundred-years village of Brigadoon, I wanted to be the Fiona he returned to. I wanted to help Jeannie pack on the evening of her wedding, to be a bridesmaid in the "Come to Me, Bend to Me" ballet. I longed to run away from my life to a palm tree-covered island in the South Pacific where it was always summer and romance would surely follow. I wanted to hand Nellie a post-shampoo towel, and most of all I wanted to be Liat and lie in Lt. Cable's arms as he sang "Younger Than Springtime" to me. I was only nine when I first saw *South Pacific*, but I had my first sexual stirrings watching Lt. Cable and Liat make love.

The musicals were an escape, a fantasy that I could almost make real by singing the songs in the cast recordings. During the afternoons after school when I was in my pre-teen years, when Mother was out playing cards or Mah-Jongg, Father was at his office, and Miss Hanna was upstairs reading or sewing on the chair in my room, I was in the living room on the second floor singing show tunes at the top of my off-key voice. From my stage in the back corner of the living room, behind an upholstered yellow chair and next to the Capehart record player, I performed for the long, yellow drapes. I moved my arms as the characters had in the shows, and walked back and forth pretending I was an actress. I knew all the words, as one might expect after listening to the same songs dozens of times. I still know them—including the entire "Soliloquy" from *Carousel*—as do my childhood friends.

Singing show tunes in my little corner carried me away from home and school into a world of happy endings. I did well at my ballet lessons, so I thought that maybe I could someday be on the stage. And amazingly, all of that singing to records eventually taught me to carry a tune.

Adapted from *Many: A Memoir of Love and Secrets*, Richard Books, 2014.

Lenox Girls

Anne Harrison

They walk in step
Their long thin legs
Stretched out in perfect rhythm,
Pacing each other
Like thoroughbreds –
And so they are
These girls, three abreast,
Lock-step striding down a summer street.
Voices high and eager
Confident and sure they walk,
Perfect creatures,
Long arms swinging
Faces open,
Drinking in the sun.
Quite sure life will be kind to them,
If they think of it at all.

The Edge of Elsewhere

Susie Kaufman

The building that Lily lives in on the southeast corner of Broadway is neither here nor there. To the west lies the great avenue with its movie theaters and Chinese restaurants, its old men reading the *Post* and feeding the pigeons, its young mothers and their fussing children. Almost anything you want can be had on these streets. On Lily's block alone, you can buy kosher meat as well as meat that God doesn't know about. You can buy tangerines, lima beans and cookies called church windows that are decorated with little dots of raspberry and apricot jam to mimic stained glass. Beyond Broadway, towards the river, the grand apartment houses on West End and Riverside Drive rise up from the asphalt, contemptuous, self-important and secretive.

To the east, there is Mr. Stern's hole-in-the wall candy store. Lily tells herself that Mr. Stern is harmless, but he's missing a right arm and a left eye, so her stomach always tightens up when she goes in there for something sweet. Once or twice, rummaging in the penny candy, she's run into the stray girl from Holy Trinity further up towards Amsterdam, a girl in a dark blue jumper with translucent freckled skin. After that, it's Puerto Rico. Lily can walk two short blocks from visiting a friend in a building on West End with a grand, hushed lobby, leather couches and uniformed doormen, to a street where men sit on stoops or stand on corners speaking percussive Spanish, merengue pouring out of open windows. The remains of dinner, efficiently collected on West End to keep the rats and cockroaches at bay, are laid out like a buffet on Amsterdam. Yellow rice and cuchifritos overflow the trash cans. Everything is out in the open. Arguments, seductions, transactions.

Lily doesn't go out of her way to walk up there, but today she has to go to the public library to research her report on Balboa. There are a lot of reports in sixth grade. She's already gone through Marconi and Paraguay. Lily actually loves libraries, and has a nascent intellectual's disdain for encyclopedias. She is intimate with the card catalogue. Still, walking those streets, she feels naked, fluoroscoped, imagining that people are looking through her. She doesn't actually see them looking because she's walking with her head down, taking in the patterns of the cracks in the sidewalk from a height of four feet and nine inches. Lily is very small and very blonde. It's not so easy to walk out of the wrought iron doors of her building and get from there to the St. Agnes branch.

In school, the Jewish kids have their own classes. It might as well be Alabama. Lily Ginzburg never sees the Puerto Rican kids except when everyone lines up before the bell rings in the morning, or when there's a fire drill. She only knows the name of one boy, Israel Bermudez, and that's just because he's famous for drowning in the lake in Central Park. This would not have happened to Balboa, who discovered the Pacific Ocean. What exactly does it mean to discover an ocean? She is pondering this question when she looks up and notices a girl wearing a cross and little gold hoops in her ears poring over an old atlas. Nothing restores Lily's sense of well-being more completely than an atlas, especially an old one with countries that have shifted out of existence. She loves the intersection of color and language, the shapes and the way they jigsaw together to form continents. Peering across the table to get a closer look, she sees that the girl is studying the Arabian Peninsula. Palestine and Trans-Jordan. It's too much, too good. She thinks, what if I pass her a piece of contraband Juicy Fruit under the table? Maybe she'll let me look at the maps with her. Just then a boy, slightly older and wearing tight pants that show everything right at Lily's eye level when he comes over, says to the girl, "Hola, Rosalia, mi chica. Cómo estás? Hay una fiesta mañana. Quieres ir conmigo?"

"Fantastico. A qué hora?"

Lily fades back into the dust and crumble of the library stacks. She can't speak Spanish and she doesn't go to parties with boys. Too smart, her mother suggests. Sometimes, Lily gets confused about the men staring at her on the street and the boys in school not liking her because she's too smart. What's that about?

The report on Balboa is a great success. Lily's presentation, complete with visual aids, is a tour de force. It is the last project of sixth grade; the last project of her grade school years. In August she'll turn twelve and in September she'll start junior high. This will, no doubt, present some challenges, but right now Lily's feeling upbeat about her future. Her best friend, Sandy Blum, calls to say her mother has proposed a fancy luncheon on Saturday for the two girls and their two mothers, complete with linen napkins, sandwiches without crusts, and lemonade. Ruthie Ginzburg and Myra Blum are both very invested in the transformation of their daughters from scrawny girls with scabby knees into young ladies equipped with all the necessary social skills. Lily's mother has some very definite ideas on this subject. Powdering your nose seems to be important, as does learning to play tennis. Lily doesn't pay too much attention to these stratagems, but she's happy to play along and pretend to be grown-up at lunch on Saturday to please her mother. She's been studying this role for several years and knows all her lines.

When Saturday arrives, Ruthie realizes that she has an appointment to have her hair whipped up into a Charlotte Russe on top of her head and will have to meet Lily at the Blums. Lily sets off up Broadway in white short shorts and a blue and white striped sleeveless t-shirt, her bare arms and legs propelling her north through the heavy June day. At 85th, she turns left and heads for Sandy's building on West End. Lily's mind is a deserted beach town. Completely empty. School is over. She's not leaving for summer camp for another two weeks. June is neither here nor there. It's not real life and it's not summer even though it's already really hot. The cool dark lobby of the Blum's building is a welcome relief. Lily presses the up button on the self-service elevator and waits for it to come down. Behind her a teenage boy, somebody's older brother, in chinos and a blue Oxford shirt, walks in and waits with her. Lily steals a peek and decides he probably goes to Bronx Science. He has that I'm-on-my-way-to-medical-school-look. The two of them stare at the descending pointer over the elevator. When the door opens, an old woman with many shopping bags shuffles out and Lily and the boy go in. The elevator door closes and the boy grabs Lily from behind and puts his hand over her mouth.

They get out at the top floor and go around to the back staircase where the boy takes her to the landing just inside the door to the roof.

For some reason she thinks of the boy as a Jeff. They do not go out on the roof where someone could see them. On the landing, Jeff stands behind her, takes off her blue and white striped sleeveless t-shirt and drops her pink underwear and white shorts down to her ankles. He positions himself a little to the left and suddenly this thing is shooting out on her left side up around the lower part of her ribcage. Because he's behind her, Lily can't see any other part of him. Just this long fleshy tube disconnected from the rest of his body. Lily has never seen a penis before. Her father, Nathan, is a soft, round, person, very prim. If she needs to get something out of the bathroom when he's in the tub, he puts a washcloth there so he looks like nothing so much as a wounded white whale repaired with a rose-colored patch.

Jeff tells Lily to rub it. He reaches around with his right hand and touches her newly minted breasts and down below. Nothing has prepared her for this experience. It's discontinuous from her life, all her previous encounters with people. She watches the movie of it from the back row, concentrating on staying in his good graces, not getting hurt. Jeff tells Lily that she's a good girl. Then abruptly, it's over. Nothing happens to mark the end. Jeff just zips up his pants and tells Lily that he's going to get in the elevator. When she hears the door closing, she can leave, run down the stairs. He has a system. Almost as an afterthought, a detail that distinguishes this assault on this particular little girl from all the others, he asks if she has any money. Lily gives him the dollar she has folded up in the tiny soft leather purse her Aunt Pauline brought her from Florence. She is absurdly relieved that he takes only the money, not the purse itself. Lily brings the leather up to her nose, sniffs and fondles it, then races down the stairs. By the time she gets to the ninth floor, she's picturing Florence on the map of Italy.

Einstein and Grace

Jan Hutchinson

1. 2/16/2004

All life is held
in a delicate glass.
A crazy magician
might any moment,
with a mad laugh,
yank away our tablecloth
to clatter our meal
against the tiled floor.
The blessings are questionable —
I mean who goes hungry
when our table is full?
All matter is transitory,
and even if earth survives,
the poor, the ill, the old forever
limp toward the cliff of night.
Still, dear Grace, pull up a chair.
Sing with me
to chase away the gloom.
Whisper your grand plan
how we can help
this sad and fragile planet,
you and I.

2. 11/14/2003

Grace and I drive slowly north
in our little blue car.
Urgent SUVs careen by us.
We'd stay home altogether
except those we love
camp out on far branches
of the tree of roadways.
So we brave the traffic,
baffled by rush and confusion,
on love's little pilgrimages.
The crazy wind buffets our car.
Leaves, snow, information, days, fly by.
We hang on to so little.
Grace has a lap robe.
She crochets as I drive.
"Love is the biggie,"
she reminds me, taking a stitch.
Grace claims Einstein said:
"Even the stuff of deep space is love."
Maybe he said it.
Maybe Grace made it up.

3. 6/13/2005

Some people write big poems
and have complicated thoughts,
but relative to Enormous Mystery
all poems are just thimbles.
Grace claims Einstein said:
"Things should be made
as simple as possible,
but no simpler."

I like to imagine
the door of impossible simplicity
opening through to the Other Side—
out into the Miraculous Everything

4. 6/20/2005

Imagine all the acres
of innerness,
vast vistas, which
on a flat day
are folded into nothing.
Grace calls out,
Guess who said
"A great truth
is a truth whose opposite
is also true?"
She's fishing from her dock,
I'm fishing from mine.
Oh that's so hard,
let me guess, Einstein?
No, she laughs across the water,
Fooled ya! Neils Bohr.
We're sitting here
on a pair a docks;
I add then:
I guess truth,
like God is a verb.
If matter is energy,
there are no nouns.
Everything whirls.
I'm dizzy Grace says,
aren't you?

5. 11/20/2009

Dark, drippy morning,
late November rain.
Some say we can't write truth
unless we leave the dark threads in.
What kind of person tries to ignore
all the suffering in the world?
Do I sing the high notes only
and fear the potholes in the road?
Grace says there are no rules:
"If it helps to imagine a safety net,
feel free."
Grace teases.
She pretends it is she
who has imagined me.
I laugh with her at us
while threads of dark November
Embroider loss across
our chests.

6. 12/28/2009

I see why
it's tempting
to imagine
a personal God.
The mind cracks
like an egg
against awareness
of the Overwhelming Mystery
and our human
insignificance
in an ever-expanding
cosmos.

Pull yourself back
into your own small
speck of consciousness.
Why not
love If-God
and imagined Grace
even if rationality
can't support them?

7. 11/28/2013

Chaos theory is a mystery,
so what's a "strange attractor?"
It's embarrassing to know so little—
less with every passing year.
Grace is encouraging.
She reminds me
wisdom comes from letting go,
digging your way out from under
weighty heaps of knowledge.
She knows squat about physics
but loves what Einstein said
about the two ways to live—
one as though nothing is a miracle,
the other as if everything is.
As my knowledge slips away,
it's a comfort to have Grace
beside me, rapt in wonder,
astonished by the endless miracles
all surrounding.

8. 6/18/2014a

Einstein, at least once,
called God
"the Old One."
Grace and I collect
synonyms for God,
which is peculiar
since, like Albert,
we're only "deeply religious
non-believers."
I suppose
to think that anyone
honest would have to
be an agnostic
is its own quirky strain
of fanaticism.
Grace says nobody
with an imaginary friend
has the right to criticize
another person's faith.
Albert says
even quantum mechanics
"hardly brings us closer
to the Old One's secrets."

9. 6/18/2014

At the Indian restaurant
Elaine blurted out:
"Everyone has to believe
in science,
or religion,
or dumb luck."
Grace was kneeling
backwards in the booth
behind her
like a child,
leaning over,
making faces,
signaling me wildly.
I smiled and winked.
Grace must trust by now
I won't choose only one.
I know we can believe
in Everything at once.
She has taught me well:
We are ephemeral, dewdrops
on the great tangled web
of Natural Law, Divine Mystery
and Cosmic Absurdity.
We and the Sufis
along with the countless planets
are whirling
through black vacuum space.
Grace and I
get the hiccups
when we even
talk about it.

10. 6/18/2014

Sometimes I feel
stretched too thin,
but Grace doesn't.
She says her pockets
are big enough
for Rumi
as well as Einstein.
We don't need
a unified field theory,
a Great Universal
Theory of Everything.
We just need to keep
in mind Rumi's line:
"This being human
is a guest house."
We keep the beds made
and the table set—
soup on a back burner,
our hearts open wide.

Haiku

JoAnne Spies

give me your radiance
old dandelion
a star hiding in the grass

PART TWO:

QUESTIONS FOR OUR MOTHERS

Two Poems

Hilde Weisert

I. Questions for Our Mothers

What we haven't asked
what we don't,
or can't ask now,
except on a page.

What we imagine they knew
but didn't say. *(How do you say
such things to a child?)*

If they are dead,
we imagine they know
everything, and would tell
the women we've become
if we find the right words
at a certain time of night.

If they are alive, we grab this chance
for a different kind of conversation.

Of course, they did know everything.
Of course, we never asked them much
except for what we needed.
Now what we need has changed.

•

All those years I asked "Who were you?"
to the mysterious woman in the photograph,
when what I really wanted to know was,
"What does who you were make me?"
No wonder you didn't answer.

This time, let the question be real.
Tell me about that other woman—
the you who has nothing to do with me.

II. To Ilona, My Step-mother

How did you stand my father?
The tantrums that drove my mother
to tears, to drink, to leave?

The red face and clenched fists
I mirrored at twenty-one, squared off
across a room, standing up to him—

didn't scare you. You laughed
as if he were a child.
How did you know he was?

Was it the actual war you'd lived through,
or just being a Hungarian
instead of a Swede? I don't know

what he deserved. I do know
you were more than I did,
loving that difficult man

until the end, bringing together
the broken family—a daughter,
a son, a father—in your home.

My question began as a joke,
but now, remembering,
I think you deserve more.

Ilona, if you will tell me,
I will listen . . .

How did you stand my father?

A Mother's Touch

Donna Lefkowitz

When I think of my mother, it's not her face I see, but her hands. Neither large nor small, nor ideally beautiful, they were practical hands. Her knuckles were enlarged by work and arthritis. She kept them clean and manicured, but her nails seldom saw polish. Her hands would dip and swoop as she worked, her fingers fluttering as if they were wings.

I loved to watch the delicate, precise movements of her hands as she worked in the kitchen, fluting a pie crust, kneading dough, or forming perfect half-moon shaped Parker House rolls. To flute a pie crust she would hold a dinner knife in her right hand, handle toward the outside of the crust pressing toward the inside against the index finger and thumb of her left hand positioned on the outside. This motion repeated at regular intervals around the circular edge of the crust formed a perfectly fluted pie crust. When she finished an apple pie she would deftly brush a little milk over the top crust with her fingers and sprinkle it with sugar to make it brown in the oven. She would roll out leftover scraps of pastry, sprinkle them with sugar and cinnamon, and bake them into a snack that would taste as good as the pies themselves. Her lemon meringue and cream pies looked as high and perfect as those from a commercial bakery, but my mother's pies tasted better.

On Mondays she did the laundry, which was heavy work in the days before automatic washers and dryers. This involved much running up and down the stairs carrying a bushel basket lined with oil cloth, or a willow basket filled with wet laundry to the backyard to be hung, and then hurried back downstairs to finish the next load. Before she had an electric washer, she used a copper boiler in the basement to soak and stir the sheets, pillowcases, and tablecloths in near-boiling water with a round wooden stick that had become bleached from years of use. She used the stick to handle the wet laundry and feed it into the manual wringer. The electric washer made the job much easier. My mother always began washing the whites and lightly soiled garments first, progressing to light colors, and finally to dark colored clothing.

The water was reused for successive loads until all of the laundry was finished. Nothing escaped her hands which smelled of bleach, bluing, sal soda and laundry soap.

Hanging the wash on the line was a very organized task. First, she would carefully wipe the lines with a soapy rag to remove whatever grime had accumulated since the last wash day. Then, if it was an especially big wash, she would string extra lines. She hung the sheets together, the towels, the shirts, the pants, the underwear and socks. She worked with little wasted motion, snapping each laundry item with a crack before hanging it with wooden clothespins. To speed up her work, she would hold several clothespins in her mouth, which allowed her to keep hanging without having to make a trip to the clothespin bag that hung on another line. When the wash was dry, she removed and folded it with equal precision. In winter the wash would be stiff and frozen and had to be hung on a wooden rack over a hot air register in the floor to thaw and finish drying.

Her ironing was a work of art. Her hands moved so swiftly you could hardly see her exact movements, the fingers of her left hand positioning, smoothing and shaping each garment as she winnowed the hot iron in and out with her right hand. The clothes and linens always smelled of the outdoors by the time they finished drying. It was the cleanest smell I knew.

As a child, I thought my mother could make anything. If someone admired what I wore, I would say, "My mother made it," even if they were admiring my shoes.

Her hands could sew anything from a dress, to automobile upholstery, to drapes. They could crochet, embroider, darn or mend. She also made raspberry jam, canned peaches, beans and even roasted whole chickens, she even knew how to store vegetables in a vegetable cellar. She could guide a steering wheel, a vacuum cleaner, broom, mop, or feather duster with equal confidence. She wrote regular letters in a graceful script that could have come from a Palmer Method Penmanship Manual. Her hands steadied us with a light touch in anticipation of a vaccination, and brought us eggnog when we were sick. Her hands soothed sweaty brows and fevered foreheads. If I close my eyes, I can still feel her fingers on my cheek.

Plum Jam

Anni Crofut

You see, some mothers are meant to die. Other peoples' mothers, but not mine.

When we were young, my mother gave my sister and me a book called My Mother is the Most Beautiful Woman in the World. It was Yugoslavian, I think. The mother in the book was ruddy-faced and plumpish in colorful gypsy garb, as was her round-cheeked daughter. My mom and I bear no similarities to the women in the book, but the title has been swimming around in my mind all these years.

My mother is not meant to die. She is not supposed to become an idea, a character in a book. This is my fifth draft of this piece of writing, and with every draft I have gotten closer to this statement.

Because, my mother is real. She is alive; she is flesh and blood. She is here now, at the end of the phone, answering with her particular and ready "Hello." She is helping me make plum jam in my kitchen, shocking me with how much sugar is required. She is showing up at my house with a dozen eggs from her chickens, some daffodils, and an article clipped from the *New York Times*.

We chat, catching up, speaking to one another in a kind of half-trot, clipping over this and that. I slow us down, wanting to go deeper. She, ever goal-oriented, moves us forward. Sometimes we hit our stride, and it is as it has always been—like running parallel, because we are so similar, and then diverging again, because we are so different. This too is as real as anything I know. I know her dread of boredom, her need for an agenda, her fear of storms, her weakness with numbers. We laugh about these things, feel despair sometimes—about the numbers thing—because I'm the same way. I am simultaneously frustrated and awed by her equanimity, and in love with it, too. I depend on it when I am sick and need reminding that I will not die from the flu, or when the prospect of global warming becomes too overwhelming, or when I have to ask if it is too early to plant cucumbers. It is there in the taste of her applesauce, the poof of her floral duvet, the veined back of her hands, her stooped figure in the garden, the valentines I find every February in my mailbox, bearing the familiar question: "Will You be Mine?"

You see, Mom, your Valentine is supposed to come next year, and the year after, and every year forever more. You are supposed to be here as you have always been, forever listening as I complain about my cramps from riding horseback, from menstruation, from falling in love, from childbirth, from menopause, from old age.

Oh, but I know that it does not work that way. I know, in fact, that you are meant to die some day, as am I. This fear of losing you is mine to witness and to bear—not yours. Acknowledging my fear, I must hold its hand, remind it that this is just the way of things, settle it softly in the place where the harder parts of love reside.

What do *you* think, Mom? Shall we take that drive up to the Clark, have lunch and discuss this draft, and the next, and the next? Or shall we look at paintings, exclaim over the red brilliance of the autumn trees, fall into our old-as-my-life half-trot rhythm? Shall we focus on today, this day, in this sweet presence of our love, not yet over?

London Asks To Be Remembered

Lisken Van Pelt Dus

Remember Aunt Pam, it says,
remember Elsa, remember

even your great-grandmother
you never knew, her shape

shrinking to no more than smoke
as the bombs she hid from in the Underground

continued to echo, refusing her
any peace but death. My mother

had been a child then, dumb
to language that could speak such things –

besides, of war, what is there to say?
Life went on. And later,

when I was a child in London, too,
I held my mother's hand

passing her old flat, walking
the same paths in the same parks.

On Sundays, I behaved my way through dinner
with great-aunts and -uncles,

and, hovering, all the absent ones –
Pam's Timmy…

their father, Frederik, dead young…
their mother, Mama Lisken,

she of the bombs, she
for whom my mother named me.

Butterflies Are Free

Joan Peronto

butterflies are free
to fly away

mother 92
tucked in a facility
called *Sweetbrook*
sight dimmed by *the macular*
is still quite spiffy
earrings hair styled
clothes pressed
a primrose in a patch of violets

she tells me when I call
she is ashamed she can't see
her plate at mealtimes
and needs an aide to whisper
carrots upper left,
potatoes lower right
in that room with china
and crystal chandeliers

she reads my face
with fingers barely touching
and I am ten again
leaning toward her
for a butterfly kiss
her lashes fluttering
like monarch wings
against my cheek

Cookies, Like You Never Tasted

Robin W. Zeamer

You never knew what mother had up her sleeve, especially late nights in the kitchen. The next morning I would pick up a sample of her creations—my mother's so called joke cookies. Some might contain traces of bourbon, hot pepper sauce, anchovies, or even soap. The ones with anchovies, as I now think about it, could have passed for a savory shortbread served with a mild soft cheese. The soap cookies were usually identifiable and smelled of lavender or peppermint. These cute little balls would eventually find their way into mother's lingerie drawer after starting out in the cookie jar. They would end up crumbling in and about all her "niceties" (as she liked to call her undergarments), and she would have to empty out the drawer, tossing all those nice niceties to the floor.

She would call out to me whenever there was any kind of household accident or mishap, however small. Invariably I would have to stop whatever I was doing, usually it was homework or talking to my best friend on our kitchen wall phone; it had the longest curly cord you've ever seen (my friend had a turquoise princess phone in her very *own* room) and yes, I would have to fix the problem for mother. It was my job to always be on call. Plus mother hated to fold. She hated to fold the laundry. She hated to make beds and she never cleaned. So there I was, often sitting on the floor of her bedroom folding each silk piece of lingerie from her drawer after first shaking out all the cookie crumbs.

By the time I was six I was a pro at housekeeping. Mother was like a drill sergeant, and even though she refused to clean the house herself, she seemed to know all about the proper methods to clean and would yell out to my sister and me exactly what and how things had to be done. We were like her slaves instead of her children. While we slaved away, she would watch us from the darkened room in our railroad flat as she briskly filed her nails. She would do this to the rhythms of old tunes she liked. She would purse her lips and wiggle her upper body to the rhythm she was playing on her nails—seemingly very pleased with herself—all the while keeping the evil eye on us. Sometimes, for her own entertainment, she would tap her fingers on her teeth to the tune of the *William Tell Overture*. We had to be very, very quiet in order to hear each and every tooth.

But the cookies she baked one morning actually smelled like real cookies. These were not "faux cookies" with a surprise taste. Oh no! This time, she had found a recipe written in her own mother's handwriting on a piece of yellow-lined paper stuck in her Betty Crocker cookbook somewhere between the casserole and meat section tabs. When she saw her mother's handwriting that morning, she wept. She said it was like a visitation from her mother, the grandmother we never knew (well, she really never was a grandmother in our lives, because she died before my sister and I were born). I had never seen mother cry like she did that morning. Oh, she excelled at the crocodile tears for sure: they appeared on command when she was frustrated or couldn't have her way. This often happened because "her way" was rarely a legitimate way in most folk's eyes, so you can only imagine! Frankly, at some point her behavior stopped being embarrassing to me. I guess this was because I just stopped caring. But when she cried this particular morning it was different. She took the old worn yellow-lined paper with her mother's handwriting on it, and wiped away her tears with it.

Then mother snapped to just like that! She whipped out the baking sheet and one of the green nesting bowls and began to follow that little recipe to a T. Then she made one batch after another, then another, and then another still. She made us collect the coffee tins stored under the sink and asked us to line them with wax paper. Six tins were filled with chocolate chip cookies and we had to fold the edges of the wax paper many times (remember, mother did not fold) "to seal in the freshness" she said, before we put the lids on the tins. You'd think mother had just transitioned into a Brownie Scout Den mother like my girlfriend Bessie's mom.

Something had changed her, you see. It had to do with her own mother. Was it a message from beyond? Maybe my mother felt her own mother's nearness so strongly that she realized she could not fool anyone nor act out anymore. Things began to change then, slowly. It was so gradual and subtle you could hardly notice, but if you looked back over time—for a month let's say—you could tell she was different. My sister and I compared notes, secretly keeping a list of the changes locked in our respective diaries. The only problem though was that very first day—the morning the change began: because mother made us deliver all six coffee tins to each neighbor's door in our tenement and we never had a chance to even *taste* the cookies. It was Mother's last triumph.

My Mother Died

Heidi Rothberg

My mother died in my living room.
My sister and I sat on either side of the bed holding her hands.
Hospice told us what to look for
And so we watched for death
The way you might wait at the window
For an invited guest.
She breathed.
And each pause promised relief that it might be over
And each new breath brought relief that it wasn't.
We left her that night and went to bed.
She died while we were sleeping.
Perhaps we held on too tightly
And our whispered permission (they told us to give her permission)
    wasn't enough.
And so she waited until we were gone and let her death be a
    private thing
And we felt bad for missing it.
My sister saw it first and didn't wake me
But I took her wedding ring because it was my living room.
They took the body wrapped in a sheet
And everything happened slow and purposefully after that.
And I kept the wedding ring even though we all wanted it
Because it was my living room.

How I (Finally)
Met My Mother

Judith Nardacci

In the hundred years since she was born, and especially since she slowly slipped away from us into a place where it was hard to reach her, I've been trying to figure my mother out. She feels to me like one of those two-sided puzzles with irregular pieces that almost (but not quite) fit the still-empty spaces. But this puzzle came without pictures on the box providing the clues needed to finish it.

The puzzle has been with me for a long time. Once in a while, I would take out a few pieces, turn them around and over, and then put them back for another day less full of "to-do" lists and urgent obligations. But recently, with the added impetus of turning 70, I've taken the box out again for closer inspection. Finally, I am beginning to make sense of it. The puzzle is nearly complete, and now I realize how different the two sides of it are. One side is full of brightness, joy, and color, while the other is dark and shadowy, full of shapes I can't quite make out, subdued patterns, things hiding behind other things. Since her death, I've begun to know my mother in a way that I never acknowledged or understood before, although I lived with her, or near her, for my entire life. I pick up one piece, then another, and glimpse how infinitely complicated my-mother-the-person really was.

Some clues emerged from her own writing, which she came to late in life, summoning the courage to sign up for writing classes for seniors. They were led by interested and sympathetic teachers who helped her find the voice she'd been lacking her whole life. She typed her assignments on an ancient manual typewriter; put together they tell (as much as I think she was able to remember and confront it) her own history.

So what was she like? As a young child she loved to read. Later, she often walked to the library in Pittsfield. She remembered elm trees shading the streets, and the "Longfellow House" on East Street. She imagined the poet still living there, writing in his study. In the summer she would bring her books into the cool shade of the house and read for hours. "I felt very much at home there, where Longfellow had once lived, and I wondered if he knew I loved his home and was glad someone cared."

My mother's mother was a gifted seamstress who was quick to laugh and was often part of a large group of friends at social gatherings. Her father was creative and generous: he played a mandolin, developed his own photographs, and had a glorious and productive garden. He would build snow forts, engage in after-supper ball games, and make candy or popcorn on Sundays with his children.

The Depression began when she was just sixteen. Although she had the security of her home and parents, their friends and neighbors, and ample food and clothing, there was little extra money for education beyond high school. She went to a business college and worked on an assembly line at General Electric for several years. As a young woman, she had an enviable figure; generous breasts, slim waist, and long, slender legs. Tall for a woman, she wore clothes well, most made by her mother, with fine tailoring and fashionable detail. In a bathing suit, she was a knockout. She rode horses and bicycles, and loved being outdoors and active. In one photo from her best friend's wedding, she's wearing an orchid gown and a wide picture hat. She looks beautiful and happy, with a big smile, curly dark hair, and laughing eyes. She wrote about the gushing compliments she and a girlfriend conspired to use to enchant their young men (and giggle about together afterward). I can just see her looking raptly up at her date, charming him with her much-rehearsed "I think you're....wonderful!"

She met my dad in her twenties and married at twenty-eight. He was ten years older, a former gymnast, a good dancer, a hard worker all his life, but from a family that was never close and certainly not happy. Their first years together must have been terribly lonely for her because my father worked long hours in a shipyard in Boston during World War II. Even then, I think she had an almost physical aversion to the telephone, and in any case it would have cost dearly to call home. Gas was rationed, so trips home were few. Still, after my brother and I were born she managed to take us back home for summer visits. One letter to my dad is full of cheerful stories about our antics and nothing about how much she must have missed him.

We moved back after the war, but I think she was still often lonely. I know she was often exhausted: she had four small children by 1951, with no disposable diapers or frozen food, a husband who worked the night shift for the extra pay, and a washing machine with a wringer that would snap buttons or grab small fingers with equal indifference. But we never missed a meal; we took long walks, and rides in her tiny car; and every day we went out after school to play until the factory whistle (or her own *whee-whooo*) signaled five o'clock. We knew warmth, supper, and Mom would be there waiting.

Until Dad retired, we lived in apartments painted, repaired and maintained by Mom and Dad themselves. She shoveled coal into the monster furnace and snow out of the driveway. She hung laundry that froze in winter and baked in summer. But even when the front yard was grassless and the side-yard a long strip of stony dirt, she planted something, even if only some transplanted wild violets. When we finally had a real yard, a row of scarlet runner beans shaded the back porch. She captured snails so we could watch them slide over plants, and caterpillars that she kept on milkweed stuck in jars until they transformed into green chrysalises at midnight (she woke us to see them) and then to gaudy butterflies she delicately released outdoors so that they could spread their wings at liberty. There was a turtle in a glass bowl, and cats in our laps. She raised all of us to love books, music, being outdoors and being active. We were all seekers, in one way or another.

I remember that sometimes, before we went to sleep, she would gather us bigger kids onto her bed, while the baby slept in the crib close by, and sing lullabies in the soft summer evenings. Cars whooshed by outside, patterns of leaves on the bedroom wall. Then we would fall asleep blanketed by comfort and peace.

Downstairs, she would labor over the "budget book", or read, or do needlework. I recall one piece of embroidery with tiny figures lifting tiny baskets under tiny green trees abundant with tiny red "French-knot"-worked apples, growing for weeks from printed patterns to minute orchard.

What else shaped her?

I turn over the puzzle and study pieces that conflict, defy, and seem impossible to reconcile. Her sociable mother, for instance, was also quick-tempered, impatient, and often "driven" (as Mom would later say about me, usually comparing me to my grandma.) Her gifted father could be blunt and unkind. She recounted things he said that must have lacerated the small soul of a sensitive child: how pretty her mother was, and how she wasn't at all like that; the size of her feet ("like shoeboxes"); how clever her *brother* was; and speculations that "surely they changed babies and we were stuck with you."

She was often ill as a young child; her love of books came from days spent in bed reading. When she walked to the library, she wrote, it was because the trolleys' "closed-in feeling and the steamy peculiar odor nearly choked [her]." She doesn't mention childhood friends. I suspect books were her main companions and comfort, when home could be a hard place to find those things. She recalled being an escape artist at the age of three, dragging the rope her mother had tied around her waist to confine her to the yard, and running away with her beloved battered Teddy Bear. A neighbor would see her "trudging along far from home", lift her up to his wagon seat, and bring her home, where no one had even missed her: "Mom was sewing and Dad was at work."

Here is the girl who was hidden from me: the one with the brother who got the new bike while she did without, and who later crashed it into a tree and blamed her. The brother who stormed into her room one day, grabbed the Teddy Bear that went everywhere with her, and pulled out its eyes. Imagining her screams, I am horrified, but her parents couldn't understand why it so affected her. It is no wonder, then, that when she was abused by her brother and a visiting male cousin, she said nothing. She always felt he was the golden child, and that she was the one her family was "stuck with." Late in life, she came to realize that in being tough with her, her father might have been trying to help her "face what was really out there, as he'd had to as a small lost boy whose mother had died when he was barely three."

Throughout my childhood, she was mostly supportive of the widely diverse interests of my siblings and me, and proud of us. She saved hundreds of our school papers, drawings, and notes. She could be very kind: when I heard a warning about breast cancer on my radio and went to her in tears, having diagnosed my budding chest as surely containing malignancy, she cuddled me and soothed my terror, containing her laughter until I was back in bed and out of earshot. But there were also times she followed me or one of my brothers up the stairs, bent on punishing us for whatever transgression we had committed. I still remember the sound of her feet on each step: if feet could impart fury, hers surely did. Sometimes she just banished us to our rooms, while she stayed below, her voice doing the punishing for what seemed like hours, while we buried our heads in our pillows. Once, talking to my adult "baby" brother about a scene like this, I heard a silence on the phone and realized he was crying at his own memory of it. Once one of my brothers foolishly announced that he liked unsweetened chocolate. I doubt he'd ever had any, but he could be persistent—*in*sistent—so she gave him a whole package and demanded he eat it. He did, and none of us ever forgot that incident.

As we got older, the house would be sometimes silent while she lay on the couch with a "headache." We tiptoed through the rooms, bringing her tea and trying to be invisible until it was over. Photos of her during her middle years show a woman in a plain housedress, her graying hair pinned back out of the way. She didn't seem to care how she looked, as long as she was tidy and clean. She began to gain weight and lose whatever confidence she had struggled to acquire. Occasionally special foods—steak, asparagus, fresh strawberries— would appear on her plate, and we'd know she was on a "diet." Now I wonder if that might have been the only way she could give herself permission for some unusual and expensive foods, which she could never have afforded to buy for all of us.

Wherever we lived in those years, the rooms downstairs were dark, the blinds closed, and the shades drawn down. She fought for privacy indoors that apartment life could not provide outside. She and my dad never went out together, and other than family, no one was ever invited over for dinner with us. But sitting with a friend over coffee? She could do that, and did, often. She was never the one who took us to school conferences, but she baked countless dozens of cookies for school events. She never went to a movie or concert or other event by herself, but took me to see "Carousel" and "Oklahoma" and art films.

When I started college, I think the inevitability of our all leaving began to affect her deeply. I got weekly letters in her tiny handwriting about doing the laundry and the ironing and taking my grandmother shopping. My friends and I found them hilarious and, I'm ashamed to admit, boring beyond words. Now I realize what little novelty and excitement were in her life then. What else did she have to write about? On my birthday that year, she and my grandmother brought me lovely presents and a carefully-chosen card (she could stand in front of a card rack for an hour). She baked me my favorite "daffodil" chiffon cake, because she knew how hard it would be for me to spend my birthday away from home.

As an older woman, she joined the senior center, became an advocate for the elderly, and started traveling with friends. She went to Florida and Mexico! And she began to write, an activity that gave her pure joy. She found something she was good at, recognized for, and healed by.

I'm beginning to understand how much I'm like her—and also how different. I wonder if her "headaches," the darkened rooms, and the furious rants formed an unrecognized obsessive-compulsive disorder and chronic depression, since all my siblings and I inherited them. One of my brothers was crippled by both; I've been lucky enough to have found a good doctor and the right medication. What would she have been like with similar care?

When I sorted through her papers after she died, it was like meeting her for the first time. I gathered some of the stories and poetry and, with my new computer, created booklets as Christmas gifts for my brothers and my two children. I wanted them to meet her, too.

To My Mother

Barbara Barak

You must meet the dead halfway
Between commitments and regrets
Firm on the cusp of loyalty
Tinged with an ache of bittersweet

The leaf for the dining room table
Is in the closet in the hall
The papers that matter
Are ordered in the den

And the attention that you paid
To the details of my life
May never be found
Again

You said you'd come back in the form of a hug
And surround me when I need you
Here I come, ready or not
To stand within your reach

You who were never much for tenderness or touch
Frozen by your own desertions and losses
Like your pain-filled body heavy from refusal
To be lifted
You held your sadness

But at that end when you'd had more than enough
And I had to help you go
You buoyed me up
With such a loving send-off

Now in vivid dreams of us
When I see you for awhile
Maybe those are your hugs
Designed to make me smile

A Second Chance

A.M. Sommers

Mom was a youthful fifty when she learned her breast cancer was terminal. On the bright side, although chemo was a failure as a life-saving measure, it did result in thicker, wavier hair. Really liking what she saw in the mirror, she decided she was too young and too good-looking to die. This decision led to an avid interest in cryonics. After spending precious days doing research on the Internet, she decided to literally place herself in the capable hands of the cryonic pioneers at Ice for Life. Her personal representative at Ice convinced her that she would look her personal best when thawed, so before being frozen she had her eyes lifted and her teeth whitened.

Today, cryonics is no longer considered voodoo science. While entering the deep freeze to wait for a cure isn't exactly mainstream, there are now quite a few former icebergs who've returned to normal life. When Mom was considering undergoing it though, the procedure it was still in its infancy. There were sketchy reports from North Korea indicating a seventy-five percent success rate with bring-backs, but they wouldn't produce any of their successes, due to what they referred to as "confidentiality" concerns. Mom was drawn to Ice for Life because they were up-front about their limitations at that time. They could absolutely guarantee that they had the technology to achieve and maintain a perfect freeze, but cryonic scientists were still fine-tuning resurrection.

At the time Mom signed up, Ice for Life was offering early test subjects a great deal. Those who signed up during Ice's research and development phase would be preserved at half price: $25,000. Ice promised to monitor cure rates for all their clients' illnesses or conditions for up to twenty-five years, while they remained, in effect, dignified popsicles.

I thought Mom's plan was just plain crazy. Dad did too, but he agreed to pay. He warned me that she had told him that I wasn't being sufficiently supportive. Well, I asked him, didn't I do everything I possibly could while she was going through treatment? I visited her every day during her hospitalization. I took my turn when she needed a ride to chemo. And I even prevented her from buying a Tina Turner "What's Love Got To Do With It" wig. He shrugged in response. He was only the messenger.

The one thing I wouldn't do, however, was talk about the Big C. After a few martinis, Mom tried to bring up her fear of dying. I couldn't take it. I would rather have had bamboo under my fingernails. I couldn't even stand to be in the same room as her when she talked about dying. Most of the time, she too, acted as if nothing major was wrong. She shopped and cooked for my father. She picked out some God-awful wallpaper and redid the front hall. She tended tomatoes. She took up Pilates and Zumba.

Our stand-off during her final warm-blooded days did not surprise me. The prickly period that mothers and their teenage daughters routinely endure was still going strong when I hit thirty, which was also the year she was diagnosed.

We were never good at heart-to-hearts. Throughout most of my childhood and adolescence, my father's drinking had made our home-life rather gothic. Mom's maternal instincts and affections were dedicated to sustaining him. He was the breadwinner. She rationalized that only if his needs were met would we have a roof over our heads, food on the table, and a reasonably current wardrobe.

She stayed up late most nights to keep Dad company and to limit his options for self-destruction. As soon as I was old enough to get myself to school, she started sleeping in. I was miffed, but she said learning self-reliance early was a gift. I wasn't allowed to have friends sleep over because she found them too noisy and irritating. I felt guilty accepting rides from my friends' mothers, because I knew Mom was unlikely to repay the favor. Or, even worse, she'd offer to pick us up after a movie or school thing and she'd either forget or be an hour late. When I needed a dress for a school dance, she'd always put off shopping until the last minute, which meant I often wound up with something depressingly tasteful or ladylike.

While I usually had a good reason to be at odds with Mom during my formative years, I would always step in to shield her when Dad was throwing punches; it was a reflex.

When Dad was behaving himself, though, he was my favorite. He was a great reporter and could easily charm his subjects, editors, and peers. His byline would be on the front page at least once a week. I identified with him. I wanted to be him, but without the alcoholism. Mom knew this and resented it, which reduced any points I might have earned for being her bodyguard. I'm fairly sure that she would have resented me anyway, at least a little. She popped me out when she was still in her teens. She had moved directly from her parents' home after her modest wedding to an "affordable" apartment with Dad. Most of her single year of freedom was spent in maternity clothes. They did manage to have some fun when I was a kid. They traveled occasionally and had their friends over to play bridge. But most of Mom's twenties were spent changing diapers, cleaning the house, and waiting for Dad to finish closing the bars.

Until I started high school, Mom never complained much about Dad's drinking or the consequences that accompanied his habit. If he came home and smashed a couple of dining room chairs, she'd just remind me that alcoholism was a disease and that Dad was a good guy. The chairs would be repaired and we'd go on as we had before. But eventually Dad started staying away for days at a time, and somebody started calling and hanging up when we answered.

That's when Mom stopped being Dad's defender and caretaker. She wanted me to know every deviant thing he had ever done. She demanded that I join her in cursing the day he was born, but I couldn't do it, wouldn't do it. Half of who I was came from him; if he was evil, what did that make me? She labeled me a traitor: first, she started calling me Benedict Arnold, then just "Benny." No more hot dinners or clean laundry for me.

We began to rhetorically hit each other where it hurt. She told me I should do something about my spare-tire butt and my saddlebag thighs. I asked if she knew what sit-ups were for. I told her to find a new hair stylist because cotton candy was not a good look for her (or anyone else).

With the combination of Dad's absences and liquor bills, money got tight. Fortunately, babysitting allowed me to buy my own clothes. Mom questioned the necessity and expense of each purchase I made. Who did I think I was, she questioned, after I had the temerity to buy pink shoes. I knew the only shopping she was doing then was for groceries; but she was old, going on forty, so I thought it didn't matter.

When I would come home from college during breaks, we were very polite to each other, but we were never close. She would ride me for sleeping past nine and then accuse me of wasting my life. I would purposely imprint my fingerprints in the dust on a tabletop and ask why, as she had nothing to do all day, her housekeeping standards had slipped. Maybe, I offered, if she cut back on her afternoon naps she'd have more time for cleaning. A decline in her wine drinking habit, I suggested, might have led to an increase in her energy levels.

Fortunately, by the time Mom got sick, Dad had been sober for several years. Their miserable marriage lapsed back into a wistful romance. Because he was estranged from his old drinking buddies, Mom became his favorite companion. When he wasn't at an AA meeting or at work, they did everything together, from grocery shopping to hitting the links. When I came home for a visit from college, I could hear them giggling like guilty, horny teenagers as they stumbled up the stairs to bed. On one hand, I was happy for them, especially for her. On the other hand, I was angry it hadn't happened years earlier; a slightly more normal childhood would have been nice.

After graduating college, I landed a reporting job at a suburban weekly outside of Chicago. After collecting some well-written—if not exciting—clips about internecine county government scandals, I moved on to the Trib's City Desk. I became the rookie police reporter, which looks exciting on TV shows, but gets old fast in real life. The hours were terrible and the deadlines inhumane. Worst of all was having to interview families of homicide victims. To them, understandably, I was one step up from vermin.

However, there was a bright spot: Ted, who covered Chicago criminal justice for the Associated Press. His job was superior to mine. Like me, he covered the police, but he was also responsible for reports on the courts, organized crime and any systemic justice problems. He was brilliant, witty and well-read. And, unlike most non-TV journalists, he was good looking.

Dad had read some of Ted's by-line because his stories went out over the national AP wire. Always professionally competitive, Dad acknowledged that Ted was a "good reporter," and conceded that Ted's writing skills *might* improve over time. Mom said she understood the appeal, but she hoped I wouldn't make the same mistakes she did.

Ted and I had been together nearly two years when Mom got sick. I went home to be with Dad when Mom had her first surgery. The post-surgery news was bad: the tumors had spread to her lymph nodes. Both chemo and radiation were prescribed. Mom took it like a champ, fought the good fight, and rarely let treatment interfere with her daily routines. Her life was now worth living, she asserted, mere cells were not going to rob her of this new, good life. Hell, she was on her second honeymoon.

Then came the cough. Those "mere cells" had spread to her lungs. Her doctors told her further treatment would not change the prognosis. That's when she became a cryonic authority, and I became a coward. I put off going home to say good-bye until the day before she checked in with Ice for Life. When Dad asked me to come home sooner, I "unselfishly" told him that I thought they should have as much time alone together as possible. He didn't argue.

The three of us went to a pricey French restaurant on the last night. Candlelight couldn't disguise that Dad looked worse than Mom, who was in fine fettle. She cracked wise about the joys of attending your own wake. Although she imbibed heavily, she never became maudlin. Thank God.

The next day, Ice sent a limo. She hugged and kissed us goodbye, gave Dad her wedding ring for safekeeping, and told me to take her jewelry box. Wearing her old work out clothes, she left the house empty-handed. Dad and I watched her driver open the car door for her and then close it after she slid in. We waved, she waved, and she was gone.

I knew it was harder for Dad than for me; he had actually liked her. I had other things to think about. My job was absorbing; Ted and I began talking marriage. I became the number two reporter at the City Hall bureau, which came with a nice raise. I worried about Dad, but other than that, life was certainly good.

Then, nearly a year later, as I began to plan my wedding, I started missing Mom. Badly. I couldn't believe it. If she were around, I told myself, she would be complaining that she was too young to be a mother-in-law. But I also knew she would have loved helping me pick a dress. I found myself trying to figure out a way to communicate with her. She wasn't, after all, really dead. I kept thinking that if I really put my mind to it, I could get through to her. There had to be a way. But, of course, there wasn't.

Ted and I became parents. We had a girl, Julia. Dad was over the moon that we named her after Mom. If he was shocked, he hid it well. By the time Julia was five, Dad had retired. He was only sixty-five, but he was worn out. Journalism was a young man's game, he said. He moved closer to us and offered to take care of Julia after school so that I could go back to work full-time. When Ted and I both worked late, we would come home and find the house clean, dinners ready to microwave, and a sweet-smelling cherub tucked in and dreaming.

I reluctantly realized that Julia would not be blessed by a perfect grandfather if Mom had not cosseted and supported Dad all those years. Her sacrifices would certainly not have won the feminist seal of approval, but given her options, she did her best. She was emblematic of her times.

As I approached forty, I did not feel even middle-aged, much less old. Although Ted shared domestic responsibilities, I still often felt stressed out. The heroic efforts of a weekly professional cleaner kept my house in order for two days a week, but we slid into sloth by day four. Julia was a joy, especially with Dad's help, but between being a mom and a reporter, I had zero free time. How, I often found myself wondering, did that young girl who gave me life manage as well as she did? How did she go on for so long without giving way to despair? It was astounding that she controlled her anger and bitterness towards Dad until I was older.

As I pulled on my Spanx each morning so I could fit into my work clothes, and styled my thinning hair with miracle products, I would flush with guilt remembering how incredibly judgmental I had been back when Mom struggled with nature's challenges.

Then I got a call from Dad, who was barely able to enunciate. Slow down, slow down I urged, concerned I might lose him to a stroke. It was good, no, great news. The fine folks at Ice For Life had obtained medical clearance; Mom was ready to thaw.

I couldn't breathe, or talk, or stand. I was getting a second chance. Julia would have a complete set of grandparents. After talking next steps with Dad, I sat there grinning and crying. Through all the happiness, I began to feel the waistband of my Spanx slicing my midriff. Hmm, I wondered. Could I possibly lose ten pounds before Mom came home?

Mother's Day

Barbara Newman

This is the first Mother's Day without my mother.

She left the earthly world eight months ago, pulled by the promise of an end to her pain, and the need to rest in total peace. I woke today, cold, a restless sleep leaving a tangled mess of blankets at my feet. A burning question led me to my morning pages.

"Is Mom more with me in death than she was in life?"

It certainly feels like she is. Her presence is like my breath. Constant. Even. Life giving. It expands and contracts. It is here. It is gone. It is here again. She is in everything. In nature. In the eyes of my children. In the French toast she taught me how to make when I was five years old.

A medley of memories stir in my mind like a favorite recipe, one that you pull out for the perfect measurements, the order of things, until you know it by heart. It's the 3-by-5 card you pass down to the next generation—to your daughter, your son, and their children if you're lucky, until they can bake the cake by heart, too.

I sit, hands poised on the keyboard, waiting to bring forth my mother's story, and mine. No longer cold, I am wearing a hole-y cashmere sweater under a newly purchased cardigan and a pair of barely worn UGGS, like warm hugs taken from my mother's closet. Things I couldn't bear to give away, like the Spode china that Mom would lovingly unwrap once a year like a treasured gift. It graced her Thanksgiving table, the one she loved to set before she became a displaced guest at someone else's table. The pink and gold pattern, made in England, is now stacked in carefully packed boxes in my closet, waiting to make an appearance. They take up a lot of space, and weigh a lot. What weighs heavier is the question in my heart, "Will this ever be used again? Or will it collect the dust of the past?"

Yesterday, I got my hair colored. My mother had a thing about my hair, as many mothers do with their daughters. I thought about cutting it and said, "No, Mom likes it long." I don't know if I would have made that conscious choice if she were still alive. But now, after her death, many of my decisions start with WWMMD (What Would My Mother Do). Does she care anymore, now that she's somewhere in the ether? Does the third dimension matter, now that she's in the 5th, or 9th or maybe even 10th? I doubt if she's thinking about setting the table with fine china; I bet she doesn't give a crap about whether or not I let my hair go grey. She has more important things to do.

Death is not a period at the end of a sentence. It is more like a comma, a pause. Perhaps even more like ellipses. In her death, Mom is connecting the dots, like a master astrologer mapping the starry sky. All of a sudden the patterns make sense and the geometry becomes sacred. Through an angelic messenger, Mom has told me that in her soul-life she can become the perfect mother…the mother she always wanted to be. She can right the wrongs, be forgiven, and be nothing but pure beauty. The only thing on her dance card now is love.

I feel her love. My mother is here now in a way that she couldn't be before. All the shadows in her and her life have disappeared. She is only light. When she was in human form, she longed to know the truth, to know what was real. She struggled. She asked a lot of questions and dug deep to find the answers. Now she has them. She is an enlightened mother, and my experience as her daughter has also changed. The little girl in me is healing. Young Barbara is looking into her happy Mom's eyes and taking in the joy of being her daughter. She is loving being loved. Her past story is getting a rewrite; and whatever ancestral pain was lodged in her DNA is being released and replaced by a gentle sweetness, the nectar of love.

I had my mom for 56 years. It is only now that I know for sure that life is eternal. She is not gone. She is more alive than ever. The question that got me out of bed far before the sun rose has been answered. All I needed was a beacon of Mom's light to see it.

I'm Still Mom

Jana Laiz

Mom? Ma!
I swear I hear it, but when I look around all I see is my pit-bull. Can you talk?

He cocks his head like dogs do when you ask them something totally stupid. It's just my cavernous house echoing… memories.

The sound of videogames blaring from the next room…the sound of piano practice, wrong keys and frustration, Arthur, Malcolm in the Middle, Buffy The Vampire Slayer, the sound of laughter, of play dates, of children making mischief.

Mom, can I use the laundry basket? For what? I would ask, dumping the clean clothes onto the couch. And outside it would go, two children sitting squished in it, speeding down the snow-covered slide like a luge. Again and again.

Now the house feels hollow. I put on Pharrell Williams' "Happy" and try to get that way, dancing around the room by myself, but it feels kind of fake. My dog watches me. I'm embarrassed.

We used to listen to Thistle & Shamrock every Sunday night and my kids and I would have our very own Ceilidh, jigging around the kitchen.

I shut their bedroom doors now; heat costs too much. I peek in my daughter's room and see on her bed the sock doll I made for her. We made it together when she was in first grade. For years, she couldn't sleep without that doll. She didn't take it with her when she moved to New York to study.

I look in my son's room, his art hanging, sketch books on the bedside table inviting me to look. I could, but I don't.

The bathroom wall has heights and ages written on it in pencil in the corner. Sometimes I stand against it, imagining my tiny children, their backs close, feet jammed onto the floor, heads perfectly straight, for honesty's sake.

My house is vast now. No husband either. That happened. My puppy looks at me expectantly. I call myself Mama. Come to Mama, be a good boy for Mama, come have cuddles with Mama. Pathetic.

I'm still Mom. I know I am. But my purpose seems to have up and moved out, and now I have to reinvent myself. And that's what I'll do. What I have to do. And yet…

Now every text is a birthday present. Every phone call a call to celebrate. And spring breaks are a wonderland.

I imagine them on subway trains, in class, at rehearsal. Are they drinking coffee with friends somewhere? Are they thinking about me? I doubt it. But then the familiar "boing boing" comes from my iPhone. It's my daughter calling first thing this morning. My birthday. And then the doorbell ringtone… my son.

I'm still Mom.

I of the Beholder

Janet Reich Elsbach

Has anyone ever said something so true that you wanted to punch them? Here is what someone said to me, and its piercing truth was so piercing and true that I wanted to get all up in their face and say RRRRAAAAAHHRR go away with that thing I wish I had never heard but will now have ringing in my goddamn ears for the rest of my life.

"You know," she said, "your daughters are not going to think they are beautiful because you tell them they are. They are going to think they are beautiful if you believe in your own beauty."

Oooh, the witch. You know the fretful sigh you let out as you see yourself in the mirror, those few times when you don't avert your eyes from your own reflection? Stop doing that. Stop bashing your thighs with an impatient hand when you put on your bathing suit. Stop making hilarious remarks about the state of your thrice-post-partum, dearly departed "abdominals." And don't just stop saying it. Stop thinking it, too. You know they have radar for that. "I know when you are mad even if you don't say anything," said a little child I know to his mother, "because I can hear it with my tummy."

When my girls were little and I was a terrible ogress about junk food, sometimes I would say "My grandchildren! My grandchildren!" and threaten to bore them with the same story, again, about how the cells they were building now would make the milk their own babies drank many years hence. But it was more than preservatives and food coloring that we needed to avoid. My daughter's daughters will be nourished by the sense of beauty I have in myself, which came from my mother, and that I will pass to them.

My grandmother, a belle of the 1920's, bound her generous bosom so she could mimic the wraith-like profile in vogue at that time. The poor jugs never recovered, though the style certainly moved on. I don't know if she told my adorable, ringlet-headed, saucer-eyed mother that she was a beautiful child; I do know she told her she was too skinny as a young girl, and then later made it known that it was a shame my dad had the prettier legs in the couple. My mother has always told me I was lovely, but I can faithfully mimic her grimace as she patted her neck in the mirror while I watched her put on her make-up. She was probably about the age I am now when she started that squinty neck-pat, along with the fretful conversations about the bags under her eyes.

By this point I have racked up years of 'do as I say, not as I do' beauty self-assessment for my girls. Is it too late to change my tune? Here is what my therapist friend says: "Let's imagine, that the person speaking is not you, but a friend you care about. Now let's imagine she is talking about whether or not she should quit smoking. Would you tell this friend that the moment to quit had passed?" Well, duh.

Now that I have wiry, unpredictable hairs sproinking randomly out of my head and neck, now that my belly is not an area of my body so much as it is an item, independent, that must be hauled up in one hand and dropped down the front of my waistband, now is the time to start believing in my own gorgeousness? Whoa. Let's slow down a notch here.

First let's examine my credibility factor. Recently I had to supply a photo of myself for public use. It occurred to me that I look a lot like Karl Malden, or perhaps Jerry Lewis, in the photo I chose or any other photo, really. This was just an honest, objective assessment; the pictures spoke for themselves. A friend was in a similar predicament. She produced two gorgeous snapshots of herself, which did not surprise me, because she is gorgeous. "Oh," she said, truly unhappily, "I take a terrible photo." That is an unreliable opinion, I said to myself. By which I meant, she is CRAY. ZEE. Because look—she is as gorgeous in this picture as she is in that picture as she is in person. This was my honest, objective opinion.

Wait. How is it that she is crazy, but I am just honest? "You are beautiful!" she said to me. *She thinks this because she loves me*, I said to myself, understanding instantly that in my accounting system, this rendered her assessment less credible. "You're crazy to think otherwise!" she said. Hey, now! That's pretty funny talk coming from a crazy lady. *You can't even tell that YOU are beautiful, dollface.*

Hmm.

So, that brings us to calculating and adjusting for the love factor. I can't imagine for one second that I could ever look at my children and see anything but beauty—clean or dirty, rested or exhausted, young or old—the sight of them makes my heart soar and I feel quite sure that it always will, whatever changes time creates. My children are always beautiful to me, and, as my little boy reminds me often, I am to them. He thinks I am beautiful. Maybe he thinks this because he loves me so much that the sight of me makes him glad, and I could look like Karl Malden's homelier cousin and he'd feel the same way. But regardless, when I complain about what I see in the mirror, it's clear that it insults him.

An insult, by its medical definition, is something that causes damage to tissue, and sons or daughters, *in utero* or out. We are building their tissue from the moment they are ours; building the matter that will sustain them and the lives that spin from theirs, traced back through ours to the whole miraculous chain of cellular artistry that makes people and trees and walruses and hummingbirds. To be alive, really, is to be beautiful, but the daily bombardment of age-defying lip-plumpers modeled by already-perfect-yet-Photoshopped-anyway twenty-year-olds helps us forget that beauty has nothing whatsoever to do with what they're selling, or defining.

All those old saws are true! Beauty IS more than skin deep. It does come from within. We tell ourselves we are ugly in the same tone we tell ourselves that we are stupid or failures, because there is really no fundamental difference. When you nail the math problem or the metaphor, first of all, you don't care what you look like because you are immersed in what you are capable of, and second of all, you look badass and gorgeous because that luminous, golden core of capability and confidence is beaming out of you from every angle and curve. What we want our daughters to believe about their physical beauty runs through the same pipes as the intelligence and strength and success we'd like them to define, not via comparison to a fickle cultural standard, but for themselves.

Beauty absolutely does lie in the eye of the beholder, where it belongs, whether you are looking at your daughter or at yourself in the mirror. It is very, very hard to speak as admiringly to yourself as you would to your daughter. But—isn't this always the way?—it is about ten times as important as it is hard to do.

After all, their tummies are listening.

PART THREE:

LOOKING FOR LOVE

Recipes from a Weekend of Love

Carolyn Fabricant

I. Chopped Liver

Eschew the new
pretenders who
prefer their liver
moussed/pureed
devoid of flavor
(baby food
slurped burped)

Ech! Blech!

Embrace instead
the old believers
golden-toothed
their mini-cleavers
chopping orbs
to quivering pieces
puddled down
in schmaltz
flash-fried
(still pink inside)
with onions browned
then spritzed
(not soused!)
with sherry/soy
plus minced boiled egg
that's just enough for

texture rough when
stuff's all thickly
squashed together
with a *fork*

*(Ignore the cuisinart
you dork!)*

The master's game
is gimme truth let's
mound some on
these crackers Ruth
fix eyes upon
the Ritz-borne prize
refuse disguise
of wretched hue
sing praises to
the Master's name
(Whoever's yours)
And *chew*

Unh *ugnh UNGH!*
Oh *ooh* OOH!

Who knew?

II. Stuffed Breasts

Butterfly your breasts
and lay them flat
with metal mallet
pound them thin
in plastic wrap
(no toothy grin!
firm discipline!)
fingers probing flesh
exploring depth
of skin within

Ah stuffing! key
to gustatory fantasy
fingerlickin chicken
unlocks lust in us
oh yes

Engorge
with savories
fried onion garlic
chopped chorizo
pepper flakes and
mix with parsley
toasted almonds
fresh bread crumbs
a jumbo egg
manchego cheese

Your phallic forms
prepared to please
(though function's
necessarily delayed)
secure the seams with
toothpicks neatly splayed

Roll round in
flour egg and
panko beds
(respectively)
sauté to golden
every side

(remember when
you rode astride
and sucked my
fingertips?)

Remove to blot
then quickly bake
(three fifty)
minutes eight to ten
indulge in
memories of sin

Inhale

Behold roulades
the diner's perfect mate!

Exhale

Slicing them
diagonally (but
not too thin)
arrange on plates
with style designed
for pause before
a sacrifice
then point

(a plunge restrained)
your steaming morsels
one by one
to salivating jaws
with grace

(Have we grown old
recalling now
so long ago
our kneeling
squealing
some nights
twice?)

III. Scrambled Eggs

Last night you
stirred me slow
so slow and easy
ecstasy slipped in
surprisingly

At dawn
I break our eggs
as carefully
as you broke me
whip them gently
(gently!)
deftly blending in
some heavy cream
a pinch of pecorino
dash of pepper too

You watch me work
your eyes aglow
the ample butter
slipping slow
and easy
round enamel
scarcely warmed

But then
desire seizes me
again a sudden
need a greed to
bring to head
jack up the heat
force fork to riot
feverishly
like stomping grapes
with urgent feet
dump clotted lumps
on plates (come! eat!)

 No no you whisper
(tongue to ear)
too tough my dear
begin again
deploy the wooden spoon
keep heat on lowest low
and standing there
recall moon's melody
the rhythm easy
swaying slow
stop   wait

stir languidly

Repeat
Repeat
Repeat

Stop wait
crescendo comes
in creaming curds
so delicate
you'll ache with pleasure
at their melting
on your tongue

Keep faith
my dearest one
this ecstasy is
soft and easy
birthing
simply slow

Last night
you scrambled me
so subtly
sweetly
tenderly
you broke me
utterly

Aphrodite & Ares

Sahra Bateson Brubeck

Between her thumb and forefinger rested a single tendril of golden hair. She played with it, allowing her fingers to fondle the curl like soft twine, braiding it tightly and setting it loose into the autumn wind. From afar the scene would appear romantic. Her gestures would be interpreted as seductive, the look in her eye perceived as a call to the hearts and bodies of young men. She appeared this way because this is what they wanted to see in her. Warriors took pride in the conquest that was her beauty. They joked amongst themselves in candle-lit tents, telling one another the intricacies of violating the delicate space that separated her warm lips. Each man who came across her dreamt of the very tendril that she held between her fingertips. In their dreams her hair was intertwined with their fingers, and her flesh pressed against their palms. They dreamt and they pursued, until she felt as though the skin of her scalp was being pulled at by all the hands of the world; and the curls she once embraced in her own warmth hung flat with the weight of their yearning.

How lucky she was, thought the other girls, to be so beautiful. But how could luck ever come to describe the pain that is embedded in such grace? Luck was not for her, nor was love, for love was no more than the fruition of a desire that did not speak to the mind, but satisfied only the body. She was rarely spoken to and never heard. Her words hung in high places, echoing in the skyline like the final breath of a hymn. When dusk settled on the horizon, she watched as the earth made way for clouds of red and orange to dissolve on her cheekbones. Even the seasons catered to a destiny that she resisted, as summer gave her skin a warmer golden glow. She fought against the beauty that sprung forth from her eyes each morning, cursing the jade that lingered endlessly beneath her eyelids. Eventually, she removed every mirror from her home, hiding herself from the image that her suitors sought so pitilessly. Every moment she spent in the company of another depleted the enormous supply of love that she was born to unleash on the world. Aphrodite came to hide from the eyes of others, escaping their gaze like the moon so often escapes the glare of the sun.

It was only in herself and in the eyes of Ares that she witnessed her true reflection. At night they lay together in the comfort of a darkened room. With the shades drawn and the candles burned out, they sought solace in the sound of each other's breath. Aphrodite began by whispering her thoughts into the safety of the almost empty room. She tilted her head back, allowing her jaw to drop slightly and let the part between her lips open wider, releasing a galaxy of sonnets that had been brewing behind barred teeth. He would lie next to her, touching only the tips of her fingers to remind her that he was there, a figment of tenderness in a world of bitter touch. When she was done speaking, he kissed the lips from which poetry was birthed, feeling the vibration of her words as they resonated on her tongue. With closed eyes, he sunk weightlessly into the beauty of her words, coating his slender spirit in a nectar of rhythmic rapture.

In return he wrote her letters. He memorized every syllable of her songs, and transcribed each conversation into a few lines, leaving her the summary of an evening on a sliver of parchment. She hung the bits of paper in her windowsill, so the peek of dawn would illuminate relics of the night. Sunlight seeped through the rounded form of his handwriting, causing each vowel to fill with the light of sorrowful remembrance.

Despair nestled into her thoughts when his absence brought on a wave of new suitors. His notes could not protect her from the boys that sought manhood in the curve of her flesh. Warriors pounded down the doors of her home to see the skin that they had heard so much about. One after another, they wrote her love poems; each one a mockery of the letters he left for her, mimicking the cadence of Ares' affection. In all of their professions of love, there was not a drop of genuine care. Aphrodite called Ares' name, shouting the words they had once spoken so softly to one another into the barren sky. His disappearance made little sense to her. But to the Gods of Olympus, the absence of Ares was no more than a strategic maneuver. They combined their powers, creating a protective shield around her home, which kept only Ares from seeking her presence.

There was another who hungered for her love, a man by the name of Hephaestus, to whom the Gods were indebted. He held the Goddess Hera, wife of Zeus, captive in the mortal realm, threatening the state of the world with her death. The conditions of her release required Aphrodite to devote herself to the act of giving this strange man love. He desired a depth of affection similar to that which Ares received from her summery caress. For no other reason than the unforeseen disappearance of Ares, Aphrodite deliberately crumbled into a state of acceptance, allowing the hollow love of Hephaestus to encompass her heart.

In the night he held her with a heavy grip, keeping her frame from swaying away from his sweat-stained chest. He removed the notes that dangled in her window, stealing the light of reminiscent dawns from the room. Her poetry was replaced with the sound of a dense grunting that emanated from his coiled stomach. Nightfall always came too soon, inevitably causing memories and faint images of Ares to surface and take hold of Aphrodite's thoughts. When the stars peeked from beneath the black cloak of night sky, she used their light to search for Ares' silhouette. Aphrodite stood on the terrace of her home, watching the perimeter of her land for a sign of his presence. She felt that he was always somewhere near, lingering in the thin space between tangibility and intangibility. What she sensed was true. He too, watched for the faintest flicker of her presence, always keeping an eye on the outskirts of her home. But the Gods do not cast spells that are easily broken. Their powers are far beyond any form of sorcery, and their eyes were just as steadily placed on the whereabouts of Aphrodite as Ares' once were.

Time waxed and waned, gently guiding Aphrodite away from the days of Ares' affection. The voice of Hephaestus was perched on her shoulder, constantly humming a deceptive tune of devotion into her ear. He praised her beauty every morning, whispering small obscenities that gathered in the darkest corners of her room. Soon the ceiling was coated with shadows of her beauty. They frolicked there in the corners of the room and crevices of her thought; and the more he spoke of her beauty, the greater their army became. She thought that the shadows were only there to remind her of what she was to the world. Their method of slow encroachment was strategic, preparing her for the moment when she was no longer a being at all, but a mere outline of what beauty was meant to be. "Unearthly," he said, as he gazed at her features shamelessly. Over time he memorized the inviting curve of her bottom lip and the small arch that rose on the edges of her lashes. But he could never master the art of interpreting her expressions. All of Aphrodite's God-given characteristics that he treasured so dearly lost their appeal when she bent and warped them into features of her own making. Even her smile eventually lost its simplicity. The calming bend of her lips was overpowered by the look in her eyes. When he contemplated the grace of her smooth skin, he wished to see only the flesh that had been marked by his touch. Without the imprint of his thick fingers on her arms, he could not love her.

Each night, before Hephaestus and Aphrodite retreated to separate dream worlds, he turned to her and asked, "Do you belong to me?" to which she was forced to reply "Yes." Never once did he mutter, "I love you," especially not in his dreams. Sometimes she admired this aspect of Hephaestus. He knew that she could not be fooled by such plentiful words, for they came from a barren tongue. So, he was never obliged to fake a form of warmth that he was incapable of possessing. There was no need to woo or seduce, no desire to set her free in a city of falsities. Instead, he used his words like a coarse rope, binding her frame to his sturdy chest. He did not care to use words of love, for they too were created by the Goddess Aphrodite. How, after all, could a mortal man of hatred speak a language created by the immortal figure of love? He would do better to speak the only truth he knew, which was one of dominance.

It was no coincidence that Hephaestus' trade was that of a blacksmith. The swell of muscle that surfaced on his hands as he pounded away at folded metals was ever present. When he touched Aphrodite's face, she felt his fingers searching for a way to remold her features. His thumb would find the bow of her jaw and press deeper, causing her face to take on a thinner shape. With his other hand, Hephaestus grappled with the excess flesh that gathered in the twist of her waist. He squeezed at her core, pushing her organs into the center of her stomach, until she was sculpted into a different woman by the strength of his forearm. Each day he set off to work in his shop, pummeling hot metals into cold, sharp weaponry; and each day he returned home, entering Aphrodite's house with the sole intention of bending her back into shape.

Over time the Gods grew bored of monitoring Aphrodite's actions. They retreated to the realm of their own troubles, and forgot to maintain the seal that kept Ares from crossing over the perimeter of her land. Ignorance blinded them from seeing that Ares had never returned to his own home. He still waited patiently at the gates of Aphrodite's castle, listening for her voice. Though her voice never came, one day a sudden and unknown sound settled on the ground beneath him. Like a clap of thunder, the sound resonated in wind, and nested in the branches of nearby trees. There was no rain, no sign of weary clouds, but a storm of winds formed nonetheless. Air tore upwards and downwards, clawing away at the translucent fabric that the Gods had hung around Aphrodite's home. Threads that held the barrier together drifted to the ground, landing on Ares' eager feet. He made his way through the gates, inhaling the nostalgic scent of half-blossomed anemone. The scent of Aphrodite's garden always clung to her hair, and in the springtime her fingertips were often stained reddish brown with fertile soil. Fresh earth took refuge in the slight crevice between her fingertips and her fingernails, giving her the natural scent of a flower in bloom.

As he neared the doors of her home, Ares firmly held on to the memories he and Aphrodite shared. He could hardly feel his own feet beneath the weight of anticipation. Slow steps rapidly turned into a steady run, until he reached the stairs that led to the opening of her house. Without knocking, he threw the doors open, allowing them to rattle and slam against the walls.

When Aphrodite heard the violent sound that reverberated from below her bedchambers, she believed it to be a sign of Hephaestus' arrival. The haste of Ares' footsteps was foreign to her, an attribute that did not fit the steadiness of his character. She sat motionless on her bed, awaiting the dense tones of Hephaestus' voice to beckon her away from the comfort of her own company.

But when she met eyes with the figure standing in her doorway, the fear that had kept her silent and cold for so long was instantly chiseled away. Ares embraced the small of her waist, tenderly drawing out the hidden lines of her smile. The round edges of his knuckles burrowed in the dips of her spine, as he recited poetry that he had memorized in her absence. He told her of the many days that were put to rest to the tune of her sonnets. Dusk would not turn to night without her words to comfort the forlorn sky.

They lay together on a bed of heather linen, watching as the sun surrendered its brightness to the dim quiver of moonlight. Aphrodite's fingers never ventured far from Ares' skin. On his chest she etched a new poem; it was one of forgiveness, of rebirth, of reconciliation. She pressed the tip of her forefinger against his abdomen, tracing the shape of each letter into the contours of his muscle. Aphrodite's poem hovered like breath between their bodies. *Let us fall from the land of the sublime, let us teach soil to catch flame, let us disappear with the constellations, let us be no more than memory, let us be freed from time.*

Aphrodite and Ares believed that they were alone with one another. They took time for granted, twisting and wrinkling the sheets. All the while their eyes remained shut. Aphrodite's pulse was fastened to the rhythm of his heavy breath, her thoughts running like liquid honey, embalming the room with remembrance. She did not think to check the doorway, nor did she even worry that Hephaestus would return from the stables before midnight. In Ares' presence, the sense of fear and paranoia that Aphrodite had grown accustomed to was abandoned. The room regained its familiarity, becoming a moonlit sanctuary for the two displaced divinities.

Hephaestus, however, had long anticipated the arrival of this moment. Knowing that the Gods were often preoccupied, he had decided to take matters into his own hands long ago. One morning, while Aphrodite was off tending to her garden, he hung a chain of translucent gossamer above the bed. Every thin vine of twisted metal that comprised the chain was infused with somber witchery of his own making. With his anvil, Hephaestus had beaten the name of Ares into the wiring of the chain, causing it to shudder and collapse in the presence of his nemesis. Hephaestus did not need the aid of those who meddled with herbs and trinkets; the depraved fall of his clenched fist was imbued with such fury that he needed no evil but his own. Only the sound of ringing platinum sheets could calm him, masking his temper with an honorable trade.

The chain was met with white starlight. It hovered above their bodies, aglow with the ghost of midnight skies. Slowly, it sunk towards the curve of Ares' spine. As the chain drew closer, its metals grew hot in the light of an unforgiving moon, releasing a shimmer that radiated against the lovers' closed eyelids. The light awoke them from their state, but it was a warning that did not come soon enough. With their lips and fingers intertwined, the chain gave way to a sudden drop. A lace of platinum landed on Ares' back, trapping the weight of his body against Aphrodite's frame. He struggled to get loose, but the chain would not allow the slightest of movements to emanate from his body. Beneath a blanket of gossamer they cried in unison.

Two Poems

Marie-Elizabeth Mali

I. To Construct of Silence a World

To find a home in silence, to breathe it
like air, to love it like a parent, a God.

•

For months after he left I howled
from room to room, the brightness
unbearable. I needed more sky
for ballast as I crossed this ocean.

•

Longing drives the ongoing conversation
with something I used to call God but now

know is probably myself. Longing for love
grafted onto desire for God because to admit

I was lonely, that I missed my father,
that I feared no man would ever love me

the way I needed, with just enough absence
to make me want him but not so much

that I feel abandoned, was too embarrassing.
Who else could get the balance right besides God?

•

To construct of silence a world.
A world I must leave to connect with others,
others who make noise and have needs
different than mine.

•

I made a self out of a cracked bowl and filled
the cracks with gold dust to make them beautiful.

One day the gold-veined bowl fell and shattered.

Silence is the only part that can't break, the space
inside the bowl that makes a bowl a bowl.

II. The Body Is an Entry for Danger

Washed up on the beach, dozens of moon jellies,
their horseshoe-shaped gonads picked clean by gulls.
A disappearing chronology of desire drawn in sand
at the edge of the sea. Death is an aphrodisiac
for jellyfish, who spawn and spawn as their pulsation
wanes and stops. After I ran out of air diving
in a ripping current at 80 feet, I shared
my friend's remaining air, which wasn't much,
as we ascended the line, my head on his shoulder,
his arm around my waist, and while I felt love
for him in that moment, sex was nowhere near
my mind, nor did it arrive when, his air level close
to zero, I switched to share another friend's air
for the last 20 feet, and when, all of us safe, we surfaced,
the only thing I wanted from my lover on the boat
was to be held and warmed so the shaking would stop.
It wasn't until later, after a meal and another dive
during which the heart-race started at the slightest hint
of current, so I had to stop, hold a rock, count to six
during each inhale and exhale, afraid to suck my air
too fast, afraid the panic would make me do something
stupid, like kill myself by dashing to the surface
or swimming straight into a hammerhead's mouth,
not until after I survived that dive, and told nobody
about how I talked myself out of dying, did I open
my body to him, grateful I still had a body to share,
grateful for his touch, for my nerves that worked
for something besides panic and tears, for my body
that will, by choice, never bear children, but will,
with great pleasure, pretend to make them until it stops.

A Constellation?
Help Me Find
the Big Dipper

Emma Flowers

Spoon me, please.
Spoon-feed me love
and kindness
and streetlights
and gin and tonics.

Don't check to see what time it is,
please, I'd prefer not to know.

Pick me up with two fingers
(gently) (please)
Drop me (plop) (splash?)
in the river
in the song
right into a
moving car
into this silly dream

Say to me,
You look familiar, I think
I found a piece of your soul last
week, when I was walking
home.

Smile. Let the lines
between our smiles
connect
Watch the way they circle each other, first,
like lions
A fun game of connect-the-dots.

New smile-map is ready now. Press start
to begin
navigating.

The Whooper Swans

Lydia Littlefield

One of our favorite family stories has to do with an afternoon when my newlywed parents were in Scotland doing graduate work. Both of them were writers and students of English Literature; the details of their stories were good and many of them have stuck. I have added bits, such as the one where her arm is threaded through his. I like to paint in details like that, even if they may not be true.

His name was Tom; she had several names: Anne, her given name; Nancy, her childhood nickname; and Hank, the name given to her by her college chums, a play on her maiden name of Henry. My parents were wonderful people, and I consider myself to be very fortunate to be their daughter, even though we all weathered some very difficult storms.

•

The walk down the hill toward the Edinburgh docks had all of the elements you might see in a great literary moment: her arm threaded through his, their athletic strides in harmony, the setting sun casting salmon-colored shots across the tops of the distant trees down near the water. It was unusual for them to have left the tearoom at such an early hour. Their usual habit was to take a budget version of high tea at about three and stay at the tearoom reading for a while. Then they'd go across the way to the pub for a night of drinking with the locals, some of whom, also fellows at the university, were their friends. They'd all sit around, tossing bits of Shakespeare and Chaucer and Donne at each other, catching them on the sharp points of their rapier wits, reveling in their good fortune to have survived the War and landed here, in this dark, poetic city. The heat from the coal fires in those public rooms was free, unlike that from the awful gas heater in their quirky, dank flat. Every night they stayed as long as they could, not only to soak up the heat, but to distract themselves from vague feelings of displacement and uncertainty about the future.

This was their second year of marriage. They had hardly known each other, really, when they married; their courtship was conducted almost entirely through the mail. She had been back at home, just outside of Philadelphia, rolling bandages and dreaming of escape from her family, after her heady experience writing about Joyce's *Ulysses* at Mount Holyoke. He had been serving in the Pacific after his graduation from Dartmouth. Their writing abilities far surpassed their interpersonal relationship skills. Edinburgh would be the gritty surface upon which they would strike the match of their paired literary geniuses. The marriage was sure to thrive on their combined creative fuel.

That day, she had looked up from her book and noticed an unusual light through the window. She suggested a walk down to the docks. He was never one to pass up a romantic moment. Even as relative newlyweds among the hills and valleys of post-war Scotland, romantic moments were becoming harder and harder to come by. Maire, the woman who had served them their tea, and who had served them most of their suppers these past three months, nodded to them when they gestured toward their things at the corner table as they moved toward the door. They'd be right back.

It was cold, early November, and the stones of the street were dark grey and damp, like almost everything else in Edinburgh. The smoke of a thousand coal fires was lifted by a stiff breeze. This was a rare light that drew the young couple, as if through a straw, down to the wind-faceted water.

It wasn't until they had cleared the pier building that they saw the two tremendous swans swimming across the harbor, moving directly towards the dock. They were a mated pair of whooper swans. My parents stood, with the setting sun behind them, and watched as the swans slowly made their way across that bit of the Firth of Forth, Edinburgh's great estuary that leads to the River Forth and then on to the North Sea.

It was so unusual to see the sun at all, and here they were looking at a landscape that could have been painted by Turner if he had added to his palette paint made from cooked lobster shells. The swans, which they knew to be white, were pink and a soft bluish grey, with an intensity of golden beak and coal black eye that riveted. And when my parents looked at one another they noticed that they, too, were rimmed with copper gilding, as were the roof ridges, towers and steeples behind them.

The swans swam into the shadow created by the dock, and instantly the brilliant colors were sucked out of the picture. The white feathers were a bit dingy after all, and it turned out that the swans were coming across the firth not to make a grand appearance, but rather, to be in the lee of the docks, to pass the time out of the prevailing wind.

Tom and Hank stood in their tweedy woolens, shivering even though they still had the last of the sun upon them. They held each other as they watched the swans. It didn't last long. There was a blast from the ferry dock down the way, and the cob took that as a sign to go. He lifted his long neck and opened his wings, mustering vast reserves of energy as he lifted himself up out of the water. Tom and Hank estimated that the wingspread was at least seven feet. The pen followed after her mate, and off they flew to the east, their feathers once again doused in the colors of a variegated golden rose.

The two aspiring writers went back to their dinner by the fire; they finished their year in Edinburgh the next spring, and they went home to create a life for themselves. But try as they did, for almost twenty years, they never learned how to create the kind of life together that they had hoped for. The brilliant colors in their minds turned out to be a palette of grays, and that was not enough to keep them afloat.

When All Else Fails

Audrey Kalman

We didn't see much of my dad after that Christmas in 1994 when he stood outside for what seemed like hours, pounding and wailing at the locked door. The pounding and wailing went on as my mother wrenched open a drawer, clanged a metal stockpot into the sink, and filled it with water.

We knew what that meant: spaghetti. And not the kind where an old Italian nonna poured hours of love into handmade meatballs and sauce from scratch, but the new American kind you made because it was the fastest, easiest thing to put on the table when all else failed. If you were my mother, you would serve it when under stress, which usually meant you couldn't remember to stir while it was cooking or time it properly, so the spaghetti—Ronzoni from a cardboard box—would come out with large segments stuck together like a bundle of cable wires. The sauce—Ronzoni from a jar—might fall victim to uneven heating in the microwave, one spot scalding your tongue and another barely warmed. And the Kraft Parmesan cheese would come from a cardboard container with a white plastic built-in shaker.

The pounding and wailing stopped as we helped my mother clear the dishes, but not before we had heard some words we weren't meant to hear. Julie, CeeCee, and I began making more noise than we needed to. We didn't notice the exact moment when the sounds outside stopped. It was as if our father had dissolved like a particle in water or dwindled like the light of a dying star you barely notice until it's no longer there.

Our lives went on. I expected divorce would come. That didn't happen. My father moved a few miles away to a cruddy apartment over a hardware store at the edge of town. Without a divorce, there was no need for child support or alimony. My father kept depositing his paychecks into the joint bank account, showing up at Cee-Cee's chorus concerts, and taking Julie out for ice cream. He thought ice cream was too childish for me, so instead he invited me to breakfast at the diner down the street from his apartment. I refused to go.

I was starting to understand that a daughter might never comprehend what goes on between her parents. Now I see that my father was preserving hope—hope that my mother would change her mind, hope that he could change to suit her; so he continued going to concerts and plays and birthday parties, hoping that one day we would be a family again.

My mother hung on to hope, too. They both kept that filament of hope flickering until one day, a couple of years later, my father drove his big rig straight into an oncoming school bus.

It happened in December, midway through my sophomore year at Berkeley. We never got the details. Was it a suicide attempt? Was he drunk? Was it just an accident? Was he dead? No, but he barely made it.

It *could* have been an accident. It happened outside Chicago at dusk on a winter's eve. A slippery road might have been involved and also jumpy shadows and winking lights. My mother knew something had happened when my father failed to show up for the Christmas concert in which Cee-Cee had a solo. By this time we were used to the politeness between them, the way my father sat next to my mother with his big shoulders hunched inward, making sure never to touch her. But we also were accustomed to having him around for these events. Sometimes he even took us to dinner afterwards.

I wasn't there when it happened. I was halfway across the country, in the middle of finals, planning to spend winter break in Berkeley working to help with tuition for next semester. When I heard about what happened that night, I imagined my mother sitting alone beside the seat she had saved for my father. Maybe she leaned over to ask if Julie had heard from him. Later she called his apartment: no answer. On Monday she called the trucking company and they told her about the accident.

He never came back to his apartment. Eventually, when the rent had gone unpaid for a month, the landlord moved his belongings into storage. When nobody had heard from him for six months after that, the landlord tracked down my mother to see if she wanted to take over payment for the storage facility. If not, he'd give my father's stuff to charity.

I was home for the summer by then and privy to my mother's rebirth. In the months after the accident she cut her hair and lost ten pounds. She still smoked, but now held the cigarette in a way that showed off her newly manicured nails. I listened to her half of the conversation with the landlord. "No, I haven't heard from him… How much a month? Forget it. Just get rid of it."

Finally, then, came the divorce. A decree formalized by the law: "Willful desertion for one year." And, for good measure, "Habitual Intemperance."

And that's what frightens me most: to be descended from a willful deserter.

•

Sean and I had a beautiful little wedding. That's what everyone called it: a beautiful little wedding. Of course it was beautiful—it was at the Mark Hopkins Hotel. And not in any old ballroom, but at The Top of the Mark with a view over San Francisco in all directions.

If we'd stuck to the tradition of the bride's family paying, we'd have gotten married at City Hall with dinner at Max's afterwards. Instead, I felt like Cinderella at the ball. Sean and I had made our wedding plans curled up together on the angular brown sofa in his apartment. I remember his hand coming to my mouth as I opened it to object to the cost, his fingers trapping the "but" behind my lips. Sean had beautiful fingers. I used to tease him that if he left the legal field he could make a living as a hand model. With those lovely fingers he stroked me into docility. "The money's not an issue," he said. "I want to do this right."

I wanted to believe he was doing it up for me, for us—the eight-piece jazz band, the caviar appetizers, the most expensive champagne. Sean passed out twenties from the pocket of his tuxedo to make sure the reception, which had already been paid for with an astronomical check, ran smoothly.

It was a small wedding that would have been smaller if not for the show Sean wanted to stage for the law firm's senior partners. And for the junior ones swimming like frantic sperm toward the prize of senior partner. They slurped our champagne and ordered mixed drinks at our hosted bar and danced with their wives and dates on the parquet floor. They took up four of the eight dinner tables. If not for my sister, Julie, and her husband and two kids, we wouldn't have had enough family to fill the head table.

There were signs and portents, if you believe in such things. Like the weather. At the time we laughed at the rain that started early in the afternoon and streamed down as guests arrived. What did we expect on Valentine's Day in San Francisco? Everyone said it would make for a good story. We'd never forget our wedding day!

The rain continued as we vowed to hold each other forever close in sickness and in health. As we ascended to the Top of the Mark for cocktail hour, we were afforded not a sparkling 360-degree view of the city, but clusters of buildings hulking in the fog.

We made it through the honeymoon and a few months of what looked like marital bliss. I moved into Sean's rectilinear apartment—but only for a little while, Sean assured me. We were going to buy a house. I felt so grown up riding in the back of the real estate agent's cream-colored Mercedes. Like I had finally arrived. We held hands as we wandered through the split-level rancher on a cul-de-sac twenty minutes south of the city. Real estate agent in tow, we scowled at another couple, the competition. We got the house.

Then the changes began, or at least that's when I began to notice them. At first they were so subtle and gone so soon I couldn't be sure I had seen anything. An outburst here, a scowl there. His face would shift as if someone had shaken a kaleidoscope behind his eyes. His voice would sound as if something were pinching his throat. Instead of watching a movie with me, Sean would disappear into the bedroom off the kitchen that he had turned into a home office.

"And he's gained weight," I complained to my former roommate.

"Awww," she said. "That's kind of cute."

One morning, I awoke to find him still in bed at 7:30 on a weekday—Sean the go-getter, who normally rose at 5:30 to hit the gym even if he'd been at the office late the night before. I rolled toward him, not sure whether to plan breakfast or feel for a fever. He lay inert against me.

I found the Lithium kind of by accident.

•

"I'll tell you the rest when we get married," Sean had said the night he proposed. And so he had, though not with words.

I called in sick that morning and held him until he woke up.

"What's wrong, honey?" I whispered. No answer. Only now we were married. Now I had rights.

When he shrugged me off and went to take a shower, I did not sit idle. I cinched my bathrobe around my waist and headed downstairs to make breakfast.

Yes, I did open the refrigerator and take out eggs, bread, butter, and milk. Yes, I put the kettle on to boil. But after that, I walked the few steps into Sean's office, where I never went without him. Although I heard the shower running upstairs, I half expected his leather chair to swivel around revealing him facing me with his elbows resting on the chair's arms and his hands pressed together under his chin.

I hesitated before the desk. Then I became that shrewish wife of movies, sliding open desk drawers, thrusting my hands into the pockets of his abandoned jacket, and finally flipping open the leather briefcase.

I served the prescription bottle alongside his plate of French toast. He looked at me with the orange juice glass halfway to his open mouth. I watched Sean with the same detached curiosity with which I had so often observed my father. What would he do? What would happen next?

Sean set down the orange juice glass, closed his mouth, dropped his forehead to the table, and began to cry. We made it past that bump in the road. It was really more like a sinkhole, but we navigated past it. He returned to his therapist. He got back on the Lithium and swore he would take it every day like he was supposed to.

"No fucking around, I promise. I love you, Eve," he said, for the first and only time in the six years we were together.

Then, without discussing it, we started trying to have a baby.

•

One can rarely imagine the truth about what goes on behind the stucco walls of a neighbor's house. "That nice young couple two doors down," is what we were to 86-year-old Mary Crowley, who waved at us from her window. To Sean's colleagues, I was the cute wife of the up-and-coming law partner. To my colleagues, I was a manager of projects, known for *getting stuff done*, whipping people into shape—even the senior execs who didn't like to be told what to do, but who often needed a swift kick disguised as a gentle nudge. A woman who moved from office to car to freeway to house, where I disappeared behind my wall of stucco.

Looking in on that one particular night you wouldn't have seen anything out of the ordinary. The wife is in bed when the lawyer pulls into the garage at 10:24. There's nothing unusual about that; all young lawyers work late. But something is different on this night. A whiff of something in the air, perfume the wife has never worn. The lawyer is inscrutable as he strips down and steps into the shower.

The wife, in bed but not asleep, hears him begin to sing. That's the end for her. That he could be singing after what she *knows* he's done. She turns toward the night table on her side of the bed and switches on the light. She is always calm in the midst of these storms. Anyone looking in would see a placid scene, because they wouldn't see the months of accumulated suspicions: the briefcase now locked, the cell phone going directly to voicemail, the increasingly erratic hours, the lovemaking less frequent and more frantic.

No one on the outside would understand why, when the husband emerges from the shower, she is no longer in the bed but standing before it, where she has placed a small overnight bag packed with one of his suits, a change of underwear and socks, and the toothbrush she snatched from the bathroom while he hummed away in the shower. They wouldn't understand what she knows in her gut, that he never truly loved her, that the words he said only once were said for himself, not for her. That the betrayal began long before the cheating.

She can't live with him for a minute longer. The only confirmation she needs that she's right about everything is the way he stands before her with the towel wrapped around his waist and says nothing, not one single word, but only narrows his eyes and makes his mouth into a line and shakes his head back and forth.

Later, if anyone asks what happened between them, the lawyer's wife will shrug and say, "It wasn't working out." And because California is a no-fault divorce state, there will be no further questions. Looking out or looking in, it will all look the same—just two people who thought things would work, but they didn't. If anyone asks, she'll tell them what comes after all else fails is another day.

Ribs (What's Taken From You to Give to Me)

Brianna Pope

"I can count your ribs," he said as his fingers ran lightly over the bony ridges. They dipped in and out of her side.

"How many are there?"

"You want me to count your ribs?"

"Yeah."

"No. I'm not going to count them."

"Say ribs again."

"Ribs."

"Mm, I'm hungry."

"You're starving," he deadpanned.

She grinned.

"Why are you smiling?"

The grin grew broader. "Seriously, stop it." Her lips contracted quickly over the gleam of slightly gray, yet perfect teeth.

"So serious today."

"Are you fucking kidding me?"

"No, you're being really serious. Kinda putting a damper on my mood."

He stood up. The plastic chair screeched along the tile.

"I'm putting a damper on your mood?" He sounded surprised, as if it were completely inconceivable. As if, the entire time he had only ever been part of the solution—not the problem.

"Yes, you are. It's, like, I didn't ask you to come in here with your black cloud."

"You're selfish." His face flushed with anger.

"I am," she agreed.

"I hate you."

"Well, that's a terrible thing to say right now. But that's fine, I hate me too."

"I hate you."

"What?"

"I HA—" He stopped. The vein in his forehead pulsed a vibrant blue. She let out a giggle. He almost started crying. "Why is this funny?"

She shrugged. "That vein—I just always want to poke it."

"You can't poke my vein." A small, bony finger reached out, ET, phone home style. He was sitting again, so close to her that her finger almost succeeded in reaching the bulge that was still slightly inflated with blood. He resisted the urge to smack her hand away; instead he took a deep breath to remind himself that he had to be gentle with her. It was times like these, times when she was in a joking mood, that he had to be reminded the most. He was unable to have fun with her the way he once did. There was some guilt that tinged his heart, but he thought that his dying sense of humor was appropriate. The way she made jokes was not.

"What if touching your vein is my last request? Then can I touch it?"

"No."

"But I'm dying. I want to touch it." Her full bottom lip stuck out. It was vaguely blue, like the rest of her skeletal body.

"You aren't dying, stop that."

"Come on, Jason. Look at me."

He had been, in fact, looking directly into her eyes at the moment she said that. He looked at the floor, unable to handle the sudden reality of her flat eyes. Spotless, with clean grout lines. A faded flower design adorned each tile. Some with leaves that stretched out to meet other flowers—some solitary, preferring to stay in the single square.

His eyes met hers again. Hers, once a green so vibrant, but no one could tell anymore because they had sunk far back into her skull. She had soft skin like a baby's, except now she had sprouted light tufts of springy dark hair all over it. There she was, propped up against the pillows, and yet she barely made an indent. She was so small under the covers, it was hard to believe that she had legs and an abdomen and arms. She appeared only to have a large, over-whelming skull, just barely covered with taut gray skin.

In that moment, Jason felt tempted to call his girlfriend beautiful, but that would have been a lie that she would have greatly appreciated. If he called her beautiful, which her personality still was, she would think that she was fine and it was fine and that what she was putting him through was fine. But it wasn't fine. It had taken him two years and eight months to realize that even all the love between them could not erase the fact of her sickness. At that point he had finally stopped thinking about what she was doing to him, focusing instead on what she was doing to herself. He realized that the pain he felt could be nothing like the pain that she felt.

He was only getting a bitter taste, but her body was literally wasting away because she was unable to believe the compliments he had given her when she was beautiful, unable to look in the mirror and see the truth with her own eyes.

It was only here, only now as she lay crumpled and slight under the starched, white sheets, that she felt perfect. When she caught glimpses of herself in reflective surfaces, she would smile and touch her overly prominent cheekbones. In private, Jason had requested only plastic utensils be given to her, and the mirror in her room had suddenly been taken down because it required "maintenance." Only sometimes did she ask to see her reflection. Perfection only gets worse, never better.

There was a soft beeping noise in the background, but it didn't annoy him. It was the only thing that made him believe Sara was alive. He stood up again.

"You're leaving?" Sara mumbled, half asleep. Jason considered it briefly. She didn't bother to fight to keep her eyelids open, partly because she had a finite supply of energy, but mostly because so many people, people forced by genetics to love her unconditionally, had left her—sick of the pain she continued to drag them through. Pain, they considered to be optional.

"No, baby, I'm not leaving." He hadn't left her bedside since he had rushed her to it. The realization triggered a wave of weariness. His mind felt the creakiness of her bones.

A nurse came in to quickly replace the depleted fluid bag and to leave fresh sheets on the back of his chair. She was the only one on Sara's nursing staff that remained firm in her belief of recovery. The only one who didn't remind him not to eat Sara's food and who made up a bed for him, even though she would always find him in Sara's. The look she gave Jason proved that she expected to see Sara's emaciated chest keep rising and falling. The nurse squeezed his shoulder and left just as quietly as she had come.

Each night it was his intention to sleep in the cot, but he would last five minutes before either climbing in with her or being asked to sleep with her. Sara had not always been particularly fond of cuddling, but his body against hers seemed necessary now. Her body was always cold. When he pressed his fingertips into her inner wrist he couldn't feel her blood flowing freely.

Jason was often visited by the horrifying image of the inside of her body being filled with tepid blood. Even with her pressed to his skin, his palm flat against the underside of her left breast, he would lie rigid and unmoving, unsure of whether or not her heart was still beating. The slight rise of her chest would scare him into thinking that it was just her soulless body bloating as it released the carbon dioxide necessary only for life outside of herself.

"I love you."

Sara didn't respond. He climbed into her bed and gingerly tucked her into the contours of his body.

"I'm sorry."

"I love you," he repeated.

Je t'adore

Teresa Gentile

My dear beloved,

You are perfect in all your imperfections,
desirable in all your disorder,
made dearer still by your messy egress in life.

The very traits you ridicule and write satirical stories to decry
are the sweetest spots to which I am drawn.
I want to quilt together the pieces of life you would erase from
   public view
and wrap myself in their human warmth.

You are one of life's many miracles.
Do not hide your brilliance
beneath the judgment of
Not Good Enough

In deeply biased admiration,
I am yours.

The Rocky Road to Happiness

Lorrin Krouss

A year and a half after my husband died, and shortly before my 43rd birthday, some friends of mine decided that I had been grieving long enough and it was now time for me to plunge head first into the icy waters of the dating scene. What none of them knew was that I had accepted my widowhood and single parent status. I was fine with being alone.

My daughter was in her second year at the University of Virginia where she had taken on a leadership role in campus politics. My son was trying to figure out how often he could smoke pot in our backyard without getting caught, while filling out college applications. I had my job in a New York City law firm, but knew that all too soon I would be thinking of the words in the Peggy Lee song, "Is that all there is?" Although the thought of going out on a date was exciting, actually going on one was something else altogether: the difference between being pregnant and having the baby.

When my friend Phyllis called to tell me that she would like to fix me up with Brad, the boss of her friend Ruthie's son, I had every intention of saying, "thanks, but no, I'm just not ready." Instead, I surprised myself and said okay. I had been married for 22 years, and as inappropriate as it might seem, I had often wondered what it would be like to spend time with a man that did not test his pulse every 15 seconds, or think he needed to go to the emergency room in the middle of the night.

Brad and I spoke on the phone several times before we made arrangements to meet. He sounded nice but just a bit rough around the edges. He told me, for example, that he was the "used car King of Bay Ridge." Brad said more than once that Phyllis had told him that this was my first date in 24 years. Every time he said this, my stomach would do a summersault.

When it was finally the Friday evening for our date, I was a nervous wreck. My hands would not stop shaking. My son, thankfully, had decided to escape my "first date" and sleep over at his friend Michael's house.

The doorbell rang. I held my breath and opened the door to meet Brad, all 300 pounds of him. He was wearing Bermuda shorts, sandals and a Hawaiian shirt covered in leaning palm trees. He looked at me as if I were a plate of hors d'oeuvres. I had nowhere to go but forward. I locked the front door behind me, followed Brad to his car and slid in, jamming myself as close to the passenger side door as possible. I noticed that the driver's side seat was pushed practically into the trunk in order to accommodate Brad's girth.

Brad drove us to a seedy-looking and dimly lit Bar and Grill in Lynbrook that was owned by his friend Rocco. Brad introduced me to Rocco as his "little lady." By now, I was feeling queasy and only ordered a club soda. Brad consumed two cheeseburgers and a mountain of fries while talking non-stop about his expensive divorce. When the check arrived, Brad pushed it towards me without pause or shame it seemed. I paid the bill, and said that I really needed to get home. I jumped out of the car the second that we pulled into my driveway.

I was still recovering from my encounter with Brad when, during a routine dental visit, Dr. Nelson suggested that I might want to meet his cousin Roger. Roger was an airline pilot who had been widowed for two years. Dr. Nelson was certain that we were a match made in heaven, especially since we had similar overbites.

Roger called a few days later. I agreed to meet him for dinner at a diner near Kennedy airport. On the evening of our date, Roger called a half hour before we were to meet and asked if instead of going out, he could stop by my house just to talk. In less than 15 minutes, I opened the door for Roger, who was still in his pilot's uniform. I noticed that he was carrying a large leather-bound album under his arm. We both sat down on my couch with the album between us. While we were trying to make small talk and laughing a bit about our similar dental problems, Roger removed his cap, jacket, tie and shoes. Then he picked up the album and placed it on his lap. He said that he had not been able to look at the pictures since his wife died, and somehow, he knew that he could share them with me.

For the next two hours, Roger gave me a detailed blow-by-blow description of the people and events captured on every single page of his son's Bar Mitzvah album. I did not know what to do and sat rigidly next to him, staring at the pictures. Just as I was warming up to his Aunt Yetta and Uncle Sol, he turned to the picture of his deceased wife and his son dancing with Grandpa Abe and burst into tears. I ran to the bathroom for tissues. When I returned, while Roger was blowing his nose and wiping his eyes, I gathered up his scattered clothing and shoes and said, "Wow! I didn't realize it was so late."

Roger thanked me for the nice evening and said that the next time we got together, he would show me the pictures of his family's last vacation at Club Med. I declined any further dates with Roger, considered finding a new dentist, and avoided flying American Airlines for several years after that.

Several weeks later, Peter the accountant received high praise from the sister-in-law of one of my closest friends. Ronda said that "Peter was a Prince." The use of the word "prince" did spark my curiosity. Peter called. He had a voice that sounded like liquid gold. I was impressed when he mentioned the name of the five-star restaurant that he wanted to take me to. I walked into the restaurant, pausing to look at the beautiful décor. I was approached by the maître d', and as soon as I said who I was meeting, he personally escorted me to the table. Peter was wearing a well-cut navy suit, white shirt and burgundy print tie. His nails were buffed and polished, and while his hair was thinning, it was perfectly cut and styled. His square-shaped, grey, tinted glasses gave him a sexy Elton John look. We began to talk and paused only long enough to order wine. After a few minutes, I noticed that beads of perspiration had started to appear on his upper lip. As the restaurant was air conditioned and a bit chilly, I wondered what was wrong. Just as I was thinking about eating poached salmon covered with baby shrimp and tomatoes, Peter leaned across the table, took both of my hands in his, looked through his tinted lenses directly into my eyes, and said in almost a stage whisper, "Would you mind going into the ladies room, taking off your panties, then coming back to the table?" I blinked as if trying to awaken from a dream. "Of course," I said, and reached under the table, retrieved my handbag and briefcase, and instead of the ladies room, headed right out the front door of the restaurant. I hailed a taxi and made it to Penn Station just in time for the 7:10 to Cedarhurst. Years later when I found out that Peter had re-married, I wondered if his bride was wearing underwear under her gown.

It should not be a surprise that I stopped dating after the Peter incident. I was now more certain than ever that remaining single was preferable. I concentrated on my children and my career, took art classes, traveled a bit, and spent quality time with friends. Then, when I least expected it, I received a phone call from a man whom I had met several times when we were both married. Andy was now divorced, and he reminded me of how many parties we had attended together over the years, at the home of mutual friends. I had a vague recollection of a nice-looking man with a warm and friendly smile.

A week after the call, I invited Andy over for some wine and cheese. This time on the other side of my door, instead of an unsavory used car salesman or an unstable pilot, stood a handsome man with straight brown hair, big brown eyes, wearing an orange sweater and perfectly pressed khaki slacks, looking a bit like Kevin Costner. My knees buckled and I felt cupid's arrow pierce my heart. We talked for hours over wine and cheese. Although we had experienced very different childhoods and had different experiences with marriage—and Andy was a diehard Yankees fan while I rooted for the Mets—what we soon learned after only a few dates was that we shared an undeniable love for each other and a desire to move forward with our lives.

A year and a half after our wine and cheese date, we were married. We have stayed together for 20 years, and today we can boast that we raised, educated and gratefully married off four children. We now have six grandchildren, three girls and three boys. We have managed some years of champagne and roses, and though many of the roses did have thorns, and sometimes the champagne was flat, I know that we are both grateful that I opened the door, and my heart, one last time.

Where Is Your Husband?

Kuukua Dzigbordi Yomekpe

Hello, My name is Adjo. I am thirty-nine. I am single. I am independent. I am African. Given the right combination of factors, I am happy most of the time. Some days I wish there was an AA-type group for women like me. Sometimes it is the sheer lack of our visibility that throws me into depression. I know we are out there, but because we don't see each other, perhaps we cave and join the married forces only to launch ourselves into permanent unhappiness. Over the years I have come to believe that marriage is not for everyone, but it takes great courage to go against the grain.

There are many theories as to why women like me exist. I am smart, highly-educated, beautiful, sexy, and a great cook. Also, Type A neat-freak, no-nonsense, impatient, brutally honest, unmarried and childless. They say we had strong female figures in our lives who overshadowed the male figures (if they were around). They say we are jaded because some guy in our past duped us. They say we are 'apuskeleke,' who just want to sleep around. They say we'll grow out of the "flawed thinking" that marriage is not for us. They say we hate men. They say we are lesbians. The list goes on.

Don't get me wrong, I too wonder sometimes. Had my parents stayed together and been the loving couple they had started out being, would I also want a marriage? Had I not been sexually molested at age seven, would I claim sexual fluidity? It was difficult to see everyone pairing off in their twenties and wonder if all was well with me. It became more concerning to others when I hit thirty and kept going, and still showed no signs of pairing off. Once I hit thirty-five, I stopped worrying about what other people thought, although I still questioned whether marriage was for me. This is my story of exploration in spite of all the pressures and social commentary. Come along with me as I share an atypical African woman's journey to sexual emancipation. I tell my story in vignettes around a handful of the partners I've experienced since I immigrated to the U.S. twenty years ago. The fact that living in the West allows me the flexibility to do some of this exploration is not lost on me. However, I believe stories like mine are more common than we think; it's just that the traditional African cultural mores keep women from sharing.

·

In Ghana, I grew up with my maternal grandmother who wouldn't even let me have boys over at our house for fear of putting ideas in my head. Having survived her own two failed marriages, she preached a gospel about the dangers of men and boys. My father used his visitations to give advice on various life issues, which almost always meant boys. My grandmother and father believed that boys were the downfall of the female, especially beautiful, mixed-race ones like my sister and me. For this reason, I kept my relationship with my first boyfriend a secret. I felt grandmother would smell it if I so much as swapped saliva with him. Our four-year relationship consisted of writing each other letters during Study Hall, stealing long hugs at 'Peace Time' during Mass, sitting next to each other during Youth Group meetings, and acting in church plays as husband and wife. After my family immigrated to the United States, we dated long-distance for a year, but it was not long before I realized that this move was permanent, and that I would need to move on. I wrote him a letter:

Dearest Kwakuvi,
You know I love you and miss you dearly, but mother says our family is going to be permanently settled in New Jersey, so I won't be returning to Ghana. I think we should break up so you can move on. I have met someone and even though I'm a bit disappointed he's not African, he's Black, and mother approves. Remember, you will always be my first love. Adjo

The response was crushing, with Kwakuvi accusing me of cheating and lying to him. I decided to ignore him and move on. God knew I was still a good Catholic virgin at twenty; if Kwakuvi didn't believe me, there wasn't much I could do. Boris was from Barbados, and with his smile, tall and solid stature, coffee-bean skin tone and Caribbean accent, I was so in love nothing could perturb me.

•

"What do you mean you are not ready for marriage?" I yelled at Boris.

"Adjo, please understand me." I winced. After six years he still hadn't learnt where to put the inflection in my name. Was this the man I really wanted to marry?

"I don't think we are ready for this sort of commitment," Boris added.

"Nigger, are you for real? You mean we've been shacking up for a year and now you've got what you want so you don't want to be married?" I spat out at him. After five years of being with him, I had felt comfortable and assured enough to relinquish my virginity, which I had been taught to guard with precision. I was sure his ambivalence had to do with me giving it up before marriage.

Smack. "I told you not to use that word with me! I'm not one of them!" As the tears welled up in my eyes, I slapped him back. We held each other and cried for a long while, knowing we weren't about to plan that Atlantis wedding our mothers talked about. When, after six years, the long-awaited marriage proposal didn't come, I was plunged into the depths of depression. I had been groomed for eighteen years in a society that had set times within which to accomplish certain goals. Key among these was marriage. I felt lost.

In hindsight, the absence of a proposal was the best thing that happened to me. I rushed off to study abroad in Haiti, Morocco and Egypt, all within a year of my break-up—places I would never have explored had I gotten married. In all these countries the men adored me because I was the color of "coca-cola." After ten years of going steady, in Morocco I allowed myself the luxury of flirting and basking in all the attention. Amid daily wooing and marriage proposals addressed to my Study Abroad director: "Madame, I give you five-hundred camel for your daughter's hand in marriage!" I came into my own female power. To top it off, there was James; we were the only two graduate assistants on this study abroad trip with twenty-five undergraduates.

"Yoo hoo James! Where are you?"

"In the shower," came his baritone voice.

"Do you need me to hand you your towel?" I had already grabbed it off the towel rack and was inching towards the shower. The chemistry was evident to both of us, and newly liberated, I flirted with pure abandon. He was a white boy. A Midwesterner. Places like Africa and Morocco, were out of his element. Alas, flirting was all he could take.

·

"I'm done with Ghanaian men! Ugh! That's it! Grandmother would rather I marry a white man anyway," I said, referring to my mulatto maternal grandmother. I looked over at my new friend for his response. Bronze skin, curly locks of dark brown hair that was a texture in a class all its own—a mixed-race Afro meets a slightly textured kinky.

"What did you say your name was?"

"I didn't," he replied, smiling so broadly I knew something was up.

"My name is Nana Sei, and I am half Ghanaian," he said "Does that disqualify me?"

Talk about open mouth, insert foot and start chewing. I'm sure my chocolate skin did overtime covering the deep, blushing red that was threatening to change my skin tones. I'd been having such a great time chatting with him until the subject of my latest break-up came up. After my break-up with Boris and the study abroad tours, I had dated about six men in succession, some simultaneously. Within a year, I had a lot of hurt men in my wake.

"It's okay," he said reaching over to squeeze my hands, which were performing multiple wringing motions in my lap. I was mortified, but I managed to survive through to a marriage proposal four years down the line.

When my third marriage proposal came, I jumped at it. The other two proposals had come from men who had met me, professed their love for me almost instantaneously, and then proceeded to ask my mother for my hand, oblivious to what I wanted. This time, Nana Sei and I had known and loved each other through some tough times. Plus, it was time to settle down; after all, I was turning thirty in a couple months and the pressure was building. We had the traditional meeting of families, after which I spent a few days trying to convince myself that this was what I wanted. Then I panicked and took the first flight I could find to the Caribbean, turning off my phone and creating a monster of a man, who lashed out repeatedly.

•

In St. Maarten, I fell in love with an Incredible Hulk who swept me off my feet with his rendition of "You Are My African Queen." He treated me like a queen for the ten days I was there. A fine man, he stood tall at six two, with about two hundred pounds of muscle, and had skin the shade of dark chocolate. In a matter of a fortnight, I had garnered another marriage proposal for my Pandora's Box. I boarded my flight back to the U.S. and signed on to an online dating site, this time in the 'women-seeking-women' section. Four marriage proposals and still single; there was something else calling for attention. I had dated one woman before.

•

Veya and I were each other's firsts. In college we had been more like acquaintances than bosom buddies. That is, until my final year when our friendship blossomed. We had thrown around terms of endearment—babe, wife, honey, darling—that were suggestive of something more than platonic friendship. After grad school, I finally got the guts to kiss her one morning while I was visiting her. It was so different from kissing boys. Something inside me responded. When she kissed me back, I knew I had to explore this other side of me. Things changed when she panicked and decided it had been just an experiment. We returned to men. We got back together and pledged a commitment. She cheated, then worried I might find out, and left in the middle of the night while we were on vacation. Head over heels, I didn't see it coming. She was gorgeous, tall and slender, and had skin crisscrossed with green veins. She was Icelandic. I came out to my mother the day Veya left me. The eventual demise of this trial-and-error first lesbian relationship left me broken hearted for a while, but pushed me to explore my sexuality broadly. So after Nana Sei, after St. Maarten, I logged in confidently to an online dating forum, creating a profile that was eye-catching. If I wasn't going to be married at thirty, I might as well check out this other side of myself.

•

Mika Ana's Profile

I love to meet new people. I love entertaining and cooking for people. I LOVE to travel, I love walking, especially beside water. I am a stickler for words and how they are spelled or used, although as I get older I learn that words are just a medium of communication and don't need to be perfect all the time. I would probably agree when others call me a mild to moderate fashionista. I love reading and writing. I dance, teach African dance, and I'm taking djembe drum lessons. I LOVE spicy foods, and foods from just about any ethnic group; I'll try anything once!

My perfect match would be someone with an identity of their own separate from mine. They would be someone who has a working knowledge (or be willing to learn) of race relations in the US as well as how the intersections of all the social "isms" in the US affect the people who are the most marginalized in our community. Overall, I am looking for: an equal, someone intelligent, who takes care of themselves, someone willing to grow, someone with an enthusiasm for new things, a kind and gentle person who sees the whole world as connected & cherishes that connection.

After reading this, I shut down my profile. I'd found the woman of my dreams and I was moving to join her in New Mexico. She had bought the ring. We'd get married legally in Vermont then drive across country together. After searching and dating for two years, I was ready to settle down. Everyone I'd dated had been white. They all thought my brown skin was so soft, like it defied their imagination of what Black skin was supposed to feel like. I was their token Black girlfriend at all their friends' gatherings. Mika Ana was brown like me. Her family had emigrated from Belize. I'd seen one picture. Her color was like that of peanut brittle. She was witty and had perfect command of the English language. It was a clear match. I was in love. She wanted our first meeting to be so special that we never even exchanged phone numbers. I didn't catch on that she was not real until it was too late.

I learned about internet scams the hard way. The email that rocked my world read:

"Dear Adjo,
On November 20th, my sister, Mika Aya, was killed. A drunk driver was driving at high speed and lost control of the vehicle, hitting the Mika Aya at the crosswalk. She was airlifted to a hospital nearby, but she suffered massive injuries and died shortly after they reached the hospital. I am very sorry. Her sister, Franceska."'

Needless to say, something died in me. I wrote back and forth with this supposed sister for months but eventually the responses I got all seemed to point to the fact that I'd been duped. Mika Ana was a hoax. I never quite figured out the person's motivation. I mourned the relationship for months, but eventually moved on, swearing off internet dating.

•

A couple of years later, I moved to Portland to do my Post Doc, and after a year of not meeting anyone, I decided to go back online. Wary of another hoax, I refused to give my real identity and pressed for a meeting after a few exchanges of emails. Intrigued by a new possibility, Zurra, we met and talked for twelve hours on our first date; we had so much in common. We read to each other in bed, finished lines of poetry for each other. She was a great sous-chef, and we used to churn out elaborate African meals together. Zurra is African, which was a bonus. My relationship with Zurra is still my longest lesbian one in the ten years since I started dating women. Having her in my life has given me the courage to come out to the rest of my nuclear family. Of course, it's taken more than 4 years for most of them to stop asking me about men and marriage. The relationship didn't last for a few reasons, an eating disorder being key among them. For a good portion our time together, I went along with whatever she wanted to do because I wanted it to work so badly.

•

A year after my break-up with Zurra, I decided to visit my mom; I hadn't been home in a while. Mom had visited us in our home twice and had totally fallen in love with Zurra. Wary that my mother would chastise me for causing the break-up, I had stayed away for a while. It was Labor Day weekend, and Newark, New Jersey was teeming with African immigrants. My mother, so proud of her daughter with the PhD, had decided to throw me a barbecue in her backyard. A number of immigrants had gathered to join her.

"Ah Adjo, are der no African men in Portland?" one woman asks.

"Do you not have time in your Post Doc? You must make time o!" another one admonishes.

"The books won't keep you warm at night or take care of you in your old age!"

"You know you aren't getting any younger!"

"Don't let the white people influence your thinking o! We are very different from them; we are Africans."

Sometimes even the men chimed in. Although we are in the Diaspora, anyone older than you must be addressed as 'bra,' 'sista,' 'auntie' or 'uncle,' following the traditions of the Continent. They feel these titles give them the right to weigh in on your life choices, comment on why you are not yet married or why you ought to begin popping out those kids.

"You should at least have a child," says Mom's neighbor, who seems to have now given up on my ever getting married.

"Ah! Don't tell her that!" retorts my biological aunt. Turning to me: "I will fast for your marriage proposal! Next year by this time, we will have your engagement!" she declares, her multiple rolls of midriff fat jiggling; she is probably shuddering at the thought of the fast. I chuckle out loud, forgetting myself and my manners.

"Or you don't want to get married?" she asks in my mother tongue, her use of which indicates her displeasure that I am laughing at such a serious matter. I quickly adjust my face, apologize, and answer in the affirmative. Who am I to tell her that I am not really interested in marriage? That honestly speaking, I can't bear the thought of living the rest of my life attached to a man? That I love my freedom too much to want to settle down with a husband and have some kids? That I couldn't begin to tell her about all the people I've been with and how they have bequeathed me a panoramic view of sexuality? She wouldn't understand. She couldn't fathom such a life. Even though she tried her hand at it, and failed a few times, she still believes marriage is part of the natural fabric of life as an African woman. And we, her offspring, are the ones to prove her right. Just because she, my mom, or for that matter about ninety percent of all the females in my family, have failed multiple times at marriage, doesn't mean that we, their offspring, won't be the success story.

•

Even though the marrying age for women is shifting every day, especially in the Western world, African women are not being encouraged to partake in this luxury of waiting until 'they know themselves, or have attained a certain level of education, or can be a true partner in a relationship, or … fill in the blank. I think those of us who find ourselves in the Diaspora have a duty to the women coming behind us—a duty to define our lives the way we truly feel called to do. The African woman in the Diaspora needs to create a new world order that has a healthy balance of tradition, self-determination and actualization.

Being in the Diaspora means new rules or relaxed old-world-order rules. No matter how hard anyone tries, it is not possible to maintain the old world order, regardless of which country you have immigrated from. Being here makes room for certain flexibility around traditions surrounding marriage, causing the rules to move from tribe-specific to country-specific, then perhaps to compromise with Africa-specific or plain Black-specific. Of course, after a certain age, families might even acquire an 'any-man-will-do-just-so-long-as-you-get-married' attitude. Despite this relaxing of traditions, there is still little room in this paradigm to shirk marriage completely, perform gender differently, or worse yet, be of a different sexual orientation.

I've focused on key partners who have created some turning points in my life; the men and women who have shaped the making of the sexually emancipated Adjo. I am staring the big 4-0 in the face as I write, and even though some of my family is still very concerned, I must say that I have never before felt so liberated. Thanks for coming along on the journey. I hope my story has inspired you to reflect on your own odyssey of sexual emancipation, or the societal pressures that have prevented you from getting there. I hope that whatever your herstory, you will be able to ask the next single woman you meet the question "What makes you tick?" rather than the standard one: "Where is your husband?"

PART FOUR:

FALLING INTO FAMILY

Breadcrumbs

Hope Fitzgerald

In life and love, I have come to depend on breadcrumbs. You know, those little signposts dropped along your path to let you know that you are, indeed, ON a path. And you never know when you're going to reach into a pocket to discover one, and then THAT breadcrumb turns out to be precisely THE one that can lead you out of the woods when it is most needed, especially when trundling down the often humbling, sometimes treacherous path called motherhood. So, here's my breadcrumb story…

It has never been easy, but it's especially hard to have been a "tween" in the last decade… coming of age in an era of confusion and instability can be fraught with dangerous precipices. One can easily fall into the void without even knowing that the cliff existed. Such was the case with My Girl as she entered 8th grade…

The summer leading into it was such a sweet one, with a balance of camp time, barn time, family time, and downtime. My 12-year-old was still very much a girl, with her slender body developing at a slower pace than her peers, and she seemed happy and carefree as she entered her last year of middle school. I secretly wondered if we might squeak through the "awkward years" relatively unscathed. We both basked in that time of delightful, easy sunshine, blissfully unaware of the looming thunderstorm, just out of sight.

One morning, three weeks into school, I noticed some unusual behavior as she got her lunch together.

"Why are you shredding up that one piece of turkey for your sandwich?"

"Um…I don't know" she said, shakily—evasively?

"What's going on? Are you feeling ok?"

"Yes, I'm fine!" (End of discussion)

I looked at her, doing a "mother-scan." Did she look thin? She most definitely looked thin. What on earth… ?

Alert now, my mind raced to put pieces together from the last few weeks—had she eaten every meal fully? Was she rushing to the bathroom after meals? Think!

Not wanting to be a helicopter parent, I had trained myself to become generally non-reactive to the little ups and downs of my kids' growing up process. This is not to say I was neglectful (at least I don't think I was), but I found it easier on the family if I stayed calm and even a tad removed from every single bump and grind. I'm telling you this to explain why I felt I was *emerging into* alarm, carefully measuring my every step in that direction. Was this an over-reactive, worst-case-scenario fear ramping up or a proper, protective, mother-instinct kicking in? Breathe, balance, *observe*...

So, I watched. She couldn't decide what to wear in the morning and complained about her clothing options. Her emotions ran from high to low, increasingly low, and my typically talkative girl became suddenly sullen. The usual pre-teen transition stuff. But she was most certainly avoiding food and started having trouble sleeping. Perhaps her behavior had aspects of "normal," but this eating thing was just so abrupt...

After a few days, the dead weight of acceptance landed, telling me that we were indeed in a crisis, and I did what any mom would do—I sprang into action. I found her a therapist, arranged for more time at the horse barn, alerted the school, and devoured *Reviving Ophelia: Saving the Selves of Adolescent Girls* by Mary Pipher.

And we descended into hell.

Even though I had caught My Girl's anorexia early on, it was on a track and timetable all its own, over which I had no control. I never knew what would happen in the next two minutes with her state of mind, so consequently I was plugged into a constant state of alert. She would swing from frozen silence to increasingly bizarre behaviors, not just about food. At times, I literally could not understand the language that blasted from her mouth, although two words did emerge repeatedly: "The Pressure."

From my reading, I came to understand what I had felt on an intuitive level—that this world offered both too much and too little for these girls. Without enough solid female role models in society (think Gloria Steinem, Sandra Day O'Connor, even Billie Jean King), they were bombarded with The Pressure *to look* and *be* a certain air-brushed way. In fact, this "beyond Barbie" iconography was woven into every aspect of their young lives, reaching them regardless of avoidance of TV, films and even the grocery check-out line. It was just THERE, in the air, and many children were suffering from it.

Not that it left me off the hook of responsibility. I had done my best to let My Girl know she was smart, capable and pretty. I didn't speak negatively about my body image and tried to model a balanced femininity. Nevertheless, I was tortured, wondering how I may have blindly failed her. My books said that this is how girls die slowly if they can't bring themselves to do it quickly, and she was already so thin. I was scrambling on a terrifying, topsy-turvy roller coaster and, despite the support of others, I felt largely alone.

One night, we reached a decibel in my car that brought me face to face with a new perception: My Girl was as lost in this as I was. In fact, I was not dealing with her so much as I was dealing with a kind of monster that had invaded her vulnerable being to prey, and stay. Aha! My feet regained steady footing as my bewilderment faded away. Now it was not a struggle with My Girl so much as an outright battle *royale* with this opportunistic Monster.

Now that I saw The Thing, I plotted my path to outsmart it. I learned its language and wily ways, and dropped landmines for it to skirt around. I spoke in one way to My Girl and in another way to It. As It strived to drink the life force from my daughter through her starvation, I sought to starve The Thing itself. I know this sounds dramatic, but it really felt as if I was in the trenches of an epic, hand-to-hand battle with this hideous beast.

Six months passed and my war with The Monster was holding a shaky steadiness, neither of us winning or losing too much ground—a victory of sorts, I guess. I had come to believe that a social element at school was a contributing factor in our story. I did my best to communicate our needs without asking for too much from the school or the other parents, whose children were also struggling. I was in a constricting position. Aside from war with The Monster, I didn't know what else to do, only that I could not give up.

One night, I bolted awake at 3 a.m. with an idea—*knowing* down to my bones. My conventional self tried to argue with the plan, but my intuition knew better and won out, even in the light of the new day. And this is where the precious bread crumb come in…

A year earlier, I had gone to visit my dear friend and (My Girl's godmother) on the set of her TV show. As her wonderful hairdresser was finishing her "do," he mentioned a road trip he had taken with his 16-year-old daughter a month before he was to be remarried in Hawaii. Out came a scrapbook of their journey that began in LA with a recalcitrant daughter who refused to speak to him. (She was not in favor of his remarriage.) He told her they were just going to keep driving north until they worked it out. In San Francisco, she muttered something. They drove on. Mendocino—a sentence. Portland, Seattle… Alaska. Three weeks later and two days before the wedding, he and *his* girl flew from Anchorage to Hawaii, and he happily entered his new life with a renewed father/daughter relationship. The breadcrumb in my pocket from the hairdresser was the permission for *me* to think innovatively. Maybe My Girl and I needed a "drive-about" with no particular destination in mind so we could just detach from the environment that the Monster was thriving in . . . ?

Knowing something and doing something are not the same thing. That very morning I walked into the head of school's office and stated my intention.

"I'm removing my daughter from school for an undetermined length of time and need some homework and access to teachers in our absence."

I may have sounded confident, but I wasn't. This non-plan plan was the thread of a promise that I was hanging onto for dear life. For both of our lives. And it sounded kinda nuts, even to me. Fortunately, the school was supportive.

However, My Girl was a bit thrown.

"What about school? Where are we going?"

"Well, we could head south where it's already spring," I suggested.

The wary Monster weighed the options while My Girl let out a flicker of a smile, tempted by warmer places.

"Okaaayyy… "

And that was that—our gamble was on. We threw our bags into the Honda Pilot and drove to my cousin in Hershey, PA. After one overnight and a tour of the chocolate factory, we started south on

Rt 81. Although still on high alert, I realized as we drove how free *I* was beginning to feel; free from norms, free from expectations, free from "The Pressure."

In the midst of a freed-up state of mind, there's much more room for epiphanies, and I had several while we drove. During the long periods of silence, I realized that this child had a rhythm that was much slower than the rest of the family. We were ever-ready, speedy bunnies, hopping around with quick banter, instantaneous decisions, and constant conversation interruptions. She, on the other hand, was more quiet, moved slowly, and took her time deliberating, even if it was over which ice cream flavor she wanted. This is not to say she was slow of mind—definitely not—but she had a pace that, I was crushed to admit, probably got her mowed over quite a bit in our household.

I also remembered that at each age, she had longed to go back to an earlier time in her life, and it occurred to me, as we barreled down the highway, that everything was just moving too darned fast for her. So, I literally took my foot off the gas and slowed down to match both the highway's speed limit and My Girl's.

I told her we would stop, eat and explore on her timeline. I handed her the Hampton Inn directory and told My Shy Girl how to call and make reservations. She was in charge, and everything would happen when and where she chose. Although I was driving, I was a passenger.

"But, where are we going?"

"I don't know."

By Virginia, My Girl had booked us a room at a Hampton Inn with a swimming pool. Our highway exit revealed a rural landscape, except for a Walmart, a diner and our trusty Hampton Inn. After a quick stop to buy bathing suits, we made a beeline for the pool. In she went, my little fish, and soon she was splashing, twirling, leaping, sliding, and bobbing. She looked like a dolphin that had finally been set free. I watched tearfully as I saw My Girl, *my real girl*, for the first time in many months. On that whiff of chlorine came the promise: "She's still in there..."

Our road trip lasted 3 weeks, covered 2,800 miles, and was filled with a daily dance of uncertainty coupled with happy surprises for both of us. Nightly swims in various pools encouraged My Girl to wriggle free from the grip of The Monster. By the time we were northbound, I beamed while listening to the light banter of her long, cheery phone call with a friend, something that would not have been possible only three weeks before. Though it would be a while before The Monster was completely defeated, that trip was the beginning of Its demise.

I can tell this story now because it has a happy ending, and because My Girl has graciously allowed me to tell it in the hopes that it will be useful to others. As her biased mother, I can say that now my girl is a beautiful, healthy, intelligent, capable, extremely sensitive young woman, who is productive and confident at college, and is able to juggle life both in the slow and fast lanes. I am immensely proud of her and grateful that she taught me, among other things, how to be more aware and adaptive to others, and that slowing down myself was really a good thing.

I make little mention of my husband, family, friends and others who greatly supported My Girl and me, without whom I don't know where we would be. I am forever deeply grateful for their wisdom and tenacity in helping us to survive. But I was asked to write this story about the mother's journey, so that is my perspective here.

I learned that acquiescing to a void called "I don't know" is not only OK, it also allowed me and my girl to give ourselves the right to create our own rules, making them up as we went along. That bread-crumb of 'permission to innovate' was a godsend to us, and now I happily pass it along to you to place in your pocket, should you ever need it.

Kind Thoughts

Rosemary Starace

All my girls grew up to be weeds.
There's the tall one strolling through grass,

she skirts the trees and flirts with sun.
And the one who never leaves the yard,

she studies the bees with her sharp blue eyes.
And the one named *rose*—they tried to offer her bouquets.

She roams along the seashore and the forest's edge,
spending her petals on the chance to be enough.

Of Royal Blood

Hester Velmans

The day I learned my Oma was a pretender to the throne of Newfoundland, it was raining inconsolably. There were rows of dripping black bikes parked in parallel racks in front of the re creation complex across the street, but the street itself was deserted. The raindrops seeping into the raw concrete of the balcony walls like grubby thumbprints were a particularly depressing sight. I longed to get away from the old-people smells and prickly sisal carpeting of my grandparents' fifties-modern Amsterdam apartment. I wanted to feel the slippery grass of my backyard, and slide down my favorite dune.

When I was little, whenever my parents had business in Amsterdam they would drop me off at Oma and Opa's on their way into the city. My grandparents lived on Edison Street in the new "South" quarter of boxy, post-war flats. The afternoons were long, unexciting and squirmy in the windowed apartment that I thought of as a fish tank, except that there weren't any fish. As in most Dutch homes, the curtains were never drawn. You could stand at the bedroom window and stare right into several identical rooms across the street, differentiated only by the plants on the windowsill. Some had showy window boxes overflowing with flowering annuals; others hid behind a downpour of shaggy green camouflage. Oma's plants were spiky, exotic, and sharp, including a beloved aspidistra, some cacti and many other kinds of barbed succulents. If you touched them, they left minuscule splinters in your fingertips that had to be removed with the same tweezers Oma used for removing the gauze from her poor, tender bunions.

How the bunions fascinated me, those bony outcroppings that projected from her feet like wings! I don't remember all that much about the rest of her; it is my grandmother's feet that bring her into focus. From my vantage point, rolling around bored out of my mind on the itchy sisal carpet, those two misshapen feet were the most prominent feature in the landscape. This was probably because in her dealings with me, Oma imbued her bunions with anxious significance, since they caused excruciating pain if jumped or stepped on by accident, which—unavoidably—happened occasionally.

Oma's feet needed lots of attention—compresses, soaking salts, and periodic applications of Campho-phenique. The bunions were so prominent that they required custom-made shoes to be built around them. There were half a dozen pairs of these beaked shoes lined up neatly along the bottom of Oma's wardrobe, each one bulging with a specially made wooden stretcher. The shoes and stretchers were the work of a Mr. de Hoorn, in his workshop in the Laressenstraat. According to Oma, Mr. de Hoorn was an angel, a savior, a genius: the most skilled cobbler and prosthesis maker in the world.

My parents often laughed about the things Oma said, but only when we were in the car driving home. They said she was really a wonderfully optimistic person, considering she had lost so much in the war—her home, her possessions, her family. My parents also thought it was too bad Oma never picked up the newspaper or a book, which might give her something worth talking about. They weren't even a little bit excited when Oma and Opa became the first people we knew to own a television. As for Oma's cooking, it was a riot. Oma proudly told us about the time she'd grabbed a can from the larder and poured it over Opa's spaghetti, only to realize it wasn't tomato sauce but an orange drink. Opa had declared it delicious.

Oma had lots of stories that made me laugh, although I had heard most of them before. "Tell me about when you were little," I begged, slipping onto her lap as I usually did to avoid the rough scrape of the orange upholstery. I tried to sit still and not bang my heels into her shins.

"Well," said Oma, "When I was little, Father, who was very strict, liked to hear my sisters sing, especially when there was company."

"But you weren't allowed to sing!" I crowed.

"No. Father would say, 'Hanna, stand in the back, behind your sisters! Keep your mouth shut!' He thought I ruined it. And I loved to sing!"

I giggled. It was true that Oma's voice was as off-key and as painfully quavery as her crooked feet. "So what did you do, Oma?" I asked mischievously

"One time, I started singing anyway, because I loved that song. Father was furious! I was sent to bed without any supper." To my wicked delight she drooped her shoulders dejectedly, as if it had happened yesterday.

The other story I craved to hear over and over was what happened when the Germans invaded our country. My Papa, just a teenager then, had cycled to the harbor at Scheveningen to try and get away. When he got there he sent a message to Oma and Opa: he and some other boys had "borrowed" a coast guard boat, and they were going to escape to England! Papa had given a stranger his bike, saying it was his to keep if he delivered the message. The fact that the boy had kept his word and delivered the message in the chaos of that terrible day was yet another of the miracles proving there was a God, according to Oma.

"And what did you do when you got Papa's note, Oma?" I demanded.

"I stood up," said Oma, pushing me off her lap sideways so that she could show me, "—we were all sitting around the dining-room table wringing our hands—and I said: 'Where my son goes, I go too.'"

"And then they said...." I prompted her.

"And then they said, 'Where Hanna goes, we go too!' And so we jumped into a taxi and we found your father at the docks—imagine, with all the crowds and all the panic! There was no more room in the boat, but your Papa shouted, 'We've got to let them come, it's my family!' The motor kept cutting out—we saw Rotterdam burning—there were warplanes overhead—oh, oh, oh..." Oma slapped her cheeks, wagging her head from side to side in a puppet-show reenactment of consternation.

"The mines!" I reminded her sternly.

"We drifted over a minefield," she continued obediently. "And the tides would have swept us out into the Atlantic Ocean, we'd never have reached England, but we didn't know that, Treasure, we were picked up by a British destroyer, and that's when the captain told your father and his friends about the tides..."

"And you just left *everything* behind!" I sighed. Some day, I was sure, I would be called on to do something heroic. I hoped I would rise to the occasion as nobly as Oma had.

"We just left everything, the dishes on the table, we didn't even do the washing up, imagine!"

I shuddered with delight, imagining the look on the Nazis' faces when confronted with all those dirty dishes.

"And Opa took the wrong suitcase?"

She nodded ruefully. "When we got to England, we opened the suitcase and instead of Opa's important papers, it was full of clothes hangers."

When they were over, Oma's stories always left me vaguely dissatisfied, as if she must have left out the best parts. I felt my insides filling up with dangerous boredom again. I had already spent a good part of the morning poring over the pictures on the dresser—cheerful snapshots of our family, fading brown photos of solemn relatives Lost in the War, and framed photographs of Queen Juliana, her husband Prince Bernhard, and the four little princesses, Beatrix, Irene, Margriet and Christina. The princesses all had blunt, short straight hair just like mine, clipped to the side with a barrette. One of them was cross-eyed and wore glasses. I sighed. I thought princesses were supposed to have long flowing curls and tiaras.

"Come, darling." Oma was rattling her keys. My grandmother carried a heavy bunch of shiny keys, like any queen of the castle would. Even the little liquor cabinet in the bookcase was kept locked, though Opa was not, to anyone's knowledge, a tippler, and visitors were few and far between. "Come help Oma look for a nail file."

I sat up. Oma was headed for the green lacquered kast in her bedroom. I knew presents were stored in there, and, seeing that Oma was the forgetful sort, there was always the hope of an over-looked birthday gift.

I watched as Oma solemnly turned the little silver key in the lock. I dragged a chair over to stand on so I could have a better look. The wardrobe reeked of Eau de Cologne and camphor. Oma kept all her medicines and the week's spending money under lock and key in that wardrobe. There were also bits and pieces of jewelry, although Oma always kept her two "best" brooches, the gold one shaped like a bow and the circle with the pearls, pinned firmly to the strap of her slip, because "you never know." Oma let me sort through a whole shelf of little boxes filled with womanly things like hairpins and hairnets, lipsticks and soaps.

"But *why* do you have so much soap, Oma?" I wheedled. I knew soap would make Oma think of Camp. Oma, in her flight from the Nazis, had landed halfway round the world in the Dutch East Indies, and there the Japanese had made her go to Camp. (When I was old enough, my parents had promised me they'd send me to camp, too. Only I knew it was a better sort of camp than Oma's. And Mrs. Zwarts' camp had been even worse. Mrs. Zwarts lived upstairs. Her tissue paper-like arm had some smudged blue numbers tattooed on it, but you weren't supposed to point.)

The worst thing about Camp was *not* that she had been separated from Opa, *not* the bad food ("Watery rice, Treasure, oh, even a plain boiled potato would have been a treat!"); not even that her lovely hair had gone white overnight; no, the *absolute worst* thing was that they hadn't had any soap. Imagine, hundreds of women sweating it out in the sweltering heat, and not one bar of soap between them!

Well, now she had plenty of soap—luscious cakes so yummy looking you were tempted to take a bite out of them. There were bottles of Eau de Cologne too, which Oma splashed on liberally to cool her neck, and jars of Elizabeth Arden products neatly stored in their original cardboard boxes. Oma spoke of Elizabeth Arden with the same reverence with which she referred to Mr. de Hoorn the shoemaker. I always assumed that Elizabeth Arden was a personal friend of hers.

At the top of the wardrobe was a shelf for hatboxes. My grandmother had been chief millinery buyer for *De Bijenkorf*, Amsterdam's largest department store, and she never went out without a cloche, fedora, or beret firmly clamped to her head. She taught me that a hat should always be worn at a jaunty angle, the more askew the better. Today she let me rummage through a box of trimmings—a heavenly collection of voile, velvety feathers, silk flowers, and hatpins.

"What's this, Oma!" I breathed, holding up a glittery circlet. It was perfect, except for a few missing rhinestones.

"Oh that!" Oma smiled. "We used to wear these over our hair, like this, see? When I was a young girl." She pulled the headband low over her brow.

"It's a diamond tiara!" I corrected her, snatching it off her thinning hair and crowning my own head with it.

"Fit for a princess!" Oma agreed, clapping her hands together. "But I *am* a princess, Treasure. Didn't I ever tell you the story?"

"*You're* a princess?" This was the first I had heard of it. If I were a princess, I would make sure everyone knew.

"I am."

I was a little skeptical. I didn't think you could be a princess at Oma's age. Nor, come to think of it, did princesses have any bunions.

But when Oma first heard she was a pretender to the throne of Newfoundland, she hadn't yet grown any bunions. She was still horning her toes into the pointy little pumps she now blamed for her deformity. At any rate, when she first heard the great news that she was a princess, she clapped her hands and patted her wobbly cheeks, as she was doing now, exclaiming, "Oh! Oh! Oh!" And then Oma danced around the piano with her sisters.

I frowned, trying to conjure up a vision of my Oma in lace pantaloons, her hair tied in a floppy bow, grabbing her sisters' hands and spurring them into the heavy-footed, bow-legged dance she often performed with me with the blandishment, "Careful, Treasure... my toes!"

I jumped down off my chair and improvised, in dance, my own version of Oma's elation.

"Ah, careful, Treasure... *ahhh!*"

Oma continued after recovering from an inadvertent collision with the bunions. She sat in the parlor, sipping tea and politely poking at one of the cream cakes Trudie, the maid, had been sent to fetch from the bakery. A distant relative had come to show Oma's father a document he had discovered deeding Newfoundland to an ancestor of ours, a Portuguese sea captain named Joseph de la Penha, who had discovered Labrador in the sixteen hundreds.

King William and Queen Mary had given him Newfoundland as a reward. But Joseph had never gone back to claim his prize.

Well! Newfoundland does come across as a tiny blob next to the vast patchwork expanses of North America, and Oma was at first a little disappointed, as any princess might be when her domain turns out to be just a scrawny backwater. But her father showed her, by flipping the pages of the atlas back to a map of Europe, that Newfoundland covered significantly more territory than the twelve provinces of the Netherlands combined.

Bigger than Holland! Even I was impressed. This arguably made my grandmother a more important royal than our own queen. And Juliana couldn't even count any real cowboys and Indians among her subjects. North America, I knew, was crawling with them.

"So what happened then, Oma?" I asked, jumping onto the bed on both knees. "Were you suddenly *awfully* rich?"

Oma crumpled her face. "Father and the other relatives who joined in the lawsuit were laughed out of court. It was much too late to stake a claim, naturally."

"So then who's the king of Newfoundland?"

"I don't think they have one."

"But they *need* a royal family," I pointed out, doing a graceful arabesque, high up on the bed.

"Never mind. It's part of Canada now. We wouldn't want to live there anyway. It's a cold and windy place, Treasure."

"Oh," I said, sinking into a gloomy plié.

"Well, maybe someday we'll try again," Oma said, giving my knees a squeeze. "But we're still princesses, you and I, no matter what!"

I laughed. Suddenly I felt unreasonably happy.

When my parents walked in on us late that giggly afternoon, we were two magnificent monarchs, our heads gloriously bedecked in dark velour adorned with trailing ostrich feathers, rhinestone pins and grape clusters, stomping around (being careful of the bunions) in a frenzied dance. The radio was playing Oma's favorite Edith Piaf song, and we were belting it out at the top of our lungs, "...*mais vous pleurrrez, Milorrd, ça, j'n'aurrrais jamais crru...* "

I caught the look exchanged by my parents.

I stopped singing, and let go of Oma's hands. I dragged the princess hat off my head and started plucking at the feathers.

Oma clomped around for a few more turns, defiantly, before waltzing over to the radio, humming off-key, to turn it off.

"Mother..." said my father, shaking his head.

"What? We were having fun!" said Oma. "Weren't we, your majesty?" she asked me, cackling.

I kept my head down, stunned by the streamlined elegance of Mama's feet in soft blue leather.

"Well!" said Mama, twisting her hair into a knot in her neck. "Time to go. Kiss your grandmother goodbye, Darling."

"Bye, Oma," I mumbled perfunctorily into Oma's damp dress.

The adults exchanged a few more words. In the patient tone I recognized as the same one they used with me, my parents were telling Oma that it would be two, maybe even three weeks before we came again. They said they knew Oma would understand that was the way it was in these busy, busy times.

Fading Into Love:
Dear Audrey

Carole Fults

Your mind has entered night time
deep and mysterious with only one or two bright stars
or flashes of light here and there.
The more brilliant beacons of moon and sun have burned out
or moved into total eclipse from which they won't return
leaving only dimmer stars to illuminate your world.
You're returning to the incomprehensible void that awaits all of us
when we cross into the ending time of our lives.
But still you remember love, and, really maybe love is what you
    are and therefore
is no effort to recall.
Your rumpled, mismatched thoughts are reflected
in your clothing and uncombed hair.
Your forgetfulness and confused thinking are compounded
by the withdrawal of your hearing and eyesight.
Yet I know who you are in there.
I remember your keen mind and insights, but maybe feeling and
    not coherent thought defines who you really are now.
Maybe your Being doesn't depend on thought at all.
Maybe Love is your only definition
Maybe that is the beautiful truth of you.

Roots, Stems and Branches: A Recollection

Linda Kaye-Moses

In this sorting, this re-collecting of the roots of my work, it feels natural to speak of those who came before, whose lives surrounded and encouraged me, before I knew to recognize it as encouragement, though there were times when it seemed most transparent and the message scrambled. This is my inheritance, my lineage, my ancestral companions in art, my 'begat.' If, in fact, I am mostly the sum of my ancestors, here are some of those whose sum I am.

My mother's father, Aaron, a Russian/Polish Jew who emigrated with his parents and siblings in the 1880's, went to the Klondike with his father when he was sixteen, seeking gold, invested in furs and, having survived the winters, mosquitoes, black flies, other miners and the eggs he sold to make money in Alaska, returned to New York, married and became a clever (and therefore, successful) merchant. He bought sculptures and paintings that, to this day, decorate the store he owned. He was an amateur violinist and pianist who wrote music and songs. His poetry and short stories were self-published in volumes given away to the customers of his store. He encouraged all seven of his children to play instruments and to participate in the literary arts. He was a wonderful teller of tales who was able to entrance his grandchildren even into their teenage years. His eldest daughter, Marion, wrote, transcribed and recorded over thirty lullabies for her son and, as a result, everyone in the family sang these songs out loud for years after they had left their cribs behind. My own children went to sleep each night hearing me sing to them the songs my aunt had written. Marion's son, in turn, became a commercial and art photographer.

My Uncle Michael wrote poetry and played guitar. He loved an audience and would gather all his siblings, his children and his nieces and nephews together and perform folk music on the guitar until it was time for us to be gathered up and stuffed into cars for our trip home, still singing of "Molly Malone's fair city." As we grew older, he shared his poetry with those of us who would listen. One of Michael's sons, Carl, played guitar, and years later, performed in coffee houses in New York City. My Aunt Violet (of the jewels and baubles fame) designed and sewed doll's fashion collections for her three nieces, complete with the obligatory wedding dress, veil and bouquet. One of Uncle Dan's grandsons has become a well-known book designer.

On my father's side of the family, Great Aunt Ann designed greeting cards and taught me to draw, among other things, beautiful cornucopia, replete with fruits and vegetables tumbling forever. Grandma Helen Anker was a seamstress who spoke three languages: English, Yiddish and German. When I was sick and had to stay in bed, her afghans surrounded me with random colors and patterns. I spent the hours when I was awake tracking the combinations of colors and trying to find my way through to her plan. I was never bored as there were never two crocheted squares in any of her afghans that were matched color for color. My earliest experiences with color and pattern came from being comfortingly swathed in them. Aunt Alfreda, Helen's daughter, was an incorrigible collector of small parts: beads, nuts and bolts, wooden items useful for building models, yarn, buttons, dried flowers, stones, shells. Even though her obsession was primarily with collecting, she did not stop at that, but went the distance to assemblage and display.

I list all of the above creative relatives and their modes of expressing their creativity, not to broadcast the wonder of it all, though I do feel that mine was a wonderfully creative family, but to emphasize the mostly unspoken encouragement, acceptance, expectation and validation of the urge to create. I was fortunate to have been given permission to bring, from disparate and separate parts, living, vibrating, coherent forms with which to make Art.

My mother, Leonora, though encouraged by the same father as her siblings, was mostly unfulfilled in her creative urges. She often expressed a desire to paint, but was tentative and unsatisfied in her attempts, almost embarrassed by this urge and always insistent on her lack of ability. She could play the piano beautifully, but would never play for others, only for herself, so certain was she that her music would be unappreciated. Somewhere in her life she accepted a personal prohibition against taking the risk of creative endeavor and acknowledging the validity of her own attempts. However, Mom invented marvelous bedtime stories that carried me away, softening the edges of the day and carrying me to where imagination reigns.

She did possess one especially remarkable creative skill, one that surpassed even her lovely piano playing and her storytelling. It was a talent that has never been recognized by galleries or museums, but which nonetheless inspired me and encouraged me to unleash my own creativity. She could doodle! The word 'doodle,' connotatively demeans an art form that is rarely appreciated. My mother's doodles should have been displayed in gilded frames. She elevated the common doodle beyond the level of casual scrawls. Her drawings convinced me of the power of the drawing pencil, of the solace to be found in allowing one's mind and hand and pencil to wander without conscious direction and to build form upon form upon form until a page is filled with astonishing marvels. The shame is that she did not respect this wondrous art and that neither of us saved a single piece of it.

Since Mom did not value her art form or her exercise of it, she did not trust Art to be a field that could seriously support, either psychologically or financially. She didn't trust her own thrusts into art, did not pursue her own artistic impulses, and, having lived through the Great Depression, was, perhaps, terrified of doing anything she perceived would not bring her obvious economic stability. Art lost in her personal battle, and it was a battle she had to fight all over again when I suggested that I wanted to study Art when I went to college.

When Mom died, I had to sort through all her papers and found that she had saved my artwork; the highlights of almost everything I had done all my life. She was impressed with my forays into the Arts. From earliest attempts to teenage years, my life in Art was salvaged and stored in a large cardboard box beneath the frame of her bed. My mother loved my artwork and praised it, displayed and treasured it. She saved very little of my other work, school papers, etc., and no report cards, although I was a strong student. She delighted in my studying piano and fostered my investigation of my own creativity.

However, she succumbed to her own fears about the relationship between Art and survival and, as I grew older, withdrew her support from my creativity. I inherited her fears, absorbing them as my own. When I was making decisions about where to go to college, my mother repeated a phrase that so many artists have heard it has almost become the mantra of mothers of hopeful artists. If you have ever been such a mother, or if you have ever had the hope of pursuing your Art, you will recognize this admonition: "Go to school and get a degree in... (Fill in the blank with any career other than Art) and then you can 'do' your art as a hobby." That advice displays a dread of the devotion needed to be successful in the Arts. This focus is made difficult, if not impossible, while engaged in another full-time career (Charles Ives, among a few others, notwithstanding). Although I loved making Art, I was very close to my mother, and her fears, expressed with determination and unflagging logic, entered my heart and mind. I went to college and became, for a time, an adequate, though discontented, Speech Therapist.

Seventeenth Summer

Susan Wozniak

Books open doors to the future, but also to the past. Today, for some reason, I remembered a book I read 50 years ago: Maureen Daly's *Seventeenth Summer*. My mother, the editor of my life, had picked it out for me when I was still in high school. I think that when she offered *Seventeenth Summer* she thought I would like it because it is about a girl who goes to college, as I was intending to do. "But don't let it give you ideas," she said as she left my room.

Books were always a minor issue between my mother and me. At the end of 6th grade, I had tested as reading on the college level. Although she was an avid reader who took us to the library every week, unsupervised reading made her nervous. When I asked her to borrow books for me from the adult reading room, she refused, first of all because it was lying and secondly because the books might give me "ideas." Did she realize that *Seventeenth Summer* was about first love? If I surprised myself this morning by remembering that book, she surprised me then by championing the story of a girl who chooses college over a suitor.

By junior year of high school, when college decisions are made, I assumed that I would apply to my local state school, the University of Michigan. Would Michigan take me? Where else should I apply? I was a student at a small Catholic high school. Academically, the school was strong. Socially, it was backward, which was fine with me, as I was a goody two-shoes with too much common sense. I never came to school with hickeys because I never dated. Although I was invited to "T-town," as Toledo, Ohio was known, to drink "3-2 beer," I never went. Travel 60 miles with a neophyte driver, inexperienced drinker, at the wheel? It sounded like a recipe for an accident, although no one I knew was ever hurt on those runs. Instead, I wrote for the school paper, sang in the glee club, was active in the drama society and entered the state-wide science fair. I was academically prepared for a Big Ten school, but how would I function socially?

During my junior year my parents accompanied me to College Night. My father was a tool-and-die grinder, but under better circumstances he might have been an engineer or a math teacher. Forced to leave school in the 8th grade because his parents were divorced, his mother was partially paralyzed with multiple sclerosis and his father was alcoholic, he was bitter. My mother was the first person in her family to graduate from high school, following the commercial course because the film *Kitty Foyle* had inspired her to become a secretary. The War intervened and she worked in a defense plant instead.

If they were uncomfortable at College Night, they hid it well. Of course, the University of Michigan was not represented because Catholic high schools disapproved of large, state universities. As we sat through presentations by Catholic girls' colleges, my life took a turn. I was impressed by one in particular, an urban school, located in Detroit, at the intersection of the wealthy Catholic and the wealthy Protestant neighborhoods, the center for the city's power elite. The mayor and the chief of police were neighborhood residents. The college, founded in the 1920s, was respected by Catholics across the country, and I was drawn in by a single sentence spoken by the director of admissions: a girl can be a leader at a women's college. My mother always had issues about my clothes and my appearance. To her, I was homely, an opinion she expressed three or four times a year, always in the most painful way possible. "Make up is for pretty girls. It makes you look like a clown." "You had better develop your personality, because no man will love you for your looks." After the college open house, my intelligence also became an issue, although there had been some foreshadowing following my first high school report card. With four B's and one A, I had just made the honor roll but, to my mother, it was a "horrible report card." She refused to sign it for two days because she was "embarrassed," but relented in time to return it to the school.

Then there was the half-hour while we waited for the Mackinaw Island ferry next to archaeologists digging at the site of Fort Michilimackinac. "I wonder if they're real archaeologists or just actors," my mother said. I tried to frame an answer about the cost of hiring actors when she exploded. I had wanted to be an archaeologist. After years of having been encouraged to study history and science, her rant surprised me. "I have one daughter and she wants to dig in the dirt. I will have to buy her a shovel for Christmas." Several months later, she came into my room and asked whether I had considered becoming a lawyer. "Your father would have made a good lawyer. He loves to talk. You need to make up for the chance he never had." Still later, she told me that I could not apply to the University of Michigan unless I intended to commute. "I am not going to pay twice for you to live." Again, I tried to respond but knew that no answer would be acceptable. I had no car. I had no driver's license because my mother forbade me to take driver's training because I would be "a terrible driver." How was I to travel the 40 miles from home to Ann Arbor, twice a day, five days a week?

I had considered applying to Radcliffe, a stretch for a blue collar girl from Detroit, but what if I had been accepted? Even if I could have put together the necessary scholarships and grants, I had no doubt my parents would have prevented me from going. I decided to save myself the application fee and the time writing an essay would take. By then, I was convinced that I was stupid and that only a Catholic college would take me, but only because I had 12 years of Catholic education. In the end, I applied to just one school, the woman's college. I was accepted. I received a one-year competitive scholarship. Good. I could go to college for a year. A month later, I received a renewable scholarship and that is when the trouble began.

The day the scholarship was awarded, I heard a noise in the kitchen of our five-room house. When I ran downstairs, I found my mother on the floor, my father standing over her with both fists clenched. He stopped speaking to the family that day. The house was largely silent for nearly six months.

School would not begin until October. I used the money I earned from my summer job to buy clothes: a burgundy A-line skirt with a matching wool cardigan, and a hunter green, sheath skirt, also with a matching cardigan. The skirts were $6 each, and my mother reprimanded me for spending so much money. She went to the S. S. Kresge store and bought me two corduroy jumpers, one black, the other kelly green. She paid a dollar for each. I also bought smart, brown loafers and a small, brown shoulder bag at Michigan's luxury department store, Jacobson's. The cost of the loafers, $15, horrified my mother, but she loved the blue herringbone Chesterfield I bought at Best & Co., and never asked the price. I found a local hairdresser who could cut the classic Vidal Sassoon five-point haircut.

In late August, a letter arrived from my college discussing the annual religious retreat, a requirement for graduation. The school suggested freshmen make their retreat before classes began in order to start the school year with friends. As the Vatican II reforms were still new, this was to be an open retreat. The priest who directed it was a man in his mid-forties, who was neither fawningly hip nor "uptight" in his approach. That night, I waited to make my confession until after the others had spoken to him.

"I'm not here to confess," I began. "I'm here to talk about my father." And then I told him my story.

"Your father is frightened," he said. "It's hard for some parents to see their children surpass them."

"But shouldn't he be happy that I am in college on scholarship? He always told us, 'Get an education so you won't have to bust your buns like I did.'"

"He probably never thought you would take him up on his challenge. He is a frightened, frightened man."

When classes started, I was nervous every day, not about the classes, but about what I would find when I returned home. I felt compelled to speak to my parents. I remember sitting on the arm of the sofa, trembling as I described what happened each day, wearing the skirts and loafers my mother disapproved of, sometimes shaking my closely cropped head.

November brought Dad-Daughter Night, a dinner dance meant to welcome fathers to our women's college. I did not want to go. I did not want to speak to my father about it at all because I was frightened of his Gothic moods. I told me mother, who thought my father might actually like the event. I spoke to him as he sat on the sofa behind the evening paper. He nodded.

Surprisingly, my father always thought of himself as a liberal. "I'm the guy who eats lunch with the Blacks and the Jews," he'd say. At the dance, I left him for a bit to talk to one of my new friends. When I sought him out, he was talking to a tall Black man with a radiant smile. I had met his daughter just once; she was a shy and serious math major who lived in the dorms. Students tended to gather together by majors, and there was a divide between resident and commuter students, generally based on money. I did, however, know her name. Her father was a letter carrier who delivered mail to my father's place of employment. They had talked together for several years but never mentioned their children. My dad was relieved to learn that someone he considered to be "a regular guy" sent his daughter to a school with a snooty reputation. That night, the silence between us finally ended.

This evening, I read several reviews of *Seventeenth Summer* online. Most young women find Angie, Daly's protagonist, stuffy and cold. They write that they know nothing about her and that her life is dull and uneventful. How eventful is anyone's life? Aren't all lives filled with "quiet desperation?" As for Angie, consider that she went to college at a time when parents didn't tell their children to go to school, a time when some girls faced violence or were forced to leave home because they opted for higher education. I know, because those ideas, those behavior patterns were still in place when I began college more than 20 years after the book was published in 1942. For myself, I admire Angie because she made a choice without giving in to anyone. Angie is a better and stronger woman than I was.

What Do You Mean Ken's Pants Zip Up the Front?

Ellen Bliss

Nobody struggles with the meaning of masculinity more than a lesbian. I should know, I come from a long line of lesbians. Literally, this may not be true, but let's face it, once you have one lesbian relative, the "aunts" come crashing in like brides-to-be at Filene's annual basement sale. You've got the current lesbian lover, the former lesbian lover, the lesbian's other lover, and her ex-lovers. You've got the lesbian friends of lovers, not to mention the honest to goodness sisters of the lovers (lesbian or not). And the queens, well, they're a whole other story.

So, I had a lot of "aunts" growing up. This was good, because I was an only child being raised by a single mother, and we didn't have many actual relatives; it was also bad, because they did kind of seem to come and go. Also bad because I didn't really have a clue about what was going on until I was in my mid-twenties. I didn't think it was unusual to call all my mother's female friends "aunt." I also didn't notice that a lot of them dressed like men. At eight years old, I thought Ken's pants zipped up the back. What did I know? What did I care?

If Chaz Bono and Donald Trump had a love child, her name would be Aunt Shirley. Aunt Shirl was a sturdy, robust woman, perhaps even burly. She had golden hair that swooped around in the most feminine masculine quiff that was possible in 1964. She was smart, she was funny, and she dressed like a man. Shirley had an apartment across the courtyard from my mother's. She shared it with Ginny, a tall, glamorous, moody blonde who wore her hair in a DA and dressed like Kim Novak (for whom she was often mistaken). They both worked in offices in THE CITY. By which I mean, in case you're not from New Jersey, Manhattan. I loved that they worked in New York because I knew it meant that they were the best at what they did. Someday, I wanted to work in New York too.

My mother was living with my Aunt Marilyn, who I knew as Aunt Shirley's sister. Sometimes my mother and I would go over to Aunt Shirley's for dinner. Eventually their friends would show up. After a while, I was handed a piece of cake and a bottle of coke and sent to the living room to watch television. I sat there straining my ears to hear their conversations. Adult talk was always far more interesting than anything on TV. Eventually I'd fall asleep watching Chiller Theatre while off in the other world, the kitchen, there was a lot of Rheingold drunk, a lot of Pall Malls smoked, a lot of laughing, sometimes even a lot of yelling (Ginny was a jealous woman) and occasionally some all-night poker.

Aunt Shirley genuinely adored kids and I adored her. She talked, she listened, and she was generous with her time. One Sunday we made a deal: I would help her clean her apartment and she would teach me how to play chess. I'm not sure that she made out well on this arrangement, but for me it was a win/win. How I loved those Sundays.

Aunt Shirley's apartment was like a Pan Am commercial, glamorous and foreign. It was filled with mementos from around the world, and I got to clean them! A painting of Big Ben and Parliament by the Thames River hung over her couch. The other wall held a street café with the Eiffel Tower in the background. I sprayed Bon Ami on the coffee table and studied those paintings: the way the light reflected on the rainy streets, the way the people sipped their drinks. How did those people get there? Someday, I thought, I'm going to go there. I'll have coffee in that café, and I'll walk across that bridge.

In the bedroom was a black lacquer suite, which included an armoire and a full-sized bed. There was just one bed. It never occurred to me to ask where Ginny slept. There was Chinese calligraphy on the wall and jade lions on the dresser. These lions captivated me. Smooth and cool to the touch, I could only imagine the splendor of the place from which they came. Gently, I wiped them clean. They seemed incredibly exotic to me, and, more importantly, an escape hatch to a beautiful world free from want and loneliness.

Shirley was the first person to lend me a book to read for pleasure. I didn't know people read books that were not required at school. I didn't know you could actually enjoy reading. She loaned me "The Good Earth." I didn't understand a lot of it, but I tried because she thought I could. Back then, I thought she was giving me her time. She knew she was giving me something far bigger, a love of reading, a key to endless possibilities.

For me, the line between masculine and feminine was blurred, even before I understood what gender meant. My Aunt Shirley was a butch lesbian, a walking contradiction in 1960s society. She believed in me and showed me that the big wide world was just waiting for me to go out and grab it. She was the ideal father. If the definition of masculinity is "the quality of looking and behaving in ways conventionally thought to be appropriate for a man or boy," then I learned many good aspects of masculinity not from a man, but from a woman. I learned that not all men go out for a pack of cigarettes and never come home, that they don't all beat you with a belt buckle. Sometimes, they nurture and encourage you and, most importantly, believe in you. Sometimes they really do love you.

Fudgsicles

Martha C. Beattie

The idea of living on the land was hard to give up. Land doesn't lose value. It was a reasonable idea. No, not just reasonable, it seemed clairvoyant, like a fast forward to what interested us most at the time: minimalist living, gardening, preserving food, cutting wood. "Boldness has genius in it." Yeah, that's how we felt about it.

There were three partners in the deal, and we bought a 100-acre lot as tenants-in-common. We went to a lawyer first. Maybe we should have gone to the bank first to get silver dollars. Then we could have tossed one into the lawyer's lap each minute of the hour we consulted with him because that was his price. The lawyer warned us that we should subdivide the lot as soon as possible. He looked at Stan and me and said, "Even then, you two will not be protected one from the other." That marked the beginning of our wedding plans.

I'm leaving out the part about the road...there was none. No road led to our new property, because the old road had been abandoned by the town years before. All that was left of it was an overgrown ditch. So the land had some challenges to it. Building the two-mile road was just the first step; there was constant upkeep because the road was always washed out. It was hard to drive up it without four-wheel-drive. Keeping that two-mile private drive passable was quite a headache and a money-sucker. Work on the land was slowgoing, and backbreaking, too.

By comparison, the marriage plans moved like a spring storm. In five years we had a four-year-old son and two-year-old twin sons. Ah... the moving we did. Looking for rentals was exhausting, and each overpriced, run-down, mish-mosh of a house we looked at inspired us with new determination to build "something" on the land. At least we owned the land.

Our lot was at the top of the hill. The view there opened up and took in the long valley beyond. Off our road was a grass and brush track that swung around to the 'building site' nestled between oaks, just below the crest of the hill. It was all wooded, and in the late spring the black flies were as thick as pollen. We had set up a screen tent, but the kids couldn't stay in the tent while their parents were outside pick-axing and digging in the dirt. It's not that we believed that a family could really live up here, it's just that, well... we owned it, so why not build a structure on it to make better use of it? Fine idea if you had extra cash. We didn't. Instead, we had a family of five and no home. We were a bit stuck, and thought that a day of hard thrashing, pounding, digging and prying out boulders might cheer us up. Faced with unappealing options, we didn't know what else to do to take charge of our lives. So there we were, digging footings, in the heat, in the bugs, in June, with the kids alternately whining and fighting.

On one hot June day, we realized we needed five gallon buckets from down in the valley at the store. Oh blessed need, to be a gopher. A little reprieve from the minute-to-minute discomfort of digging. I strapped the twins into their car seats in the back of the Jeep and slowly picked my way between the ruts going down the hill. Once I was on the town road and had the sky arching over me, I could see that the day was truly fine. Without the forest blocking it, the sun was amazingly bright. We were just coming to the new general store when I had an urge for something cold, so cold... I wanted a fudgsicle. That's all, just a fudgsicle. I thought of my toddlers in the back. It was so hot and I had been toiling in the woods for hours with black flies chewing on my ears. Why do black flies like ears so much? The black flies were not out here in the sunshine.

I needed life to be more normal, just for a moment. I pulled into the general store, stepped inside and came out with three fudgsicles. I peeled down the wrappers and gave one to each of my twin sons. "They're fudgsicles," I said, "You lick them. You can bite them too." I tucked a napkin under each chin.

Then I drove away with my elbow sticking out the window and the breeze filling the car. I gently nibbled bites of icy fudgsicle, never even turning my head back to glance at those two in the back seat with their first-ever fudgsicles. I just felt the sunny breeze on my bug bites and the cold, wet chocolatey goodness of my fudgsicle, which I ate without spilling a drop.

Too soon I reached the camp, bearing the needed buckets. I stopped, got out of the car, and looked at my children in the back. Their faces, hair, ears, and chests were covered in glistening fudgsicle. The chocolate was melting onto their laps faster than they could lick it off the sticks... I have no memory of how I cleaned them up. But I see clearly, even now, those babies with their shiny, sticky faces and the faraway look in their eyes. They were exhausted from licking those quickly melting bars. Their eyes in those brown gooey faces could barely stay open.

I like to imagine now that I veered off my script for the day and headed across town to Grandma's house, where Grandma and Grandpa had a hearty laugh before they got out the hose and the wading pool, peeled off the boys' clothes, and let them splash and flop around in the pool until the last drop of fudgsicle had vanished. Grandma would have taken their messy clothes down to the cellar and ran them through the washer and dryer. That would have been nice. But I could never have brought them to Grandma's and admitted the foolish thing I'd done, or shown that I was really in need of a grassy back yard and running water and washers and dryers. I couldn't admit that because I was busy trying to prove something else. Something time would help me forget.

Boys Don't Cry

Lisken Van Pelt Dus

I t wasn't the first time I'd ever fallen off a horse. And it certainly wasn't the first time I'd been mistaken for a boy. In fact, that was an error I actively encouraged: I wore my hair pixie-short, was as daredevil as the toughest boy in my class, and vigorously eschewed dresses or—God forbid—anything pink.

Now I was flat on my back in the dust. My balking horse had cantered off to the fence line, and my breath, which had been knocked out of me on impact, had returned to me in the form of sobs. Suddenly, I was being yelled at, a single, declarative exclamation cannoning at me from above: *¡Niños no lloran!* Boys don't cry!

My riding instructor's face seemed huge, looming over me, rough-skinned and rough-shaven. I'd never been spoken to so loudly and aggressively in all my nine years. I was shocked into obedience and stopped crying—or at least tried to. *P-pero*, I stammered back, *¡soy niña!* I'm a girl!

Instantly and astonishingly, I found myself swept up in his arms. He cradled me as he carried me past the jumps to a stone wall at the edge of the ring, where he set me down gently, all the while repeating *¡Ay, mi pobrecita!* Poor little girl! His voice was suddenly inflected softly, audibly tinged with horror that he could so have misjudged and mistreated me.

I'll admit, I wasn't above milking it. But what a revelation! For the first time in my life, I considered that it might actually be an advantage not to be a boy.

•

This was Mexico City in 1972, still very much a man's world. Women taught me and my friends, and looked after us, but for the most part, men provided for and ruled over us. From what I could see, boys had freedom and girls had compliance. Boys had adventures, and girls got to read about them. Bad behavior in either gender was punished, but seemed forgotten thereafter in boys, while a heavy fog of disappointment lingered over a girl who transgressed. From what I could tell, it was only going to get worse for me. At nine, being a tomboy was a forgivable fantasy, but the end was in sight. "Some day, you'll be glad you're a girl," my sister assured me, but I didn't believe it, and she couldn't articulate any reasons that made sense to me.

For the time being, I could only see the downsides, and my brief flash of insight into the unpleasant pressures that might accompany boyhood faded fast. The ramifications of that tumble in the ring were nothing but bad. Now that my riding teacher knew I was a girl, he was solicitous of me in ways he hadn't been before, prescribing only the smaller jumps and, worst of all, not allowing me to ride my favorite horse, a large, obstreperous animal over whom I delighted in exerting control. No longer was I out in front on our wild trail rides, where we careened over gullies, scrambled up and down the dusty sides of arroyos, and negotiated the packs of barking dogs. In any given encounter, it was anyone's guess whether your horse would shy from them, or kick them. Either way, now I watched Juan, or Davíd, or Mateo with envy as they took off on my erstwhile steed while I pummeled an aging mare with my spurs, trying to keep up.

•

Flash forward some fifteen years. I live in rural Massachusetts, and my relationship to my own gender has finally changed—thanks in part to love. I'm getting married, and my fiancé's 9-year old son is trying to act like a man. Every time a camera is pointed in his direction, he squares his face to look stoic and solemn. We're laughing, a little, but it's serious business to him. He's taken his cues and decided that to be a man is to hold your emotions in check.

A few weeks later, the three of us and some of other students are at a karate tournament. Daniel and his friends have been training for and looking forward to this for months. Kata competition has gone well, but it's time now for the kids to leave their trophies aside for a moment and enter the sparring rings. My husband and I are watching from the sidelines, eager and a little anxious to see how our students will do. Clarissa makes it through several rounds in her girls' division, proudly taking third. Richard dances through his division with his quick footwork, and also places. So far, Daniel's done well in his group, too, but suddenly his new opponent winds up with a powerful roundhouse kick that lands squarely on his jaw, knocking him to the ground. Strikes to the head are clearly forbidden by the rules, and the boy should be disqualified. Instead, and inexplicably, he's awarded the point, high-fived by his sensei, and granted the match. Meanwhile, Daniel is picking himself up from the mat. For a moment he looks at me, and I see tears forming in his eyes. Abruptly, he looks away. When he turns around again, he is expressionless.

•

We left that tournament and never went back to the circuit, opting instead to found our own tournament series that emphasizes a different set of values. But the experience opened the door to a number of conversations with our son about masculinity and machismo, and about the chasm we believe lies between them. His dad doesn't cry much, but if tears do come, he lets them out. And so, I am happy to report, does Daniel. In our world, boys do cry.

Sandbars

Jenny Laird

For the sake of anonymity, let's call him "B." B is my seventeen-year old stepson. I love B, but these days, I don't love-love him. I'm trying, but he is *so* getting in the way of any chance I might have of following the Tibetan advice to "keep my mind as vast as the sky and my daily conduct as fine as a grain of sand."

I can only assume my stepson enjoys the role of Jenny's bad-ass spiritual stumbling block because he has a knack for getting into the most trouble when his Dad is out of town. Today, B has been expelled from school for hurling a yogurt—and the trump card of curse words—at the cafeteria's little old lunch lady, and I'm the one who must fetch our wayward child from the principal's holding cell.

"Listen, B," I say, "When you use the C-word to describe one woman, you're implying that ALL women are the C-word. You know that, right?"

"Jesus, Jenny, you don't need to go all femi-nazi on me. The yogurt I threw wasn't even open," he says, staring out the window of our car, trying to ignore his autistic little brother who is in the back-seat, squealing with glee at the sound of his brother's voice.

I wish I heard what my 3-year-old son, Quinn, hears in B's voice; some buried joy, only audible to pure spirits and dogs. But I don't. The sound of B's voice only makes me cringe, bristle, or sometimes cry. I look at the his pimply cheek, a few stray hairs on his chin, the belt buckle made of bullets, and the steel studs sticking out of the shoulders of his jean jacket, literally rendering him unsafe to hug … and I think about a therapist I saw when I lived in Chicago, The therapist who helped me embrace the idea that I might actually be up to the task of packing up my entire life and moving East to marry a recently widowed man with two grieving teenage sons. I think about how serene her blue eyes looked when she told me that all I had to do was "be there with love," promising me that that would be enough. I think about her telling me that "just because something is impossible, it doesn't mean we shouldn't try," and then I think about calling her and asking for a refund.

It doesn't take a trained therapist to assess that my stepson's "acting out" while his father is away is his way of protesting abandonment. B was twelve when his Mom was killed in a car accident. Hoping to resolve an argument she'd had with her boyfriend earlier in the day, she had driven off in the middle of the night while B and his older brother were asleep in their beds. She never returned.

Because I am now the mother of a son, a sweet 3-year-old who could one day grow up to shock and disappoint me with his misogynistic language, I am considering it my duty, my gift to B's mom's memory, to make sure the C-word is extricated from her son's vocabulary.

"You wouldn't use the N-word, would you?" I say.

"That's different," he mumbles as he grabs a case of cds from the glove box and begins searching for some music he doesn't totally hate. "You guys are so lame. What is this crap? You need some Sex Pistols. Subhumans. Misfits."

What I wanted to say was: "I need another subhuman like I need a hole in the head." Instead, I blurted out, "I grew up on the Sex Pistols."

"Sex Pistols are SICK," he offers.

"Yeah, right? I mean, I saw, 'Sid and Nancy,' you know, the movie, like eight times."

I didn't. I saw it once, and I wanted to run screaming from the theatre. But I'm searching for my way across this ocean that separates my stepchild and me, and right now Sid Vicious is the only sandbar in sight.

"You wouldn't use the N-word because you know it's dehumanizing, just like the C-word. And the R-word. Those words hurt everybody, not just the person you're calling the name."

"Whatever. I'll just put on some Clapton."

I know this kid is in acute emotional pain; I know he didn't ask to move to this small town in the Berkshires after twelve "glorious" years as a New York City kid; I know he didn't ask to be motherless or for his father to re-marry and have a special needs child who needs more attention than him; I know all this and still, I can't help but lapse into fantasies of all the ways I could wipe that "whatever" look right off of his face.

The problem is, B secretly likes it when you fantasize about throwing his pierced body out of the car. He likes it when you threaten him with big burly men with duct tape whisking him off to the woods in the middle of the night, because he's desperate for you to confirm his worst suspicions: that the world is shit, that people can't be trusted and that there is no such thing as unconditional love. He is determined to push every last button in sight until his outer world reflects his inner world, so his misery will be justified and he will become a part of the natural order of things, not some crazy teenaged mutant. The problem is, he *is* a crazy teenage mutant and the only way to engage with his goodness is to hunt it down and d-r-a-g it into the light . . .

"Okay. So, who do you love most in the world ... besides your Dad?"

"I dunno ... Emma."

"And how would you feel if someone called Emma the C-word?"

"She's not one, so nobody would call her that."

"I'm sure that lunch-lady's husband feels the same way about his wife."

"No way that *bleep* is married."

"I don't want this to turn into a battle of wills, B, I just want you to understand that language is a powerful tool and you shouldn't wield it so carelessly."

"You can call a man a *bleep* too."

"Damnit, B, cut it out. And don't use the C-word in my presence again. It's disrespectful. To me. To all women. And if your brother's first word is the C- word, you will have yourself to thank."

"Yeah, except that kid is never gonna talk."

He has skipped my jugular and gone straight for my heart. As if clutching my chest, I check the rearview mirror and see Quinn wordlessly uttering sounds of delight. He is joyfully flapping his hands, his autism waving its bright red flags for all to see. He can't help it, it's his way of saying he loves a good car ride. He loves to watch the world whiz by from the safety of his raised seat, and he especially loves it when his brother rides along.

B is right. It doesn't look hopeful. Quinn and I may spend our whole lives just driving around these mountains, lost in our language-less tomb while B saunters about, foolishly trading in bounty for apathy, plenty for profanation. I may never even get to scold Quinn for using the C-word or the F-word or any other word because for some (unfathomable, make you question the intelligence of the "Infinite Intelligence") reason, my sweet boy was born without a boatload of capacities. B was given twice his share.

"Squanderer!" I shout.

"Whaaaaa?"

"Listen, Buster, I mean it, don't ever say that word around me or Quinn again or you're going to be sorry."

I see B's hackles rise, he's gearing up for things to get good. He knows I only use the word "Buster" when I'm a raging lunatic, and he knows if he goes all "Constitutional" on me, I'll completely flip my lid.

"If someone's acting like a—*bleep*—it's a free country, like The First Amendment and stuff, I have my right to call it like I see it!"

"Freedom of Speech might give you the right, but it doesn't make it right! You wanna know who verbally defiles other human beings for the fun of it? The KKK and Nazis and all the other subhumans out there! It's how we descend into barbarism, my friend, rape and torture and genocide."

"Calm down."

"Do you know how many people have died so that little old you could have your First Amendment? But hey, thanks to them, it's your 'right' to shit all over their graves."

"I have a right to tell the truth."

"Oh, yeah, I forgot, because You, B-ALL-MIGHTY, YOU are the authority on all things *bleep*."

Yup, I said it. The reviled C-word. My hopes of ever having a "vast" mind or "fine" conduct have been mangled beyond recognition. B seems to intuit this because he's sporting a humongous smile. And for a moment, he appears stripped and unguarded, or is that just me? And that's when I get a flicker . . . of transcendence. Don't worry, it's just a flicker.

A memory comes to mind in this moment. B is twelve and in the throes of grief over losing his mom. I've just flown in from Chicago and he, his dad, and I are walking in Battery Park. We are headed to the movies, but I'm keeping my distance, wary of appearing too eager, fearful of doing anything to disrespect his mother's memory. Suddenly B is running up to me, grabbing my hand and holding it as we walk.

He says, "If somebody saw us walking like this, would they think we were a family?"

"Maybe," I say, unsure of what he wants the answer to be.

"I bet they'd think you were my mom."

"They might."

"Because you have brown hair and I have brown hair … " At the time, it was the only sandbar in sight, and he leapt on it as if his life depended on it.

"Listen B," I say, "You gotta stop flipping the bird at life. You're the strongest, smartest, most able-bodied, beautiful boy I know, and you take it all for granted. Worse, you piss it all away. Like it's nothing."

"You don't understand, Jenny, she's like the worst lunch lady ever, and she wouldn't let me return my yogurt and get something else, and you guys never put enough money on my lunch card so I have like nothing to eat and it's the stupidest rule, 'cuz I didn't even open it, and she was smiling, like she was happy I'm going to starve."

"Nobody wants you to starve, kiddo. But I don't care how hungry you are, you don't get to be a jerk."

"Okay. Do you think you could drop me off in town so I can get a chicken sandwich or something?"

I don't know if I'm feeding the beast or nourishing the child, but I pull over in front of Subway and hand him a ten spot … and I think … So what if I don't get my happy ending… just because something is impossible, doesn't mean we shouldn't try.

"I only need like five," he says.

"It's all I have. Just bring me the change."

"Okay. Thanks," he says, grabbing my offering, climbing out of the car, and blowing kisses to Quinn in the backseat before he shuts the door and goes his own way.

He's seventeen years old and he still blows kisses. I love it when he does that.

PART FIVE:

COURAGE, RESILIENCE AND STRENGTH

THE POWER OF WOMEN'S VOICES AND VISIONS

Searching for the Moon: Musings on Growing Up Female

Amber Chand

I am told that my mother searched for the moon on the night of my birth.

From the window of the hospital room in which I was born, she gazed up into the African sky as a full, luminous moon lit up that warm August night. When dawn arose, she walked over to my cradle, gently placed a tiny golden spoon dipped in honey on my newborn tongue in accordance with ancient Vedic tradition, and offered me my name. Amber Chand. Moon in the Sky.

I am grateful for this name, steeped as it is in the Sanskrit roots of my Indian ancestral beginnings. It has carried me well these 64 years. Evocative and feminine, it transcends the boundaries of geography, nationality and race. Given to me by my Hindu mother on that propitious night, my name has offered me my sense of place in the world. It has become my personal touchstone.

As an Indian woman born in Uganda, raised in England, and residing in the United States for the past 40 years, I have come to see myself as a cultural hybrid; a woman of many shades, bearing witness to the pulsating rhythms of many cultures and many worlds. Most of my life, I have lived on the edge of society, an outsider looking in, bound by the inescapable fact that I am a woman—a brown skinned woman. My race and gender, inextricably bound like two devoted sisters, have offered me the enduring thread through which the tapestry of my life has been created.

My first memory of being female comes to me through the lyrics of a song that I would sing when I was only four years old. Punching the air with my small fists, I would sing out loud, "When I am a woman, I shall box men, I shall box men." The refrain was always met by applause as my parents' circle of close friends—all Indian—clapped their hands. "What a daughter you have!" they would exclaim to my mother and father. "You better watch out for her. She may never get a husband, and if she does, he better watch out. We know who will be the boss in that household!" But to me, I knew only that when I sang this song, I felt strong and brave and invincible.

Years later, as a gawky adolescent studying at a girls' private school in the heart of the English countryside, I remember sitting alone in my dormitory room, staring at my reflection in the mirror with great despair. I was the only girl of Indian descent in the school at that time, and I bemoaned my fate. "Why wasn't I born beautiful?" I complained tearfully. "Why wasn't I born with white skin? Why couldn't I look like the other girls?" The brave invincibility of my childhood had now been replaced by the sad insecurities of a teenage girl who wanted desperately to fit in, to melt into the background so that her distinct Indian features would not be noticed in this sea of pale freckled faces and small upturned noses. I yearned to be valued, to be cherished, to be told by this external world of strict English teachers and indifferent students, that I was appreciated for who I was.

Instead, I was often dismissed as a curiosity, something distinct and different from the Anglo Saxon norm. I was whisked off to elocution classes to learn to speak proper English with its crisp overtones, told repeatedly by the more popular girls that I was not pretty or smart enough, and often shunned when I walked into a room because of the color of my skin. In the eyes of my peers, I was the "Other."

One grey afternoon as a light drizzle came down and I stared at my desolate reflection in the mirror, I came to an important conclusion. To survive this fragmented world, I would need to armor myself; I would need to learn to adapt to my environment like a social chameleon and choose the skillful art of masquerade. I would pretend that I was someone I was not. I would become "more English than the English" and assume their ways, all the while hiding behind a protective mask of appropriate smiles, false bravados, and obedient gestures—the "stiff upper lip" syndrome of the dominant white culture. Little by little, over the span of my adolescent years, I lost touch with the vulnerable truth of my being and the very roots of my identity. I forgot who I was.

The crisp blue aerogram letters, postmarked with Ugandan stamps, would arrive at school regularly, and in each of them, between snippets of news from home, my mother and father would caution me: "Remember who you are, Amber. We sent you to England to be educated, not to pick up the habits of the English. Don't ever forget this."

Implicit in this parental warning was their veiled hope that with my elite Western education I would return home, eligible for marriage to a respectable young Indian man. I would sigh and put away the letters in an old mahogany box that I kept under my bed, strangely reassured that somehow my parents knew who I was and who I was to become, even though I myself did not.

Once I graduated from my English boarding school, I returned to my childhood home in Uganda. Stepping off the plane in my lemon-yellow miniskirt, chunky sandals, and bright orange dangly hoop earrings, I remember feeling a certain confidence. I was a 17-year-old social chameleon, now seemingly at ease with the ways of the English; whether listening to the Beatles and Rolling Stones, joining a Ban The Bomb protest march in London, or reciting Tennyson and Shakespeare. My parents, however, standing there at Entebbe Airport ready to receive me, were mortified. They took one look at my appearance and concluded that they had failed—for in their eyes I had become a "Westernized" woman. This conjured up numbing stereotypical images of overt independence, sexual permissiveness, spiritual indifference and wild defiance to the ways of solid tradition.

One morning, as I was breakfasting on fresh papaya and mango slices, my father announced, "Amber, your mother and I have decided it is time for you to marry. We have found you a very good man!" I gulped. "He is everything we want for you," my mother chimed in, undeterred by my surprised expression. "He's well-educated, comes from a respectable family in Delhi, with an excellent financial future, and he lives in the United States."

"But is he good looking?" I inquired, finishing up my breakfast, unimpressed by his credentials.

My parents looked aghast. "But Amber, how silly to base something as important as marriage on something as frivolous as good looks. Don't you realize that whoever you marry, when he is middle-aged he will have a bald head and a potbelly?"

Many months later, I stood behind a curtained window, peering out and waiting for this "Prince Charming" to show up at my door. He was flying in from the United States to meet me. To be frank, I did get caught up in a whirlwind of fantasy as I imagined my fate with this prospective suitor. "Will he be handsome?" I wondered. "Will he be rich? Will he carry me off my feet and take me into a world of happily ever after?" My father had gone to pick him up at the airport, and standing there behind the curtains, I watched as the car slowly made its way down our pebbled driveway. My heart beat fast with curiosity. I watched and waited. From the passenger seat, emerged a young, fairly heavy-set bespectacled man, with short wavy hair, a moustache, and the confident air of success. Oh no! He was ugly! He was no Prince Charming! My face fell and my fantasy quickly dissipated into a mist of disappointment.

I refused to marry him. My mother was bewildered. To her, echoing the voice of her generation of Indian women, finding a suitable husband was the only path to redemption, the only possible destiny for a woman.

"Don't you realize, it is the best passport to your future?" she moaned, fearing that her daughter was falling off the steady, predictable path of what it meant to be a woman. I was unmoved.

After several failed attempts at arranging my marriage, my parents finally succumbed. They knew that I was determined to chart my own course in life, to shape my own destiny and to choose my own husband, if I were to marry.

Which is what I did. But that is another story.

The Drowning Girls

Grace Rossman

Bubbles babble over pebbles, haunted gravel in the bed, eternal, crooked creek creeping into vernal pools, spools of your golden hair winding in the rapids, sinking, heavy, like your vapid mind, your effervescing tresses intertwined with stems of roses, pansies, that's for thoughts, never thought you yourself would be caught in a watery web like the one you observed in his ruined kingdom. Come now, sweet babe, don't let this cradle be your grave, I know you're tired, weathered, worn, so take this chance and be reborn.

Let this brook wash your sins away like rain. I promise I understand your pain, I feel ya, Ophelia, as you float among the coy camellia flowers. Own your power, you know you're not so meek—release the water from your lungs and speak your truth. Forsooth, my dear, don't let fear drown you in this clear cold stream, arterial. Yes, dear wench, you are ethereal, but don't forget: you're human, too.

Emerge from the icy blue and claim it—your life. Name it: the strife you turned inward on yourself, compromised your health, not knowing that this wealth of woe exists outside you. Take pride, too, in recognizing malice. You must heal your own corroded chalice and learn to fill it with the world. Let your fiery fists uncurl and I'll anoint you Saint of water, daughter of the moon and child of the universe. Shake yourself off and start rehearsing for your looming debut.

And as you lie glued to your inglorious story six feet under, you have the choice of acknowledging your blunder, swimming up to the light and reveling in the wonder of the world you gave up on. What song would you like to sing? Loosening the lump in your throat, let it ring out over the barren fields you abandoned. As you become your own champion, so will the green come back to the land—no need to wrack your brain, just stand up to your full height, like the goddess that you are—Star of Venus, mother Demeter, creature of the deep.

Kept in the keep of your own murky melancholy, recognizing your folly as you dry off slowly, long locks blowing like amber waves on the rolling hills of a nation you must learn to own. You must never condone suffering—yours or the world's. I see you mustering the passion that swirls across your eyelids when you sleep; you mustn't slumber forever to reap the benefits. You are still benevolent without your burden—try to cool the fire that threatened to burn you. It's peace you're yearning for, yawning into the vermillion dawn, you are an army one million strong.

And if you learn to bring each warrior priestess along, align the pieces, piecing together this arsenal of care, may the planet beware and be wary of the torch you carry, at your command, mountains will move, as you learn to groove to the tune you were born to play. There is no better day than today to do it. You thought you blew it; you were simply blowing bubbles, pockets of air amid the despair and the rubble, as you gurgled, garbled, when you couldn't cope, you brilliantly, lovingly gave yourself hope, Hop. Out. Now. And heal the languid landscape—you know how.

Black Clues

Joan Embree

Water taught you things. When you were five, standing on a dock with a couple of grown-ups and some other kids, all of you in bathing suits, someone said, "*brrrrr.....that water looks too cold for me*," which preposterously inspired you to jump heedlessly into the lake like some possessed and deranged creature, considering you didn't yet know how to swim. Splat! You sank like a rock, struggled to the surface, arms flailing, face contorted, kicking your feet to no avail, everyone looking down at you and shrieking with laughter, assuming you were clowning around. Thrashing wildly, embarrassed to be drowning in front of an audience, you willed your way to shore. Two lessons learned: It's humiliating to have people see you in the throes of dying. And, sometimes, you have to save your own ass.

The next week, your unusual grandmother taught you how to swim. You called her "unusual" because she had a blue or sometimes lavender rag mop head of curls, incessantly smoked Kools in a rhinestone cigarette holder like she was Greta Garbo, wore blouses so perilously décolletage you were tempted during Sunday breakfast in her basement kitchen to try and flip a piece of sausage off your fork down into her ruinous cleavage, subscribed to a magazine for morticians called *Sunnyside and Casket* and had six canaries, each named Petey, who flew unrestrained throughout her house, which pretty much put your mother in a terrible state, not just because of bird seed and poop scattered everywhere, but because they seemed to know she hated them, and so mercilessly dive-bombed her head.

One hot summer afternoon, Octavia (which is what you called your grandmother, because she wouldn't hear of any reference to old age such as Grandma) said, "Get a leg on, I'm gonna teach you to swim 'cause no one else around here seems to care anything about it. It's time you learned, for crying out loud. No dilly dallying. Put your suit on now." The two of you bounced on backcountry roads in her chocolate brown Hudson Hornet, until you came to a sign next to a swimming hole that said: No Trespassing, Private Property, and in bigger letters, **KEEP OUT**. But nothing ever stopped her.

Wading into the icy water, in her one-piece purple satin bathing suit with a pleated skirt, she let out a long *EEEEEEEEK*, as the water rose to her thighs. Then she did the doggy paddle, her head held erect in dappled forest sunlight, cutting through the water like some new form of animal life. "Come on, come on, get in the water," she called. "I don't have all day." You slid in after her, not daring to disobey, remembering you already knew how to save yourself from drowning. Later, when you thought about it, you realized that without her bullying, you could have easily developed a phobia about the water for the rest of your life. Lesson learned: Sometimes the bossy, cranky, mean people who act like they don't love you are the ones who not only love you, but get you where you need to go.

•

When you grew up, and were old enough to know better, you got involved with a bad man named Dean who wanted you to go fishing with him. You met him at a lake where he had "borrowed" someone's rowboat. You wore an elegant Laura Ashley dress. He yelled at you for dressing like a stupid bitch. He yelled at his dog, Butch, a sweet black Labrador Retriever, who was too scared to move. He picked up the trembling dog and threw him in the boat. You and Butch sat together in the boat way out in the middle of the lake. The dog was shaking and you put your arm around him as Dean ranted and raved. You and Butch looked at one another and you could have sworn he said, "We have to get out of here." So the two of you jumped into the water and swam neck to neck, him eyeballing you, making sure you were keeping up, your dress trailing behind you like a field of flowers, swimming like your lives depended on it, which they did, all the way back to the shore, Dean screaming in temper tantrum mode, shaking his fist at the two of you, neither of you paying any attention. You brought Butch home with you. Dean called the cops and said you stole his dog. You told him you'd go to jail before you'd ever give Butch back, and he could just go to goddamn hell. Finally, he stopped stalking you. He found other victims. One foolish woman after another, and a series of poor, innocent dogs. Out on the water that day you learned about terror and the unrivaled bravery and goodness of a dog. You learned how lucky you were to have escaped what some people live with their whole miserable lives, because they have no one to help them, and they haven't the will to save themselves.

•

Your best friend growing up was your next door neighbor, Zephyr Jaworski, better known as Z. He was a year older than you, and you had the notion that he spent his first year on earth waiting for you to show up. The two of you would pry up a plank on the flat bridge that ran across the front of your houses and slither down into the shallow brook that ran deep into the underbelly of your town. It was an underground cave full of bats and water snakes. He'd take your hand and pull you along the rusted rubble and sucking mud. One time you tried to take back your hand, but he held on.

"I don't want to walk down there...it's too dark," you said.

"Sure you do," he said. "It's what we have to do. Walk in the water down into the blackest darkness. It will give us magic powers so no one can ever kill us."

Z was always saying weird stuff like that. Shafts of light streamed down on you from the spaces between the bridge's slats. Head bowed, his golden hair dipping over his smoky green eyes, his hand holding yours like it was precious, your heart beating with the knowledge that he was everything: the wind twisting in the trees, a starry night, the sun and the moon. There, under the bridge, your shoulders and hips bumping as you trudged silently in the murky, sullied water, sharing the splendor of a once-in-a-lifetime first true love.

•

"You gonna get cut bad, mother fucker," men shouted outside down on the corner, shattering the morning silence. Hop, your black coonhound with a bum front leg, startled, sat upright on your bed, his long hears shivering. Your mother on the phone with your aunt angrily complaining, almost shouting, about Mr Jaworski's black rooster crowing at this ungodly hour. These loud outbursts so stark in contrast to the starched white eyelet curtains fluttering in a gentle breeze at the open window. "I'm gonna fuck you up, mother fucker!" Hop skulked up to your shoulder, nervously licked his lips. You wondered if what the men were yelling was even possible? Would someone actually fuck his own mother? And so it went, your childhood in that hardscrabble neighborhood, a black comedy, really, when you think about it, but not altogether bad, what with the high drama and heart-racing, hold-your-breath moments.

There was the time when no one else was around, and your aunt frantically asked you to go downtown and pick your grandmother up at jail. Something about shoplifting a pair of black rayon gloves from Genung's Department Store.

"I'm sure it's all a big misunderstanding," she said.

"Auntie, I'm only 13. I can't drive."

"Well, of course you can, dear. I know your father lets you drive on back roads, and I'm in too much of a state myself to drive."

It was a mystery how you knew how to back her Catalina hardback down the long, black cinder chip driveway, but you did; Hop in the passenger seat, gleaming in his black glory and sweetness.

"Hop, I'm driving!" you shouted, and "Woof woof!" he replied, enormously pleased by the outing. You parked in the A&P parking lot a block away from the police station. You didn't want to get arrested for illegal driving. Your grandmother was standing out front, a cop next to her, dumb fury slurring her face, wearing a conservative, long black coat and an English nanny hat like Mary Poppins—not her usual off-the-shoulder-flaunting-cleavage-Marilyn-Monroe look. You wondered if this was her special shoplifting outfit.

"You'll catch flies with your mouth open like that," she snarled. "What in Sam Hill took you so long? You think I want every Tom, Dick and Harry gawking at me out here?"

The cop winked at you and said "Good luck, honey. Better you than me." Hop jumped into the backseat.

"I'm too young to drive, you know."

"Too young? What's that have to do with the price of eggs?"

"Excuse me for asking, Octavia, but can't you afford to pay for things you need?"

"Don't talk nonsense. Nobody needs black gloves."

Hop started poking the back of her head with his nose. "I've about had it with this dog of yours."

"Oh, sorry. He's just excited. It's not everyday we get to drive to jail to pick someone up arrested for shoplifting."

"Shoplifting? What kind of thing is that to say to me? Haven't I been through enough?"

"But isn't that why you were arrested?"

"Listen, I paid good money for a pair of nylons, so it's not like I was robbing them blind, for Pete's sake."

"Oh," you said, knowing when to back off.

•

All through childhood you and your brother, for reasons unknown to you, were sent away for weeks at a time to stay with different people you called aunt and uncle, none of whom were actual blood relatives. All of them were Italian and connected to Aunt Clara and Uncle Sal's Restaurant. You were pretty sure they were in The Mob. Except for this one German couple who lived in a lavish house out in the country: Aunt Margaret, a kind, dowdy woman and her husband, Uncle Steen, scary with his chiseled good looks and clipped accent. You and your brother slept in twin beds out on their sunporch.

There was one black night, bull frogs croaking, a screech owl screaming, when a bat found its way inside, and clung with hairy feet to the chintz drapes. You could see a pulse beating beneath his little black body. Your brother was fast asleep. Uncle Steen came onto the porch, you didn't know why, and stood, a silent giant looming over you, then leaning down, pushing his tongue into your mouth. You were seven years old. You looked up into his face and saw that his eyes were empty black holes, his hand groping under the featherbed, but you don't remember what else, other than that he disappeared as ghostly as he had magically appeared.

Outside the window stars glowed and burned like hot coals in the black sky. The fog-streaked full moon hung in the sky, a sickly grey stain hanging over it like the underbelly of a dead fish. You got up and took your yellow cardigan off a chair and gently put it over the bat. You were worried Uncle Steen would come back and kill him, so you unclipped the screen and shook him out into the darkness. An outside lantern illuminated tender bones and tiny veins coursing with blood exquisitely etched in his outspread wings. You were happy to see him fly away, dissolving into the black night, his liberation making everything seem alright.

Be Fruitful

Heather C. Meehan

Sticky with
ripened fruit and
menstrual fluid, blood
oranges and belladonna.
I take your dose on my tongue
and slug it down.
You filled my waiting cup
when I was done with water.
You raised it to my lip—
liquid like wine,
sweet in the belly, bitter
in the
descent.
Medicine,
like abstinence, tastes
better after it's taken.
In the dark, we did not speak
but voices issued
from our chests, whispering
to one another. I
did not promise this soul,
only a silent acre
tilled and harrowed.

You were prior to all my other loves, the man
that came in the moonlight to fallow my fields, to quake
my orchards and gather
the fruit that fell. You
took my unharvested bounty,
savoring each swollen seed.
You stabbed into my
softened core
with the littlest of your fingers.
Was this what God was asking
when he bid
me to "Be Fruitful"?

Surviving the Cold

Teresa Gentile

All day I trudged through crusty snow
Moving animals to feedlots
Breaking ice in water troughs
Dragging hay and grain in wheel barrows
too heavy to cross the frozen ground.

Dreaming all day of:
stiff fingered gloves curling
round a coffee cup so hot
that it blisters my palms

Spooning scalding hot soup
into a mouth made numb
by the day long sear of subzero air

Toasting frozen toes on a
wood burning fire
'til the socks peel off
like overly crisp chicken skin.

But when evening comes
none of these warms my soul
like the heat of another body curled against mine.

Even if it is my dog.

Hand Towels

Barbara Dean

The hand towels in my grandmother's bathroom get to me every time.

There are 2 of them: brilliant, warm-toned, with wide stripes of red, alternating with cheerful orange and yellow.

They are elegant and pleasing, luxurious and tasteful.

They fit right in, in my grandmother's neat, small, simply furnished apartment on Ocean Parkway.

I have moved in with her in my senior year of high school.

I have come to get away from the cramped, chaotic, cluttered apartment in Queens where I have lived since I was 7.

Our hand towels there were worn and non-descript.

At age 17, I was still sharing a bedroom with my two younger sisters, aged seven and nine.

I couldn't stand it anymore.

Now I sleep in my grandmother's living room, a tremendous sense of peace and blissful solitude enveloping me every night.

I can breathe.

Sometimes I go into my grandmother's bedroom when she is not there.

I examine everything.

Her dark wood bureau has photographs, a jewelry box, face powder and perfume on its satiny top.

I peer into the drawers—they aren't as neat as I would like them to be, but not as bad as the drawers at home, and anyway, they look great closed.

I pick up each piece of jewelry. There are two I especially like: a solid silver hand-wrought necklace my uncle brought from Mexico, and a long necklace of delicately shaped green and blue beads.

I covet these. I think "I will inherit them when she dies." Then I feel guilty.

I put them back.

Sometimes my grandmother's sister, eight years her junior, comes
   down from her apartment on the floor above.
She is a bargain hunter par excellence. She and my grandmother
   huddle over the latest finds.
Then they turn to me.
"Show her," my grandmother demands.
My aunt proffers a terry-cloth bathrobe, festooned in strange colors,
   which if I had bought, I wouldn't be showing to anyone.
"Guess how much?" my aunt insists.
Oh, brother, I think. I shrug.
She tells me, and I know I am expected to show admiration and awe
   on my face.
So I do.
They talk at length about other purchases, other bargains, other
   shopping adventures.
It is only much later in my life that I put it all together.
They grew up poor and half-starved on the Lower East Side.
As small children, it became their job to seek out the best and
   cheapest 1- or 2-day-old bread, the best butchers' bones or
   castoffs, the best bruised and damaged fruits and vegetables.
They had to be clever, they had to be discriminating, they had to be
   winsome and appealing.
They had to have good excuses for why they couldn't pay what the
   vendor asked.
At this, they excelled.
And now, whenever they found and pursued a bargain, which was
   always, their pride burst through.
They had done it again. They had survived. They had triumphed.

Concerning Bella

Jayne Benjulian

Gravitas, the manager said,
flipping résumé pages,

he stared at the demilitarized
zone on my head from roots to ear,

white advancing south from the crown,
chestnut retreating down. He

should have known Bella, my
Romanian grandmother, she

sold pencils to the army, ran
her sons like a combat unit, chopped

liver like a samurai,
her white coils vibrating like a power

grid around her eggplant cheeks.
Zoftig: from *zaft*, juice, sap—

she had *gravitas*.

Bella, Bella, Bella,

before I knew it meant beauty,
it sounded like combat to me.

The Girls' Club

Ellen Meeropol

Flo speaks into the telephone. "But isn't today Saturday? We meet on Thursdays."

"Emergency meeting," Mimi says. "I'll pick you up in half an hour."

"What's the emergency?"

"You." Mimi pauses. "You're the emergency."

Flo is quiet for a moment before responding. "I'll be ready."

At the toot of Mimi's horn, Flo double-checks the list taped to the inside of the apartment door—coffeepot unplugged, cat fed, stove turned off, keys in hand—and then lets herself out. They are each quiet in the car. Flo tries to think what to say, but nothing comes.

Marlene, Fanny and Claire have already claimed the blue sofa at the Coffee Hut. While Mimi stands in line for their Mocha Delights, Flo sits on the loveseat across from her friends. Seven of them had met at the Women's Center in 1970, when Flo had just moved to Springfield and was pregnant with Sam. Together they had counseled rape victims, protested wars and male privilege, and raised their children. Every Sunday night they met for consciousness-raising. Now in their 70's, after losing two members of their group and several partners, they organize food brigades following a hospital discharge as efficiently as civil disobedience.

Their meeting time has changed to Thursday mornings and the conversation may be a bit more forgiving. But today is a Saturday.

"Can we talk about a name for our group?" Fanny says, like she does every meeting. "We can't be the Sunday night group any more. I've been thinking, how about the Sisterhood?"

"More like the geezerhood," Marlene mutters.

Claire shakes her head. "Sisterhood reminds me too much of the Hadassah, from when I was a kid."

"We can appropriate the name," Fanny argues. "Make it ours."

"I like the Girls' Club," Marlene says.

Flo doesn't care about the name, but pauses to consider how odd it is that when they were in their twenties and thirties they weren't allowed to call themselves girls, but now, in their seventies and eighties, it's okay. She rubs her face and touches a stiff hair. Those pesky chin bristles. Maybe she should add "Shave face" to the list on her front door, except she would hate for Sam or Zoe to see it.

Fanny won't let it go. "We are serious women and we need a serious name, one that expresses our losses—like work and our dear husbands." She looks sideways at Mimi. "Partners, I mean."

Mimi's Joanna was the most recent beloved to die, four months earlier. Sitting Shiva for her, they listened to Mimi describe how the Board of the food pantry she started in her living room four decades earlier had maneuvered her out of her director's job the week before Joanna's death.

"Out with the old guard," Marlene said that day. "That's exactly what the women's shelter trustees did to me. And after I created the project out of my own broken ribs."

Marlene still hasn't forgiven Claire's unkind response that day and she looks at Claire now. "Didn't you suggest the Deposed Dictators' Club?" Marlene's voice drips with scorn.

"She didn't mean it, Marlene," Fanny says. "And some of us chose to retire. Didn't you decide to stop working, Flo?"

Flo remembers her work, recording narration for training videos and indie documentaries. She had loved freelancing, being her own boss, but it stopped abruptly, last month or last year, when her son Sam dissolved the business. Before she lost everything, he said, but he didn't explain. No, she did not choose.

"Some of us still work for a living," Claire reminds them. She supervises night shift nurses at a community hospital every other weekend. She hasn't mentioned that administration pretty much demolished her benefits when they decreased her hours the year before. "And not all of us are tyrants on the job."

"Earth to Flo," Mimi says.

Flo looks down at her lap. These women are her dearest friends in the world, but in the last few months she often has no clue what they are talking about. That's what she should add to her list: Pay Closer Attention.

"Never mind," Mimi says. "Hey, you know what I was thinking about last night, when I couldn't sleep?"

"I saw your post on Facebook," Fanny says. "I couldn't sleep either."

Mimi ignores the interruption. "I was remembering that speech you gave in Yellow Springs, Flo, about child care and the feminist movement."

Oh, Flo remembers *that*. The feminist-socialist women's conference. "I was nursing Sam and the conference food collective wouldn't let me drink milk with meals. They insisted that milk was just for coffee. Remember *that* part?"

Mimi laughs. "Do I ever. You got up on stage without your shirt, Sammy hanging on your tit, and let them have it about the right of feminists to have kids if we wanted to. How those kids had to be part of our revolution."

"Even the boys." Flo laughs too. "What a hoot that was!"

This is just one of the reasons Flo loves Mimi so much. Nobody else, not even Sam or Zoe, can remind Flo of who she is beyond the memory lapses and chin hairs. No one else remembers every demonstration, every political meeting, every endless argument about the primary contradiction and is feminism a bourgeois sidetrack.

"That's exactly my point." Fanny smacks her hand against the coffee table. "We need a name to reflect our history and who we really are."

Who exactly are we, Flo wonders. Who is she?

"Wait a minute," Marlene says. "Aren't we here because of some kind of emergency?"

Mimi nods. "Yes. We're here to talk about Flo's … problem."

Flo looks at her lap and tries to name the conflicting feelings that swell up in her throat, making it hard to swallow. Annoyance that Fanny won't shut up about naming their group. Irritation at how bossy Mimi can be, sticking her nose in other people's business. Gratitude that her friends came because she has a problem.

What *is* her problem? Something is wrong but she can't quite identify it. Words have always been her friends but now they desert her. Without her words, who is she?

Claire reaches across the table and pats Flo's knee. "What's going on?"

"And how can we help?" Marlene adds.

Next to her on the sofa, Mimi leans close and takes Flo's hand. "Do you want to tell them, or should I?"

Flo's face burns with the heat of their stares. "You," she says.

Mimi looks from one woman to the next, around the circle. "Flo has been having problems with her memory."

Fanny jumps right in. "Of course she has. At our age we all have lapses."

Claire shuts her up with a glance. Claire takes her role as the group's health professional seriously.

"These are more serious," Mimi says. "One day last week she forgot where she lived and couldn't get home. A cop rescued her and brought her to Sam's apartment."

Flo closes her eyes, remembering the nubby surface of the curb where she sat waiting for a clue about which direction to walk. How ashamed she felt when the cop talked to her like a little lost girl.

"The thing is," Mimi continues, "Flo has been diagnosed with Alzheimer's."

"The dreaded A," Marlene says softly.

Flo knows that word. When Mimi pauses and takes a sip of her mocha, Flo sees that her own mug is full. She isn't thirsty.

"Sam has decided that Flo can't live alone any longer," Mimi continues. "He's been looking at assisted living facilities. The place he's chosen is nice, but Flo doesn't want to go."

Her voice trails away. The silence stretches on and on. Flo can't think of a time they've been quiet for this long, not since after the artery in Joanna's head ballooned and burst without warning, and they were all stunned into the stillness of inarticulate grief. This is like a death too, she thinks. It's the demise of her brain they are mourning.

Claire reaches across the table again and takes Flo's other hand. "I imagine you're feeling pretty bad about the diagnosis, Flo?"

A distant section of her brain flares and pulses. Flo pictures a thought being born and growing into life. Clumsily, like when Sam was an infant and first discovered that his fingers could move to his mouth and he could suck them and it felt good. Her thought feels good too, if she can just hold onto it long enough to form it into words and push them through her mouth.

"Does it ever happen to you," Flo says, "that all of a sudden you don't know where you are?" She falters and hesitates. Even with the lists, her brain misplaces stuff—eyeglasses and ideas and even essential things like where she lives and how to get there.

But losing words is the worst. What's left when the words are gone? When she loses words, her heart races and she breathes faster and faster until she thinks she'll die of breathlessness and dizziness and sometimes the thought swells and bursts, leaking shards of broken letters from her useless head.

"Flo?" Mimi says.

So she tries again. "Landmarks disappear," she says. "You know how you try to grab onto something familiar—a house or corner store or park bench? You dig your fingernails into the surface of the world but it turns slippery and you're lost, you know?"

She can tell by their faces that they don't.

"We'll come to you," Marlene says. "Have our weekly meetings in the place, you know, where you'll be living."

"I'll make a schedule," Claire adds. "We'll visit and bring you food, and treats."

"Nothing is settled yet," Mimi says. "But I thought you would all want to know. And it didn't seem right to talk about Flo without her being here."

That's the problem, isn't it? Even when she is right here, sitting with her best friends, it happens. The words she needs are sliding out of their sentences, tumbling from their paragraphs, and soon they'll be gone and she'll be lost.

Mimi squeezes her hand.

But maybe not alone.

Second Opinion

Sondra Zeidenstein

Yesterday a doctor with a classic Russian name
interpreted the MRI of my left shoulder.
He wore dark pants and a bright blue,
not very fashionable, jersey
I imagined had been shipped from family in Russia.
He was tall, well-proportioned, graceful.
That is what I focused on, how pleasing
he looked in the office with just room for me
on a narrow table and George on a chair.

He stood, relaxed, facing me, and told me
my left shoulder was the exact duplicate in damage
of my right which had been MRI'd almost two years ago,
same total tear, no tendon to hold the shoulder joint
in place, more space for degenerative arthritis to flourish.
Nothing new. *Oh dear.* But he spoke in such a clear,
pleasant voice I kept imagining the Russian grandma
who adored him, raised him to be soft spoken,
with no need to impress.

No one really knows, he said, what is the cause
of such damage when there has been no trauma. It can happen.
It is believed, I think he said, that tendons have a life span
of their own and sometimes it is shorter than the person's life.
My tendons, he conjectured, had thinned slowly as I aged
until they finally separated. *If you need me for something more,*
he offered, just call. I shook the doctor's large hand.
As we left, I wept a bit. George did too.
Then we shared a donut

and I gathered my courage around me again.
I can make salads, I can empty the dishwasher,
I can swim on my back, I can look at Josef Albers'
colored squares at the Morgan in New York City
and think of them for days. I can read. I can laugh,
sometimes I can stop myself from worry
about children and grandchildren. *Life as it is.*
I think I can face dying, though I can't say I'm ready.
I'm just trying to be prepared. There's a difference.

The Story of
Harriet Ferment

Sally-Jane Heit

This is the story of Harriet Ferment.
Do you want to know the most important thing about Harriet?
She is afraid to die.
She doesn't say so
She just is!
She never goes to funerals.
Her mother died.
She didn't go.
Her father died.
She didn't go.
Every time she sees an old person she cries.
Old is dead.
She is terrified.
She thinks if she never gets old, she won't die.
So she wants to have all her parts re-done.
But she can't because she thinks she might die on the operating table.
Everyone thinks she loves life.
She doesn't.
She loves death.
Not that stupid Brad Pitt movie, Joe Death.
Was that stupid or what?
She was obsessed with the idea of death.

Harriet had an early experience with death.
When Harriet was three, her mother disappeared.
One day Harriet's father said he was bringing her mother home.
How could that be?
You die and you could come back?

Harriet's mother was coming back from the dead.

When her mother came into the house, she looked beautiful.

She carried a big basket.

She placed the basket on the sofa.

Her mother was going to pick Harriet up and hug and kiss her.

She didn't.

Instead, she picked a blanket out of the basket.

She hugged the blanket.

She kissed the blanket.

The blanket cried.

This was very strange.

Harriet realized her mother had bought her a crying doll.

She had always wanted a crying doll.

Her mother sat on the sofa, the blanket still in her arms.

"Harriet!" she said, "Sit next to me."

Harriet sat.

Her mother held the blanket so Harriet could look into it.

It was a very funny crying doll.

All red…all scrunched up.

The doll cried and cried and cried and cried.

Harriet thanked her mother for her present.

Her mother and father laughed.

Harriet laughed.

She loved to laugh with her mother and father.

Her father said, "Harriet, this is not a present.

This is your new baby sister, Rona."

He laughed again.

Harriet laughed again, too.

Harriet's mother stopped laughing.

"Harriet!" she said. "This is what is meant by a gorgeous baby."

The blanket still cried.

Her mother put her doll back in the basket.

Harriet asked her mother to pick her up.

"Later," she said, "I have to make formula."

Her mother asked her to watch her baby sister.

Harriet had never watched a baby sister.

At first, she wanted to.

She really tried.

But, Rona, her crying doll sister, wouldn't stop crying.

She looked at her.

She didn't think she was gorgeous.

She was red and scrunchy.

Harriet climbed into the basket.

She sat on Rona, the crying doll.

Her mother and father returned.

They screamed.

Her father pulled her out of the basket.

He shook her.

He shook her hard.

Her mother screamed.

Her mother pushed Harriet away.

Her mother picked up the blanket.

She kissed and hugged it.

It was going to be all right.

Any minute they were going to take Rona back.

They would bring her a real crying doll.

Harriet didn't realize it, but this was her first experience of death.

Harriet couldn't explain death.

She only knew that as with her mother's disappearance.

One moment you were there and then you weren't.

Most nights she dreamed of disappearing.

When she began to menstruate she was sure she was bleeding to
    death.

When she married, she mixed it all together.

A little blood, a little sex, a little death.

She was a good girl.

She didn't understand what she had done wrong.

She didn't want to die.

She didn't understand how it happened.

She was pregnant.

She went into labor.

Each contraction brought her closer to death.

But she didn't die.
Now she had her own crying blanket.

Harriet's life was rich and full and only hurt when she breathed.
As Nina grew, Harriet died many times.
Nina went from a crying blanket to a grunting teenager.
Harriet had to protect Nina from dying.
If she planned every detail of Nina's life, she would not die.
But Nina rebelled.
Harriet didn't understand.
Didn't Nina understand?
If she followed Harriet's list, she wouldn't die.
Nina had her own list.
Nina did not want to go to college.
She wanted to marry Dong Chow, the Chinese Muslim produce
    manager of the Big Y.

Now Nina was pregnant.
Harriet was anxious.
How was she going to keep Nina from dying?
Nina had her baby in the spiritual co-op she and her husband had
    founded and didn't die.
Well, Harriet needed to rewrite her list.
She did.
She asked her husband if she could go to law school.
He asked Harriet if they could do "it."
Every time she had sex she dreamed she disappeared.
She was sure she had died and returned.
She graduated law school.
She passed the bar.
On her 20th wedding anniversary, her husband ran away with her
    sister, Rona.
Harriet wanted to die.
But she didn't.

Death was everywhere.
Her father died.

Her mother died.
Her husband left.
Her daughter moved away.
They all disappeared.
She was afraid to close her eyes.
She knew if she did, she was dead.
Keeping her eyes open was a full time job.
It was exhausting.
Her almost best friends since second grade, Marcia and Edith,
    recommended their therapist.
Harriet refused.
She didn't have any problems.
Not like Marcia and Edith.
Marcia had four husbands and hated all men.
Edith had one husband and loved all men.
Harriet took more classes…basket weaving, re-forestation.
She went on more spiritual retreats.
She swam with more dolphins.
She thought she heard something crack.
She thought it was acid reflux.
It wasn't.
Everyone tried to help.
Nina asked her to babysit for her daughter
    Morning-Light-As-A-Feather.
Marcia asked her to join a ménage with her new girlfriend.
Edith made an appointment for her with her dental hygienist who
    was a fantastic flosser.
When she asked her newspaper delivery boy, Mykos
    Catastraphanes, when he got off from work, she began, ever so
    slowly, to disappear.
She went to a therapist.
The therapist asked her to close her eyes.
She could not.
She did not want to die.
The therapist never said a word.
Not one word.
Harriet thought this was funny.

She laughed.
She never laughed so hard.
Therapy was better than a Marx Brothers' movie.
She started to break up.
Like her cell phone.
She couldn't help herself.
She was sooo tired.
Her eyes just closed.
All by themselves.
She didn't die.
She gave in.

I wonder what will become of Harriet.
I confess.
I willingly acknowledge many similarities between myself and
    Harriet.
I wonder, if I am going to die someday anyway, can I, maybe, enjoy
    life?
I will have to talk that over with Harriet.
In the meantime, I have devised a new daily regimen.
The alarm goes off.
I do not get out of bed.
I pick up my right hand.
I put my left hand on the inside of my right hand's wrist.
Son of a bitch!
It's working.

Betty's Brain

Jan Krause Greene

In the last moment before she lost consciousness, Betty wondered who she would be when she awoke. She and her husband Mark had discussed this many times before agreeing to the experimental procedure that, if all went well, would save her from the ravages of Alzheimer's disease. They had carefully assessed their options, examining each projection of their future life together in minute detail, as if they could take their love, their desires, their children's reactions and examine each under the lens of a microscope—reducing the incredible complexity of human life to a collection of cells pulsing and vibrating against each other. They had convinced themselves because they felt, in the end, they had no other choice. They believed they could bring order and predictability to the rest of their life together if they could save Betty's brain from the rapid and inevitable deterioration of early-onset Alzheimer's.

Betty had agreed to be the first person to have the neural stem cells of another human transplanted into her own brain after her daughter and son-in-law offered to donate stem cells from their newborn son. Knowing that she would be transplanted with cells that would bear some of her own genetic material was comforting, and it was encouraging to know that the cells were from a newborn. It was frightening not to know whether these cells would change her from the person she had been to some new version of herself, but in the final analysis, both Betty and Mark had concluded that this prospect was less frightening than the new version of herself that Alzheimer's promised.

As the surgical nurse inserted Betty's IV line, Mark gently kissed her forehead. "I love you, Betty," he said. "I will always love you … no matter what." He meant what he said, but they both knew she would be easier to love if she was still Betty, the Betty he had lived with and loved for 26 years. This had been the deciding factor for them—betting on the fact that Alzheimer's would take away more of the Betty he loved than having another person's stem cells in her brain would. It was a risk and they both knew it. The night before, while making love, Mark had vowed to stick by her no matter what the outcome.

Three months earlier, sitting in the researcher's office, Betty and Mark and their daughter, Karen, had listened to two neuroscientists and one surgeon explain the procedure. Sitting in a straight-backed armless chair, Betty had clutched the worn leather strap of her pocket book and unconsciously tapped her right foot against the leg of the chair while the surgeon gently touched her head, outlining the incision he would make. He pointed to an area behind her ear, calling it "the point of entry" as he detailed the process of inserting healthy newborn stem cells into her ravaged brain.

Karen sat on a small faded blue couch looking nervous and instinctively rubbing her large belly as if to protect the growing life inside her. She looked from her parents to the doctor. When the surgeon asked if she had any concerns, all she could say was, "If you can promise me it won't hurt my baby, I will do anything to save my mother."

Mark, sitting beside Karen, also asked for reassurance that his unborn grandchild would not be hurt in any way. The surgeon assured him that there was no risk to the baby. Feeling only slightly relieved, he asked the question that had been plaguing him. He wanted to know if infant stem cells had personality traits. Was there a chance that implanting neural stem cells from another person would drastically change his wife's personality? The question scared him so much that he had refrained from asking it until now. The doctors, it turned out, did not know the answer to his question. The research community would be studying Betty to help find the answer.

Karen looked at Betty to see her reaction, but Betty's face was passive. She was, as her family described it, "in a state." Although she had been fully engaged in the conversation just a few moments before, Betty's mind had now drifted to a place known only to her. She stared blankly ahead, slack-jawed and unaware of her surroundings. Her hands, no longer tightly gripping her handbag, rested on her knees. She didn't look worried, or happy, or sad. She appeared emotionless. Karen averted her gaze. It broke her heart to see her mother this way.

At the hospital on the day of her surgery, Betty didn't remember this visit to the doctor. She didn't remember the many long conversations she and Mark had had, agonizing together over whether or not to volunteer for this experimental cure. But she still remembered Mark and Karen and her two sons, and still loved each of them fiercely even though sometimes when they were all together she felt bewildered by all the talking and laughing, and the crying too.

Betty's loss of memory had been getting worse each day. As her neurologist had predicted, early-onset Alzheimer's progressed rapidly. Yet there were days when her mind seemed clear and sharp—days when her sense of humor was quick and her comments witty. These good days made the bad days harder for her family. They wanted to understand what was really happening inside her brain. Why could she think clearly one day and forget how to put her shoes on the next day?

Mark had once heard Alzheimer's described as a "long goodbye." It seemed so terribly accurate to him as he witnessed his wife losing pieces of herself, bit by bit, day by day. He was shocked to realize that with every bit of her that disappeared, she took a little piece of him too. The shared memories, the knowing looks that once conveyed meaning without the need of words, the simple understanding of who he was because of who they were together—he was losing all of this, just as Betty was losing herself. Because of this the choice was easier. They would take this chance because they had each already lost so much of themselves to the war in Betty's brain.

Mark pictured Betty's brain as a battlefield where healthy neurons were waging a valiant battle against the foot soldiers of Alzheimer's—amyloid plaque and tangles of tau protein gone cruelly awry. Doctors had explained to him that the clumps of plaque and tangles of protein prevent vital nutrients from being transported to brain cells, hindering them from sending messages to each other. He pictured the healthy neurons stretching and straining to connect with each other.

He wanted these healthy cells to win this battle more than he had ever wanted anyone to win anything. He believed his survival depended on it, because he believed these neurons made it possible for the rest of Betty's brain to love him. He hoped that their grandson's stem cells could supply the ammunition needed to win the war that was being waged inside her brain—a war that had started without provocation, without a declaration of war, without anyone even knowing when the first battle had begun. It had started with the slightest hint that something was amiss when Betty couldn't remember how to bid her hand in bridge. Mark had jokingly called it a senior moment, even though Betty was only 49.

Betty lay on the operating table, surrounded by nurses, neuro surgeons, and anesthesiologists. An audience watched from the viewing chamber above the operating room. Although they could see inside her brain, none of them could see inside her mind. What was it experiencing as thousands of healthy stem cells were implanted in her brain? Would Betty ever be able to recount it to them? When she regained consciousness would it be obvious that the experiment had worked? Would lost memories be restored? Could she begin to accumulate new ones?

•

Betty felt as if she was emerging from a warm liquid. She longed to be held. She wanted to suckle at her mother's breast. She wanted to be enveloped in loving arms. But first she had to keep going into this scary place. She crawled slowly through a thorny path, struggling to get through the tangle of briars and clumps of rust-colored mud. The further she went, the easier it got. She felt stronger as she made her way to a distant clearing. She felt alive in a way she could not describe. There was something waiting in the sunlight. As she got closer, she recognized it. It was her past. She embraced it lovingly and then continued on to the glowing, pulsing path waiting just beyond. When she reached the path, she stood up and took her first step. She knew just where she was going. The path led to the rest of her life and she couldn't wait to get there.

I Found I Had Neglected Thirst

Rosemary Starace

(for B.G.)

And so,
under the nightstand,
next to my ear,
a porcelain bowl,
full as the moon,
set down.

And thirst came
a hundred times
to the night's kindness,
tapping its rapid and delicate code,
a lullaby of tongues.

Just that day wild turkeys
had come pecking to your winter yard.
You phoned me, your voice was crackling,
you were glad-handing seed from your doorstep—
and into the absurdity of the telephone
clipped to your breast,
you let them coo for me
their long hunger.

Years before, we'd listened in
on what the healer called
a spirit wind
coursing through a woman's heart.
It made a sound like the moon intoning!
It was then I flushed
with the permanent fullness
of this lifetime's longing.

And once, I tell you, lost in mountains,
I slept on the path desire followed.
And the deer came leaping over me
to the near stream and drank all night
of that gleaming moon-chamber.

And in the night, too, Jesus came,
whom I don't know, and he told me
there was nothing
that he brought to save us
but his thirst.

Four Poems

Ruth Irupé Sanabria

I. The Collapse of Greta Oto

The EMT administered as much salvia as he thought her body
   could process
but she kept driveling on about salvation and memory.
Earlier that week a concerned citizen had snitched. The report read
   that she was ruining the landscape with her limp-winged hobble.
No one could ask her about her day; she'd kept blathering,
"some confuse salvation and saving souls
with managing massive emptiness in the yards.
Memory is spayed,
nothing flowers robust and sweet."
She had been captured easily.
Like all minds that surrender, she had always struggled with her
   proclivity
to be limp-winged but had managed it well until the day she sank
into an editorial reveling in the recent death of her mother
and condemning her mother's friends for having *"revered the 'fire*
   of subversion'
the way deer venerate the sweet, dark-pink flesh
and smooth, sturdy canes of a thorn-less raspberry bush…
When the Beast of Memory spews his fire, may they all burn!"
Now, strapped down to the stretcher, spiracle mask fogging up,
there was no point in holding back truth when the Admitting
   Chair asked
what she thought about fire, so she confessed; her heart feared
the transmutation of an era into a fragment of a puzzle.
"It says in your chart that your first and only mission
through the Throat of Silence landed you here,"
the Admitting Chair mumbled while checking the strength of her thorax.

"Mining memory's throat is a solitary practice only in theory,"
he whispered so as to not to be overheard, then closed the chart and
    scuttled away.
A window came in and placed an extra blanket on her bed,
"Here, just in case."
"Window!" She called out, *"My caterpillars? The fire? The Beast of
    Memory?"*
The window upped the oxygen, leaned in, *"Breathe up.*
You've got to abandon that 'work.'
With wings as transparent as yours,
you have no business mining memory's throat.
Who's going to pull you from the long silence next time?"
"But, my babies. Did they make it?!"
"You need to sort your realities if you want to get out of here."

II. Ars Poetica

Story takes her skin. Story takes her bones;
she finds her toes and her fingertips.
When she speaks, like salmon running,
the dead and the living converge.
The river of memory rocks
the hunger of claws and tongues.
Electricity swallows itself back
through its double prod picana,
bullets dislodge themselves from
their chore of destroying
the same day over and over again,
and from the caverns of fear and revision,
skin resurrects the skin.
Each sentence closes in,
the crawl of split skin
sealing its red, wet avulsion.
The enormity of the pending night scares the seven assassins on trial.
They understand that in hell, they will eat their own throats.

III. The Cardinal Delivers Us

Baptize the cardinal in our yard
when I ask: *where is my mother?*
marvel at the cardinal you've named
for she flew to us
an ember among the ovenbirds.
What truths can a cardinal sing?
A bird knows a bird's song
attracts its own fate, not ours.
We are a swirl of red feathers on a canvas.
We are a scarlet flutter in a poem.
I'd climb the almond tree,
climb the brick wall,
and follow the cat
to learn how the cat finishes the cardinal.

IV. Latin American Women Writing In Exile

"*You Can't Drown The Fire.* That's stupid!"
The gas station attendant spat and pumped our gas.
The poet I most admired at that time,
my tio's girlfriend, spoke back,
"Her mother edited this book!"
The gas station attendant kept pumping.
I was the only other person in the car.
He waited for me.
My mother's book of embers, its cover,
Frida's Self Portrait #2, smoldered
in my hands; my face incandesced.
"I don't care who your mother is,
you *can* drown the fire."
"You're going let him say that?"
The worst part of that minute was
that the car had no air conditioning
and he had the basis of a philosophical argument:

water makes us and beats us.
Our most fetid fluids coax life to come again
and quiet our inexhaustible loneliness.
Then, we disappear.
And with good luck, we will swim
in the pool of a human being's memory.
We will travel down a sad cheek,
kiss it and kiss it
before evanescing. We will become
fog on another's windows.
We will morph
into this morning's breathtaking dew,
into the unforeseen
drizzles and downpours; we will reincarnate
in the wet breath of the offspring's offspring
who is telling a story.

Three Poems

Raquel Partnoy

I. Friendship

Fear became our best friend.
He came dressed up as if he were coming to a party,
a long heavy silk tunic covering his body,
wearing the most expensive death-smell perfume.
He brought a huge baggage of books by his big brother Terror
and installed himself in our house
to help.

A model of friendship:
Our real friends were friends of his
and our supposed friends also befriended him;
he wouldn't let them come to our house.

A paragon of virtues:
Wherever we went he seized our arms and scolded us.
He wouldn't let us open our mouths when we searched for our
daughter.
When we went to talk to military chaplains he spoke for us;
when we went to police stations he spoke for us;
when we went to the army headquarters he spoke for us.

An example of solidarity:
If we were awake he would be awake to keep us company;
if we were asleep he would inhabit our dreams.
He managed to take my brushes and work with me;
he didn't let my son study alone for a single minute
and accompanied my husband to his classes at the university.

He stayed at our home for five long months,
until my daughter and her husband "appeared" and were sent to jail.

Since then he never has forgotten to visit us.

II. The Dolls

Three generations of dolls lie on my bed
Our girl plays house, plays baby with them:
her rag doll Pepona, dirty and discolored;
Lulú, her mother's naked and over-bathed doll;
my blue-eyed malcriado with a broken leg.
All play family with her, she talks to them.
She answers for them, attaching together
the puzzle pieces of her little life.

Our dolls are spread on the floors
all over the house. I paint these dolls
lying on the streets of this city's port,
sharing memories with the samovar
on the small table,
pushed by the wind,
swinging in the sky with our little child.

Like our dolls, we three generations are puppets in the hands of a
crazy puppeteer, lives flying at random in this heavy air.

III. Red horizons

In my city of red horizons that trap the winds and shelter the wings
   of monsters,
where a white salt marsh bars the land from bearing fruit, and the
   tamarisk bush houses fear,
there are people who envision new skies to keep on living.

In my city of windows blurred by the dust of indifference and the
   gray complicity of silence,
where streets have kept the indelible prints of the angel of death,
   prints of genocidal boots,
there are people who vanish from the earth,
who were never allowed to meet new skies.

In my city of gloomy parks, where churches are siblings to the killer
   crows, to terror,
where outrageous spokespersons poison the air and break all
   dreams that sprout anew,
there are people who never chose to live under new skies.

Aunt Nkoumou and the Panthers

Pauline Dongala

The story I am about to tell is about my aunt. Aunty Nkoumou lived her entire life in the village of Bikie in the Congo. She was an aunt to all the children in our extended family and did not have a chance to have children of her own. She used to dress in traditional African attire, wrapping one piece of cloth around her waist and another around her torso. She always had a wrap to cover her head, and she walked barefoot. She suffered from leprosy and was physically challenged; her walking was slowed down by her condition. Aunt Nkoumou was a quiet person, not distracted by many things. With no concerns of taking care of a household, she kept her energy and had time to sharpen her spiritual gifts. She was thought of as a mystical person. I personally thought of her as a powerful woman who always empowered other women. Because she was among the elders, she was very respected by other women of the family. She once said to me, "Wherever you go, don't let anybody look down on you." When I heard those words coming from her mouth, I felt like I was receiving a huge electroshock that boosted my self-esteem.

In the village of Bikie, many different clans and families lived together. There were the Basimbingui, Basimaka, Basiniata, Babumu and others. My mother said that in the 1940's, when she was about twelve years old, our men were attacked by a group of men from a neighboring village. The cause of the fighting was that my family was accused of placing a curse on a woman who was married to my cousin. They had lost so many children that my cousin's wife left her husband's village, Bikie, to go back to her own village and family. When she went back, her family consulted a Nganga (a medium and healer) who said that the bad influence was coming from her husband's family. In the meantime, her family kept the woman; her family did not want to give her back to my mother's cousin.

My cousin loved his wife, and so he began visiting her in her village. At the beginning, his wife's family told him about the *mampoh*. A mampoh is a revelation given by the Nganga. Ngangas are considered to be intermediaries between the spirit of the unknown and the ordinary world of humans. Each Nganga has a specific domain of action or activities. Many kinds of Ngangas exist, such as the Nganga Mukissi, who work with water influences, and the Nganga Lungu, who heal fractures. There are Nganga for many other kinds of healing and for providing fetish objects filled with power and intention.

His in-laws did not welcome my mother's cousin during his visits to his wife in her village. Once his in-laws said to him, "We don't want you to come here anymore; our daughter is now free of your family's influence. We are ready to pay back the dowry you and your family gave for her wedding." My mother's cousin was not happy about his wife's family's attitude. He saw himself diminished by the condescending verbal abuse. Rumors followed that he was to be beaten and attacked if he showed up again in their village.

The gossip spread all the way to my mother's village. There was a rumor that he would be killed. One day, my mother's cousin sent a message to his wife that his family wanted to meet his wife's family to settle the dispute in front of the chiefs. Her family rejected the offer and promised to come attack my mother's village if he stubbornly kept seeking his wife. In the meantime my mother's cousin was seeking help in every possible way. The gossip about his search reached the far village.

The African dawn is silent; one hears only the call of the rooster or the song of the early birds, which played the role of clocks to remind people that the protector spirits, the Bafu, are gone and it is time for humans to wake up. It is in that time that the body is completely relaxed, and the soul begins to rise up, to catch from the dreams the experiences that the body cannot physically see because our daytime vision is blocked and blurred by distraction and lack of readiness. It was in this dreamy and foggy time that my mother's cousin and other members of the family heard noises all around outside their house. The noise hypnotized everybody and made them wonder what was going on. Then it became clear even to my relatives who were half-awake that they were being attacked.

The group outside was hurling insults against my mother's clan, against their men, and against the targeted cousin. The attackers started banging at the gate and screaming loudly. "Come out, we are here to fight." The first person who came out from the housing compound was my mother's cousin. The group grabbed him and started beating him. Then my mother's entire family jumped into the fight. The group that came from the far village was equipped with poles. They had come ready to fight their enemies, while my mother's family never dreamed of being attacked that morning. They had thought only of having a normal morning, where morning rituals were to take place, such as calls to spirits, greetings, prayers, river showers, and the cooking of the early meal that preceded the day's work.

My mom's family was beaten. Their men were humiliated. The scene of the fight drew many people. It was a profound insult for a well-respected family to be caught in such a situation. My mother's sister Nkumu was in despair. She distanced herself from the crowd as if she were in a trance. She faced the forest and turned her back to the fighting scene. With her legs wide apart, she raised both arms above her head. Her face changed; her look became focused and powerful. The color of her eyes also changed. She started shouting, calling the names of her clan as if it were a mantra; then she called the names of deceased members of the family, then many long singing vowels. My mother said she repeated everything and gestured for about seven minutes. She called to the ancestors for help saying, "Your people are being massacred, your men are betrayed, your men have lost their honor."

Suddenly three panthers came out of the jungle, walking slowly and roaring. They were strong, fat adult panthers. The movement of the panthers was unusual; they lined up one behind the other, and walked slowly through the village. None of the panthers attacked any of the people gathered, though panthers are usually very aggressive animals. On that day they just walked peacefully. Seeing the three animals, the crowd stopped fighting and dispersed within minutes.

Nkoumou kept chanting while the three animals crossed the village and returned to the jungle.

My mother's cousin never got his wife back, but there were no more attacks on the village. My mother's clan in Bikie understood that the ancestors or Bafu did not want them to keep fighting for that marriage. The whole village recognized the message. Even before this incident, my mother's sister was considered a powerful woman. After the incident of the panthers, it was widely known that she could summon powers of the ancestors and other forces from the world of spirits.

In summoning the Panthers, Aunt Nkoumou saved the entire village. She was capable of stopping a fight that could have been very ferocious, leading to a mass killing within the two contentious families. But even though Aunt Nkoumou was famous, like many other women in the family, the weight of the traditional values colored the way she was viewed. Most of the family did not recognize the power that she or other women manifested. Men of the community often used the prefix "moua," which means "sub," and then added the word "woman," implying that women were sub-people.

Today, when I look back at female family members who have been influential in my clan, I think of them as movers and shakers. The light and insight they brought were sometimes more significant than that which came from the macho side of the family. What made people fearful of women like her? Only those who weren't ready to see a woman leader in the family disapproved of her notable presence. Similarly, another aunt of that generation was called "Tractor" in a disparaging way, because she always had a flourishing harvest every year. She was a strong woman who harvested bags of cassava and peanut that were twice or three times the size of those harvested by the rest of women in the village. She attracted the jealousy of men. Tales and gossip said that she had mystical powers and spirits that were stealing other people's chances of producing more crops. She was very proud of herself, but in the eyes of men, she was only a woman.

Men received more respect than Aunt "Tractor." They had many wives and bore many children. Those men were the people in command in the family. Throughout my entire childhood I never saw a female chief of the village. Wise women were respected and called elders, but they never led a village. They were given roles such as counselors to other women or midwives. They were healers but not leaders.

Today, we still see history repeat itself in many ways; the past and the present teach us to look within ourselves, and to recognize that it is often people's fears of women's power that prevent the women of the world from thriving.

No One Knew

Maggie Katz

No one knew.
Not my husband.
Not my mother.
Not my best friend.
No one knew the fear I'd been hiding for 10 years.

It first gripped me one day when I was eight years old. I was standing on the tarmac at JFK airport, the Air Canada prop plane towering behind my mother, my 10-year-old brother, and me, as we said goodbye. It was a hot July afternoon in the late 1960's and the clouds of dust that swirled around us smelled of stinky exhaust fumes. I could feel my brother's eagerness to get on with the good-byes and fly for the first time. Not me. I was anxious and upset. I didn't want to leave my mother, and I didn't want to go away. I loved my cousins, aunts and uncles in Canada, but that didn't make leaving any easier.

I stood in my 1960's Jackie Kennedy Pill Box suit with the swirling ruby- colored paisley fabric. Blonde, like me, my brother stood beside me in his blue seer-sucker shorts and suit jacket.

The stewardess beckoned to us with quick waves of her hand, impatient to get us on board. It was time to go, to say goodbye. She was tidy, buttoned up with no soft edges in her Air Canada navy polyester suit. Her bleach-blonde beehive hairdo stayed perfectly in place despite the strong wind that came from the plane's engines. My stomach lurched and I felt sick. I moved forward and gave my mother a hug and kiss.

Then, obediently, I walked to the white metal stairs that folded down like an accordion from the airplane door. I climbed the steps designed for people with much longer legs. I had a flashback of little John Kennedy Jr., a small boy walking down steps like the ones I was climbing, holding onto his mama's hand.

I wanted my mama to hold my hand. Hot tears started to spill down my cheeks as I climbed.

At the entrance to the plane, I turned and looked back at my mother, shielding my eyes from the sun and also hiding my tears. I wanted to be strong and brave.

I knew she needed me to be all those things for her sake as well as mine. I forced a smile, gave a last wave, and turned around again, feeling the anxiety of separation overwhelm me. Stepping into the plane, I felt like I was heading off to another galaxy. I was afraid I'd never come back.

The First Class passengers swam in a blur of tears like I was underwater. I heard murmurs and soft clucks of concern. Instead of welcoming their sympathy, I was miserable. Ashamed. Head down, I followed the brown leather heels of my brother's shoes. The stewardess pointed to our seats. In a falsely warm voice she asked, "Would you like some 7up? Coke? Coloring books?"

I turned my face to the window to hide my tears while my brother answered for both of us, happily agreeing to everything offered. He was excited to fly and go on an adventure.

The engines whirred, then burst into screams of raging power. They seemed like roaring dragons to me, dragons that were tearing my heart out. The plane surged forward into the sky, and we left home and my mother behind.

My uneasy relationship with flying was born. I did not feel safe. Engines throttled at takeoff brought back gut-wrenching memories of partings. Anxiety blossomed like a mushroom cloud.

Fast forward to 2002, one year after 9/11. I hadn't flown in nine years, since an airplane scare I'd had just before the end of my Peace Corps service with my husband in the Marshall Islands. It was just before I had become pregnant with our daughter.

After 9/11, I began having frequent, hellish nightmares of going down in plane crashes with the twin towers collapsing on me. I was too embarrassed to speak about my fear of flying to anyone. I missed traveling to faraway places, missed having exotic adventures, but I couldn't get past it.

As our daughter grew, my husband suggested we fly to places we'd never been. I knew what to say to end the discussion, to keep myself safe: "No, let's save our money." He'd happily acquiesce, pleased at this new turn in my thinking. Until then he'd been the budget-conscious one.

I applied for a job at The College Internship Program, a program to support young adults with learning differences. The interview was going well, until the director said the job would involve a few overnight trips a year. "Not many," he continued breezily. "You'll fly to conferences and be gone three to five days." He knew I had an 8-year-old.

My stomach knotted up as he smiled kindly and asked, "Would that work for you?"

I felt queasy. Fly and leave my daughter at the same time?

"Uhh, yes," I nodded, "that could work." I smiled wanly, feeling my chest starting to tighten.

That night I told my husband about the fabulous job. It was all great, except for one problem: I had to take some trips. He focused on the details of how to get our daughter to and from school while he was at work. "We'll figure it out," he said reassuringly.

I got the job. It was work I loved, and I easily revolved around my daughter's school schedule. I even had summers off. Perfect! Except that I had to fly. I had a few months to figure it out.

I bought *The Anxiety and Phobia Workbook, A Step-By-Step Program for Curing Yourself of Extreme Anxiety, Panic Attacks and Phobias* by Edmund Bourne. I liked the dedication: "*This book is dedicated to anyone who has struggled with anxiety or an incomprehensible fear.*" I studied the chapter on "Visualization," which began on a hopeful note: "You may or may not be able to will your way to a particular goal, yet repeatedly visualizing the attainment of that goal has a good chance of bringing exactly what you seek."

I followed the guidelines, imagining myself driving to the airport, walking through security, sitting in the waiting area before the flight, and stepping into the plane, and walking to my seat. During my practice sessions, my heart raced, my palms got sweaty, and my mouth went dry. But with more practice I noticed subtle shifts, and the symptoms of my anxiety began to lessen. I thought I could do it. I had to do it.

But the week of my flight I couldn't sleep. Plane crash nightmares continued to haunt me. I needed more visualization practice!

On the day of my flight, I was filled with anxiety but made it to my seat. Uneasy and shaky, I waited for take-off but the plane didn't move. We waited and waited. Something was wrong. Finally, the Captain's voice came over the speakers. "Ladies and gentlemen, this is your Captain. I'm sorry for the delay, but we will be delayed a little longer. We have a little part we need to repair."

No! No! No! This couldn't be happening. Please God, No! Why did he have to tell us? I didn't want to know about broken parts.

He came on again. "Ladies and Gentlemen, this is your Captain. We've decided we are not going to fix the part."

Oh my God. That sounded worse. My heart raced as I went into high alert. I started to sweat with fear.

Another five minutes passed. He came on again. "Ladies and gentlemen, we've decided we are going to fix the part. I apologize for the further delay."

I took a deep breath of relief, trying to unclench my jangled nerves. Another five minutes passed and then the Captain came on yet again. "Ladies and gentlemen, we're not going to fix the part after all. It's just the starter motor. We'll be fine."

The starter motor! That didn't sound like something you could do without!

Fear rising like a tidal wave filled my gut and chest. My superb ability to "visualize" went into high gear, but not to my benefit. I envisioned the engines choking out at 40,000 feet, with no "starter motor." I saw the whole scene in an instant, we were crashing, screaming, sobbing, on the verge of death! I began an internal face-off, my rational versus my irrational selves at war.

"I've got to get off this plane!"

"No, you can do it. Stay on the plane."

"No, I can't, I have to get off the plane."

"Stay on the plane. You can do it."

"No, I can't."

I snapped. Hands fumbling, I tore at the seat belt. The latch popped open. I jumped up, scooting past both businessmen beside me. I walked quickly up the long aisle to the front of the plane.

I felt 250 pairs of eyes boring into my back, but I didn't care. I was getting off. I'd never have to see them again. I reached the front, startling the two male flight attendants who jumped in their small fold down seats. One was tall and thin, the other short. They looked up, eyes widening.

"Ma'am, we've closed the door. You must sit down. You must go back to your seat," the short one said.

"No. I want to get off the plane," I said in a quietly determined voice.

"Ma'am, the door is shut. We are leaving the gate. You must sit down."

"I want to get off," I repeated.

We had a short standoff, staring at one another. I didn't move. The steward surprised me by reaching above his head and pulling a phone receiver down off the wall.

"Captain," he sighed, "We have a woman who wants to get off the plane."

He did something else I didn't expect. He handed me the phone.

"Hello?" I said in a small voice, feeling very much like the scared 8-year-old girl I'd been on my first flight.

"Hello, what is your name?" The pilot had a kind baritone voice. His tone was warm and calming, as though he had all day to talk to me and walk me patiently through my fear. As though it didn't matter that there were 250 passengers waiting and the control tower had given the "go ahead" for take-off.

"Maggie, Maggie Katz," I said.

"Well, Maggie," he said in a voice like warm mahogany. "Tell me, what's the problem?"

"I, um, want to get off the plane."

"And why is that?"

I gulped, "Uh, I don't feel safe."

"Let me tell you something, Maggie. First, I'm the father of three teenage sons, and I have a wife I love very much. I would never do anything that would compromise my making it home. Equally important Maggie, I would never, ever, do anything that would put my passengers in danger."

"Oh," I said.

"The starter motor sounds like an important piece of equipment, but it's not."

"Oh," I said again.

"We don't need it to take off, fly, or land," he said.

"Oh," I said, beginning to feel reassured.

"We don't need it at all. It's like if the CD player in your car broke. You can still drive the car. You just can't use your CD player."

"Oh." I felt lighter, calmer.

"So, Maggie, what do you think? Do you think you can fly?"

"Yes."

"Are you sure?"

"Yes. I'm sure." I knew I could.

"Okay, that's great."

"Thank you. Thank you so much." My voice wobbled, my eyes filling with tears.

"You're welcome," he said, and his warm voice clicked off.

I handed the phone back to the flight attendant and braced myself to face the 250 passengers behind me, who must have been sure I was a nut case, or worse, a terrorist. Flushed with embarrassment, like when I was eight, I dropped my gaze to the floor, and started the long walk back to my seat, using my peripheral vision so I wouldn't have to look anyone in the eye. When I finally got there, I slid back past both businessmen.

"Sorry," I whispered.

I buckled up, pursed my lips, and looked out at the tarmac to hide my mortification. But inside I felt calm.

The Captain came over the speakers. "Ladies and Gentlemen, I want to share something with you ...." He went on to repeat what he'd told me about the starter engine and how it wasn't needed to fly. I felt a collective whoosh, a release of air as the passengers breathed sighs of relief. Shoulders and bellies relaxed and the tension left the plane. I felt less foolish.

Three times during the flight, the flight attendant came to check on me.

"Are you alright ma'am?" he kept asking.

I flushed pink each time, my ears red, my cheeks burning. I smiled and nodded, assuring him, "Yes, I'm fine."

The flight went smoothly and we landed safely. I was alive. I waited to be the last passenger to get off the plane so I could thank the pilot. I walked up the aisle beaming like a new bride. As I did, I saw the tall, slim flight attendant elbow the captain, nodding his head at me.

The Captain, a tall, portly man with an athletic frame, towered above me. I felt short before him, yet whole and strong. Our eyes met. There was an instant connection. We each broke into a broad, open smile.

"Maggie?" he asked.

I nodded.

"How was it?"

"Good. Thanks to you, I was fine! Thank you so much for your kindness!"

As I stepped off the plane I wanted to do a victory dance and shout with joy, "I did it! I made it!" My life opened up once again. Adventure beckoned.

Goodnight

Casey Anne Hall

Here lie the wanderers, the ones without rest.
Here lie the thinkers, the jailers, the best.
Here lie the ones with the stones in their shoes
who let themselves lie, but never to lose.
Here lies the girl, the sneerer, the cruel,
Here lies the boy, who thought he was, too.
Here lies your maker, who did try to see
if he could indeed make you the best you could be.
Say goodnight to your soldiers,
and all their good work.
Visit their battlefields,
where they no longer lurk.
Goodnight to the leaders,
goodnight to the slaves.
Goodnight to the smithies,
getting up from their lathes.
Their weapon is broken now,
shattered by fate.
You must really be going now,
lest you be late.
But one final goodnight,
will bring rest to them all,
farewell to the one
who tried to cushion
your fall.

A Hard Story

Leigh Strimbeck

"That was a hard story you told," she wrote to me in an email. She was a playwright and a storyteller. It was only a few weeks after and here I was, emailing someone I didn't know all that well about what had happened. "A hard story," she called it. And she was right; but I didn't see it as a story yet, even though I found myself telling it over and over again to anyone who would listen.

There are so many things I don't remember about that time, but this is what I can't forget:

I was walking to my doctor's office feeling smug, almost 20 weeks pregnant and barely showing. I attributed this to yoga and careful eating. The walk was about a mile through the small town I had lived in for ten years while I worked with a regional ensemble theater company. Having recently married, I no longer lived there and had moved over an hour away to be with my husband, Joe. But I was back to work on a collaborative project with the company and happy to be among friends as I started this new chapter in my life. Proud of my small pregnant belly, I strode along Main Street, past the local hardware store and diner, up a hill, the college on the right, student housing on the left, up another little hill and into a one-story medical building.

My doctor was a rare breed, a general practitioner who still delivered babies. I had been seeing him for years about ailments big and small. He was gentle, smart, and he had a dry wit. When I got married, I made an appointment with him and said, "Joe and I want to have a baby, and we wondered if you had any, you know, advice?" There was an extended pause. "I think you'll figure it out," he replied in his laconic Midwestern way. I took the whole enterprise so seriously that it took me some time before I saw how funny his advice was. I did get pregnant right away, but miscarried soon after, during the opening week of a play I was directing, after we had announced my pregnancy to the world. I spotted all week, and after the final dress rehearsal, I miscarried in the middle of the night. I went to see my doctor with the tissue I had passed in the middle of the night in a snack-size plastic bag. There was the snap of the garbage can when he tossed it out. I grilled him with questions trying to find out what I might have done wrong. Decaf coffee? Too much exercise? The stress of directing a play? He had no answers. "When you're ready, try again."

I got pregnant again, quite soon after. This time we waited until after the first trimester to tell any of our friends and family. I am glad all this happened in the years before social media. I checked in for my appointment, 20 weeks and feeling great. I had felt the baby move for the first time that week. A fluttering like a butterfly, like a tiny goldfish swimming by. The examination at the office was routine. I don't remember if there were any tests, but I do recall that when we parted, he mentioned that he was going on vacation that very Friday afternoon, so I was surprised when, later that day, he called me. He could be very droll, but on this call his voice was quiet and direct. I was staying in guest-artist housing, which also happened to be an ex-boyfriend's apartment. I leaned against the doorjamb of the kitchen and twisted the long, coiled phone cord between my fingers. He had concerns, he said. The fetus wasn't big enough and he wanted me to go to a major medical center two hours west, as soon as possible. He had already called the medical center and had scheduled us for Monday morning. I called Joe. We spoke to our family. We all knew that it was serious, that there could be a hard decision right around the corner.

We passed a long weekend, during which I performed in the show that I had come to town to do. When we got to the Medical Center, I had an ultrasound. The technician said, "I want you to listen closely, because I'm going to say some sobering things." I don't remember the rest, but I do remember that I got dressed and we were ushered out in the hallway to wait to see another doctor. Then there was a sound, a howling sound, and it was coming from me. Joe sat close and held me as I convulsed forward, bent at the waist. I couldn't have controlled that sound any more than I could have controlled a baby that was crowning. Suddenly, a private room was found for us to wait in, instead of the hallway with all the other pregnant women.

There are words that brand themselves on your heart. Semi-lobar holoprosencephaly. The brain was mostly fluid, the hemispheres not fusing, the umbilical cord incomplete. Here's what's going to happen, they said: this baby will die in utero, be stillborn, or there's a 5% chance of life which will be a maximum of five months on life support, no feeding, smiling, sitting up—living briefly and painfully, only to die. Stillbirths are complicated, I was told, especially at my age.

"Please," we said. "Tell us what you would do; don't mince words. We are pro-choice."

The doctor said that if it were his wife or his daughter, he would advise her to terminate. He was straightforward and clear. It was a teaching hospital, and he had asked us if an intern could be in the room. I remember that I felt bad for the intern having to be part of this in any way. I gripped the arm of the chair, industrial blue fabric, trying to hold myself together for the conversation. But it wasn't a hard decision. I was losing my second pregnancy; we were losing our second chance at being parents, one way or the other. I was already 36. We chose sooner rather than later, termination rather than stillbirth.

As soon as the decision was made, the doctor concluded by saying, "We're a state-funded hospital. We can't have a role in any part of this decision."

We stood up, and as we left the room a nurse opened a cupboard and handed us a photocopy of a brochure with information about a clinic in Philadelphia that performed second-trimester abortions. We asked to use the office phone and were told we could not, to please leave. Down the elevator we went, and called the Philadelphia clinic from the bank of payphones in the lobby. We must have been in some kind of shock. It didn't occur to us to research, to step back and look around for the best place to go. The brochure said Philadelphia, and to Philadelphia we would go. We never should have stayed in Pennsylvania. This was 1994, and much of the experience we were about to have was because of Pennsylvania Governor Casey and his determined efforts to eradicate all abortion.

The next day we drove down and found the clinic on the second floor of a nondescript building. The halls were shabby and dim, lined with boxes outside of the flimsy doors with taped-on signs that read "Biohazard, blood samples only"—NO DRUGS in this box. The waiting room was full. No one made eye contact; the TV prattled and flashed from a high corner. Once the process started, I was rushed from room to room: urine samples, blood samples, the ultrasound with a pizza menu on top, and gel from another patient still on the wand, the wand sweeping over my belly confirming the beating heart, the tiny flickering I had already felt. It seemed like the nurses were barking at me until finally I said, "Please, we wanted this pregnancy, please stop yelling."

We were then ushered into a room to sign a stack of papers. We were required by law to name the fetus and to pay for its cremation. In the last room there was a group of people waiting for "counseling," also required by law. A full-color beautifully produced booklet of photographs of a healthy fetus in every stage of development up through birth was put into our hands, for us to keep. The person who ran the brief session read the statements that he was required to read. He seemed to realize that all of us in that situation had a different difficult tale and no one needed judgment and shame, though he was required to provide it, as well as to underscore that we could die by seeking this procedure.

At this point, the conditions in this office seemed so marginal that Joe and I considered leaving. It didn't seem clean or safe. But we agreed not to walk out until we met with the doctor, one of the very few in the state who would do this surgery, or any abortion procedure at all. He was staggering under lawsuits and harassment. He was so radical that he apparently hadn't had time to change his haircut since the 70's; one of the nurses told me his nickname was Disco Doc. She said not to worry. He was very good.

We liked him and appreciated the time he took speaking with us. When we found out that the actual procedure would be in a nearby hospital we decided to continue. Then, as required by law, we were sent away for 24 hours to make sure we knew what we were doing, in case we wanted to change our minds. I felt like I was being patted on the head by the state, treated like someone with cognitive difficulties. There, there little girl, are you *sure* you know what you want? We went back to the Comfort Inn in Philadelphia to "consider our decision," which meant going out to dinner and talking about getting through this, talking about what we might do if we couldn't have a successful pregnancy, ever.

When we returned the next day, the nurse inserted laminaria (which I was told was a kind of algae) into my cervix to begin dilation and sent us back to the Comfort Inn to wait. For pain, I was prescribed one Percocet, plus they told me I could take Aleve. We walked out of the clinic and I felt fine, but while we were filling the prescription at the pharmacy a wave of dizziness hit me, and the pain began. On the car ride back to the hotel I had to press my feet up against the dashboard as the contractions came. Joe held me up to walk me into the hotel, but still I hobbled forward, bent over in cramping pain. Needless to say, there was no sleep that night. I held off taking the Percocet until midnight and spent most of the night lying on my back on the floor, pressing a rolled up washcloth into my lower back to ease the pain. I watched a mother-daughter beauty pageant. Out of the window I could see the lights arching through the darkness on a bridge into the city. Joe mostly slept, which was fine by me. I've always thought if there are two of you, at least one should be rested, especially when the hard stuff hits.

The next morning, we were back at 6 a.m. to check into the hospital as instructed. Even at that early hour the waiting room was filled with bodies. There were no seats available. We were part of a group of people waiting for appointments all over the hospital, not just for Disco Doc, all of us waiting for the next phase of our medical journeys. We were told to find a place and wait, so we sat on the floor, as some of the others were doing. In too much pain to argue, I continued to labor, writhing on the floor for about an hour and a half, until it was too much and Joe went off to complain. "My wife is in labor," he said. At last a bed was offered.

The worst part of the next stage was that the person putting in my IV line took multiple stabs to get it right. Not what I needed at that point. Finally, someone else took over and did it in one go. When I was wheeled into the operating room, I looked up at the doctor and said, "I hope you got a lot of sleep last night." Then they pushed the anesthetic into my veins, the kindest act, and I didn't come to until I was going up an elevator into the recovery room.

After a recovery period of a few hours (I remember that the patient in the bed next to me was a 14-year-old girl who had also just had an abortion) we drove two hours north back home to the Scranton area, which I would later learn was considered the "home of the pro-life movement." We were in a hurry to get home. There are no words for a time like this, or if there are, they are simple: "Are you hungry? Do you want to lie down? Does it hurt?"

When we got home, Joe said he was going to mow the lawn, but first we had to do something else. We may have paid for a cremation, but that was meant to be a punishment, not a part of true grieving. Without discussion we went into the woods behind our house and held a ceremony, burying an avocado, because I had craved them so during that pregnancy and sprinkled the little mound of dirt with rose petals. Joe looked down at the ground and cried.

I went to lie down and the next phase soon hit. There is a whole new kind of hurt when half of your body fills with milk for a baby and half of your body bleeds the loss. My breasts swelled up and were as hard as rocks. Ice packs helped, and more ibuprofen, but the only thing to be done was wait it out. Lying in bed, that same afternoon as the surgery, I talked to a few people on the phone. I tried to explain what we had been through, but I was so angry and baffled that it colored everything I said.

It had been just a week since I walked up the hill to the doctor's office on that beautiful summer day, feeling so proud of what little weight I had gained, of how much energy I had. Naively, I had thought I would come home, rest, and drive an hour to the theater the next day to perform. But when I got out of bed the next morning and was overcome by dizziness, I called the stage manager. He was matter of fact, and had already lined up an understudy earlier in the week when I told him what was happening and where we were going. I didn't know I would feel so weak. How could I know? I knew nothing about these situations, never knew how common these losses are until they happen to you and everyone wants to tell you their story. "I had four miscarriages." "I had two, and then a stillbirth, then my first daughter."

So many people wanted to show me they understood by telling me a story of their own loss. One friend met me for lunch and told me a long, explicit story of her cat dying, including the burial and the blood coming out of the cat's mouth. That was the story that did me in, and I promised myself I wasn't going to listen to any more stories for a while, no matter how well-intentioned, and no matter how hard someone was trying to connect. This was my story. It happened to me. And I needed to sort it out, to rinse it over and over again like the dirtiest laundry until I could wear it soft and dry like a threadbare shirt.

Over time, as I told the story, we heard there was a clinic in Vermont that specialized in second trimester abortions where I would have been treated with respect and care, even tenderness. Over time, I talked about it to a newspaper reporter and found myself on the receiving end of threatening hate mail. Over time, I gave birth to our first son, and 18 months after that, our second son. I had no birth plan with either of them, and have no heroic birth tales to tell. I had them both in hospitals. They both were full-term and healthy.

There are so many things I don't remember about that time, but I will tell you what I do remember: in the worst of it there is a story writing itself, and that story is yours for the rest of time. I told mine until I couldn't anymore, and then Joe took it up. One night at dinner, we sat with another couple we were getting to know. The husband made a casual remark about "those people who have abortions." And Joe told him the whole story while I sat suddenly still: palms damp, breath trapped, heart knocking in my chest to escape, all of me contracting and expanding as he told our hard story.

Why I Chant

Diane Kavanaugh-Black

(For Mary, and in memory of Judy and Tommy)

I have always been told I don't sing well. In a group, I jump to the note next to me and then waver, unsure, if a different note croons closer to my ear. I'll attempt snippets with my car CD player or part of a hymn I've hummed a hundred times before, but only when fairly confident I will land correctly. Even then, I wibble and wobble.

At yoga school last year, chant began our day. I had to open my mouth and make sound come out. On target or out of key, it didn't matter. First thing, we intoned "the resonance of the universe," Om, followed by three Sanskrit stanzas of the Student-Teacher Mantra. Almost sixty of us perched our sit-bones on little black cushions while, out the window, sunrise pinked the eastern sky. Mountain fog dissipated into the evergreens. Our eyes remained closed, or followed the lines on a large-print poster up front. The mantra song felt strange to many, and made us itch and wiggle like little kids. Over twelve days the chant became more familiar.

During the month-long break between school sessions, I committed to continue, using a grainy digital video recorded one morning. At that point, I needed to be led. By the third stanza, my throat usually hurt. I tried again and again every daybreak, with a vocalization some mornings tentative and froggy, other times expansively bouncing off the yoga room walls. Breath slowed and deepened out of necessity; chant warmed my throat and warmed my thoughts toward myself.

Deeper breath invited gentle movement and heat. Tears dribbled into my mouth as Om came out. Heart-thumps of happiness surprised me. I recognized unwanted thoughts and let them float away. Finally, calm replaced my nausea and frustration. This was not just a tune.

When we returned to our final training session, I heard my morning voice steady and confident.

Out of school now, why do I do it?

•

One afternoon I sat in my kitchen, which reeked of cooking detritus. Basil stems and onion ends needed to be taken to the trash; cabbage bits and tea leaves sogged in the sink; crumbs sprinkled the table and floor. I was home early because my therapist had forgotten our appointment–*what deep things does THAT say about me?* I half-joked to myself as I looked around the kitchen and unpacked my bag.

On the way home, I had stopped at the used bookstore and found two paperbacks for the lake vacation I'd planned with my best friend. At my messy table I acknowledged to myself that she and I would have to put off that vacation. Her brother was sick. Instead she would drive five hours back and forth to him a couple days a week, and then to doctors and hospitals in search of diagnosis, prognosis, the plan, whatever that plan might be, however long it might take. Because of love.

Mourning her losses and mine, I asked myself: How can I make my life like a vacation without a trip? *Give yourself permission*, my therapist might have said. Stay up late and crush basil into pesto, cut watermelon and freeze grapes for hot afternoon snacking, wash lettuce. Toss out a sprouting sweet potato, notice the sticky floor under my feet, acknowledge I ate maybe one too many pieces of the blueberry buckle baked in the beautiful dark. *Feel it all.*

Earlier, I had given the therapist some of that blueberry buckle as we laughed over the scheduling error. Now I thought, *I would send some to my best friend if I could fly it there.* In the midst of her pain, she'd mailed me a royal blue Pashmina shawl, with a card reading: *Wrap yourself in this hug from me.*

I want to take her to the lake we'd planned to visit, hear the loons and go on long photo safaris in search of wild flowers and angles of light, and huff the thickly oxygenated Canadian forest air. Drape myself like a scarf around her sad, sad shoulders. Feed her blueberry buckle and sip Chambord into the evening, watch the hummingbirds and mist dance in over the beach.

·

That's why I chant.

I chant to create space, to take in distress and delight. I chant, holding close my best friend and her gravely ill brother. I chant and remember my friend Judy who died two years ago. I remember all the deaths I've known. I chant, love gliding out of me. I chant into lakes and ponds and rivers and creeks, up the farmland and mountains, through the cumulus and wispy and mackerel skies. I chant into my cells: skin and fat and muscle and bone; lungs, intestines, heart. Into my toes and fingers. Through my navel: center of gravity, center of balance, center of self. Then out again and out again. Stretch, release. Expand, contract.

Time passes and I am inhaling, vibrating, exhaling, feeling.

Time passes; I am in my breath and in my body so time is inconsequential.

Chanting beckons me back to the yoga mat and back to myself.

Chanting opens me with sound.

So most mornings, I chant.

An Unusually Warm November

Jana Laiz

It's early November and the bank clock announces a balmy seventy degrees. I shake my head in disgust, car window rolled down several inches. Arriving at the post office, the chatty postman says, "Good morning! What a day! I would love to be outside today!" The wind is up, leaves swirling on the too warm breeze and instead of agreeing with him, which I actually do, I say something like, "It's too weird, unnatural." He looks at me, disappointed, probably thinking what a downer I am. One of those environmentalists. "Leave the door open on your way out," he calls, trying to stay upbeat amidst my gloomy protestations.

The day is magnificent, he's right. The sky is wrapped in shades of dusky blue and gray. The sunlight is hitting the trees in that almost divine way, bathing the leaves in color; light here, dark there, forcing me to pull my car over and just look. Last night had been warm and full of stars when my puppy needed to go out. The howling wind had woken us both up. I padded out in only my nightgown and slippers. No need for even a robe. My pup and I looked up, watching clouds scudding across the star-dotted sky. He cocked his head as he listened to the coyotes yipping far off in the distance. So warm, so strange and new, yet oddly comforting.

It's been said that while we were busy discussing climate change, climate changed.

I've fought so hard against this change for most of my life; running from one protest march to the next to save the whales, to stop big oil, to decrease our carbon footprint. I've reduced, reused, recycled, composted, bought gas-sipping cars, climbed on soapboxes, asked people to turn off their idling engines, angering them in the process, written eco-themed novels, and tried to live the most conscious life I could.

I've been thinking a lot about my postman. Does he not get the implications of this unnaturally warm November? Isn't he worried about floods and storms and landslides, hurricanes and wild fires burning out of control? Do the plea-filled envelopes he delivers, adorned with photographs of ailing bats and drowning polar bears, move him not at all?

Or is he simply a person living in the moment and enjoying a beautiful day? Is he merely being present when someone walks into the post office flushed and windswept, with only a windbreaker for protection when in the past they would be swathed in wool and down? And if so, is there anything wrong with that? Is it a sign of naïveté? Ignorance? Denial? Is he a Zen master in disguise teaching me to enjoy the sun on my face and a cup of coffee on my deck, sitting on furniture that normally would have been stored away in preparation for a long cold winter?

I picked a violet the other day. Just a lone violet growing in the November grass. I put it in a tiny vase and admired its purple perfection, all the while being disturbed by its late presence. Today, I watch my two dogs basking in the sun, my twelve-year-old dachshund, blissfully rolling in the warm still-green grass while the puppy gnaws on the stump of a dead tree, both oblivious to global warming or whatever this new paradigm signifies. They are simply enjoying a warm November day. My puppy looks up from his stump to watch a yellow butterfly flutter past. A butterfly. In November.

There are two woodstoves in my house that have been lit twice since my wood was delivered. By this time years past I would have gone through a quarter of a cord. So how do I come to terms with this change? Do I adapt? Fight it? Accept it? Complain? I'm not sure. I do know that when the winter winds blast in from Canada, I'm ready for the Costa Rican Pacific. I'm not a hypocrite, but I don't want to be a purveyor of doom. Change is definitely happening. There's no denying that the world is heating up. But today, on this unusually warm November day, from where I sit, it's beautiful.

There's a story of a man falling off a cliff to his death. On his way down he sees a flower growing from a rock and smiles. Can I be that guy?

I think I'll go to the post office and get some clarity. And my mail.

When the Sky Fell

Yvette "Jamuna" Sirker

An August morning
in America
South of the Mason Dixon line.
Above oil slicks like rainbows riding the waves of the
Gulf of Mexico.
Come Mr. Tally Man. Tally me bananas
On the northernmost tip of the Third World.
Day-o.
I woke up to groaning;
Air conditioner fighting to push out
the heaviest heat morning could imagine.
Day-ay-ay-o.
I peeked outside to make sure the sky was still there. Been doing
    that for a while now.
Saw steam rising off Miss Beth's black tar roof.
        Miss Beth
        Lucille Ball red hair
        Porch-time stories of the old days:
        soda fountains and root beer floats;
        cool fall evenings on the oak-tree tire-swing.
        Her husband who drank and smoked too much.
        After she kicked him out
        Her eyes stopped watering.
        Miss Beth
        Her wine-soaked cackle made pigeons scatter.
As I checked on Old Mr. Sky, there he was: Mr. Menacing Sun just
    glaring.
I snatched up the paper/news/fishwrap:
War
Oil
Soldiers dying in a desert

Earth choking on greed
Oceans boiling
Earth poised to strike back.
The usual.
But The Lady Spinning in the Gulf?
She was gonna strike somewhere else
This time. The fishwrap said.
So I kicked back to watch my ceiling fan spin instead.
To listen to neighborhood birds fussin'
Cat-in-heat making all the boy cats real nervous. Dogs yappin' at
  rats scurrying along power lines.
And a Bag Lady lookin' up at me:
>   *Do you see the sun's rain pouring into my skin?*
>   *I feel it all over*
>   *My skin loves drinking sun's rain.*

There she was just relaxin' next to her shopping cart
while everyone else was workin' or fixin' to.
Sweaty men hammering
on that black tar roof.
>   (Never thought so much could happen on roof tops until ….)

Detective Guidry, in his rearview mirror, spit-combing back his
  cow lick.
Nurse Claire pulling up her white knee-high stockings.
A smile and wave as she turns the corner.
>   (To the hospital where …)

Beaux and Dave taking last puffs of morning high.
Then they step out into the world of fried seafood, brown cork trays,
  white ceramic coffee cups and martini lunches.
The sign in the window flashes red: RESTAURANT OPEN.
As I walked to work, briefcase in hand, I noticed Ol' Cousin Cloud
  passin' by watchin'. Just like momma watched me and my sista
  play patty cake on the front porch after summer evening supper.

Bag Lady, following me, looked up too:
>   *Do you see Ol' Mr. Sky's watchin' eyes? No?*
>   *Funny thing about Ol' Miss Water*
>   *She likes to return to familiar places.*

When the Sky Fell • *Yvette "Jamuna" Sirker* • 228

Funny how we ignore Bag Ladies
even when they speak the truth.

Round the corner came Miss Wind
Blowin' my hair all about my face.
Miss Wind was angry.
>   *I'm mad as hell*
>   *trying to suck all that heat*
>   *up out of the water!*
>   *It's too much!*
She's angry.

Bag Lady spoke to me again:

>   *I admire your trees.*
>   *When the wind blows?*
>   *They reach out and dance.*
>   *In the winter?*
>   *Me, I put on all my clothes.*
>   *I mean everything I own.*
>   *Tryin' to stay warm.*
>   *Move around a lot, too.*
>   *But trees?*
>   *When Miss Winter comes*
>   *Them trees get naked.*
>   *And stand perfectly still.*
>   *Audacious.*
>   *Naked and still in the winter.*

So I said, to no one in particular,
>   *You ever noticed Momma Magnolia sitting in brown ladies' hair,*
>   *putting a silk dress to shame?*
>   *Ever seen blades of grass sweatin' first thing in the morning?*
>   *The coolest part of the day?*
>   *I used to think, That don't make no kinda sense.*
>   *But now*
>   *I think my banana trees' spring flowers fill my home*

with the smell of happy southern women
on a porch swing sipping bourbon and laughing.

Bag Lady, chasing behind me, piped in:
> *Beware*
> *I mean beware*
> *The Lady in the Gulf?*
> *She's one helluva kind of woman.*
> *Beware is all I gotta say.*

Then, Miss Wind said:
> *I'm in a tizzy.*
> *It's SO HOT!*
> *Feels like hot flashes baby and you know that's crazy.*
> *Feels like hell is comin' straight up through the ground.*
> *Got me spinnin'*

Momma Earth piped in:
> *I hear ya baby.*
> *Look at me!!*
> *I'm a mess!*
> *They done messed me up ya hear?*
> *I'm so angry!*
> *But you watch ...*

Bag Lady replied:
> *I'm watchin' honey.*
Then Miss Wind took to **spinnin'**.
I mean **spinnin'** and **spinnin'**!

Bag Lady asked me if I wanted a cup of tea, securi-tea. I wrinkled my brow and went on my way. Taking small, slow steps.

I prefer a peaceful wind, me. When I wanna catch the spirit? I feel an about-to-rain breeze on my cheeks. Or I breathe in Sweet Olive. Yeah. Into my whole body. Sweet Olive is fresh green laughter when a lover wets your check with desirous lips.

In my mind's eye I danced the merengue. Small, passionate, earthy, proud steps. But with my chin lifted up and away from Bag Lady, I failed to notice the heavy iron clamps
Around my ankles.

Then, **Yemaya** showed up.
I shoulda suspected right then and there.
Yemaya was dancing,
thanking the water
like she does.
> Thank you river below us,
> Lake above us,
> Gulf just beyond the swamps.

Yemaya was dancing too.
Then,
she took off her mask.
As she did, Momma Earth went back to fussin':
> I ain't no slave
> Y'all done messed with the wrong lady!
> Sellin' my body out to the highest bidder?
> So they can fill me with filth to make a buck?
> Oh hell no!
> Y'all done messed with the wrong lady!

But I was busy noticing the butt-crack-showing delivery-boy-mother-fucker reekin' of cigarettes and shrimp. *Shrimp man!* He shouted to restaurant kitchen door. Then he turned to me. Look at that big-as-a-cat rat just struttin' along, said butt-crack. *Not scared of nothin'. Like he owns the whole neighborhood. It's a rat's world, bruh. I'm tellin' ya.*

Meanwhile, my attention was drawn to early morning PhD's and Masters Degrees headin' in to wait tables ...
THEN,
Miss Wind got together with Ole Miss Water
And honey,
It wasn't nothin' nice.

Together they tumbled
And rumbled
And sweated
And regretted the times in the past
When they left us alone.
And while we was going about our
fixin' to workness
Miss Wind and Ole Miss Water
Blended, brewed, united, fused,
crossbred, incorporated, conglomerated
Until …
There she was
Shimmying her gold lamé cocktail dress right up her curvaceous hips.
A beehive swirling above
Her huge EYE
Striking a pose
Smiling
Pleased
     Yes, honey. Momma's comin' to the rescue

Stepping back to relish in her beauty
she reached for her sash,
pulling it over her beehive and down
with great ceremony.
Stripper-slow
the sash came to rest across one shoulder.
It read: Miss America
She sang:
     Here I come, MISS Katrina!

That's when the sky fell

Solstice Dreams

Jennifer Browdy

All week the energy of the summer solstice seemed to build in me. After a few days of rain, the sun burst through, and we had a series of clear, low-humidity days in which it appeared that you could see the plants growing happily, stretching their roots down into the soil and their leaves up towards the bright sky.

On the day of the solstice, I spent a lot of time out in the garden, planting vegetables and annuals, weeding flowerbeds, mulching, staking, and tending. That evening, in honor of the longest day of the year, my son and I took a hike up a local mountain and sat on a rock ledge facing west as the sun slowly and majestically dropped towards the horizon.

We were happy to find some friends up there—a caterpillar with beautiful markings, making its way up an oak sapling, and a pair of orange-and-black butterflies, sunning themselves just like we were.

As we walked down the mountain in the last rays of sunshine, I couldn't help thinking about the strong contrast between the peaceful, lovely landscape of my home ground, where for many of us the most urgent question of the day is "what shall we have for dinner?" or "what movie shall we watch tonight?" and the social landscapes that cry out to me every day when I read the news headlines—arid, violent, rigid, harsh.

This summer solstice, as I sit in my peaceful green American haven, the Middle East is again descending into crazed sectarian violence. The news reports telling us that "militias are organizing" or "a bomb exploded in a market" focus on the politicians playing the mad chess game of war and the young men drawn into the armies as battlefield pawns. No mention is made of the mothers, sisters and grandmothers of those politicians and young men. The women rarely surface in the headlines, and when they do, the news is not good: a woman who dared to go out to a rally stripped and gang-raped, for example.

We hear about women obliquely in the reporting about the incredible surge of refugees living in camps in recent years; of the millions of people living in refugee camps under United Nations supervision, half are children—which means that a high percentage of the other half is probably mothers and grandmothers. But that is an inference I am making by reading between the lines; those women are invisible in the official story.

I have to recognize the incredible privilege I have as an American woman, living in the heart of the heavily guarded gated community that this country has become. Other people around the world are paying the price for the peace and plenty I have here in my home. And not just people—the animals and insects and birds and forests are paying the hugest price of all to allow me to maintain my privileged lifestyle.

How long can I continue to live comfortably with this knowledge?

The more time goes on, the more I see how prescient J.R.R. Tolkien was with his *Lord of the Rings* series. Berkshire County, where I live, is indeed "the Shire" of legend—peaceful, productive, green and jolly. Outside our borders, far, far away, the armies of Mordor are mobilizing in the midst of lands laid waste by the industries of the Dark Lord. Few in the Shire are worried; the chance of those nasty people and industries actually coming here seem remote indeed.

In *Lord of the Rings*, it is Gandalf the wizard who serves as the bridge between these two very different landscapes. He gives Bilbo, and later Frodo, the charge of becoming the change agents who can make all the difference. The fight against the Dark Lord is fought on many fronts, but the quest to destroy the Ring of Power is paramount, and in order to destroy the ring, Frodo must journey to the heart of the dark Empire itself.

I can't escape the feeling that here in the quiet Shire where I live, ordinary people like me are being called upon, as Bilbo and Frodo were, to step up to the immense and dangerous challenge of resisting the darkness that is brewing on our borders. But in our case, there does not seem to be a Gandalf who can give us a mission and guide us as we set off on the quest. Not even the wisest leaders of the environmental and peace movements seem to be able to provide that kind of guidance. Worldwide, the leaders who claim to know with absolute certainty what is right and what to do are precisely the ones who are fomenting war and leading us down the path to environmental and civilizational suicide.

That must be why I am trying to tune out the mad blaring of the news and listen to what the Earth herself is telling me. When I look out into the green world stretching up towards our beneficent Sun, or glowing brightly under our sweet white Moon, I can see and hear the harmony that life on Earth evolved to sing. Put water and sunlight together, wait a few billion years, and you get this incredible lush planet, pulsating with life.

Human beings have flourished so well that now we have become overpopulated, an invasive species that is destructively taking over every last niche on the planet. In a normal terrestrial cycle, we would go bust, our civilization would collapse, and with time the earth and the sun would gradually rebuild life in endlessly new creative forms.

Is that what is coming? Or will we be able to be the Gandalfs of our own generation, waking ourselves up out of our complacency here in the beautiful American Shire, and conquering the inner and outer Dark Lords that are laying waste to the planet?

On this summer solstice, as I walk down the mountainside in the peaceful dusk, my mind is buzzing with questions. What is the quest that is mine to carry out? Who will be my companions? Do women have a special role to play? What should our priorities be? I have to believe that if we at least start asking these questions, with the greater good of the Earth in mind, perhaps the answers will emerge in time to set humanity on a better path.

Woman Wondering

Suzanne Fowle

Batman would be more interesting if he possessed bat-like qualities. Why doesn't he sleep upside down or eat insects? He might feel empowered by adding mosquitoes to a peanut butter and jelly sandwich, or by scrambling moths into his eggs. And what about echolocation? Wouldn't it make sense for Batman to be able to use sonar to find his way in the dark?

What about Wonder Woman and her biology? She has also been denied the true, innate powers of her name. Does she ever incubate and birth a baby? Do her breasts ever produce milk? No. Her breasts and hips appear to be only for decoration, for filling out the costume. But what is more powerful than the uterus, with which we push our large-headed offspring through a relatively tiny opening? Anyone with the name "Wonder Woman" should have a uterus that could leap over a building in a single bound.

An authentic Wonder Woman would have menstrual blood so rich in nutrients it could revitalize a desert. "Just one drop will fertilize an acre of crops," would go the jingle. She would adorn her "third eye" with a drop of menstrual blood, Hindu-style, because this is the sixth chakra, the place of intuition and knowing. That would give her more authority than a predictably starred and striped leotard. That would command attention.

Forget the bullet-deflecting bracelets and the shooting tiara. Please. The real Wonder Woman would shoot breast milk so accurately and so tastily it would stop people in their tracks, make them as docile as Dorothy in a field of poppies. She would shoot it right into their mouths, stopping kidnappers in mid-crime and causing bank robbers to drop their moneybags.

Let's think about and redesign her feet, her connection to the ground. The spike-heeled go-go boots have got to go. Authentic Wonder Woman needs to be planted firmly on the earth to do her work.

Our new Super Heroine would have elephant-like powers in her feet. Elephant feet are sensitized to pick up seismic, underground signals from miles away, like the forehead of a whale. They can even distinguish between types of signals. The new and improved Wonder Woman would be able to feel and interpret quiet rumblings underground. She would detect silent strife this way, feeling the subtlest vibrations with her soft, wide, non-dainty feet.

Perpetual compassion would be one of her greatest talents. When this Super Heroine locates an injured human spirit, she would not try to subdue or calm the person right away. Instead, she would keep her charge safe as she allows the airing of pain. She would not tell her charge to "be strong" – that tired, old piece of advice we give to stave off emotion – because she would know that it takes strength and courage to feel deeply.

This is the magical part: once the flares of pain have subsided, she would give the injured person the feeling that he or she is being held, hugged, by moonlight. The moonlight would not mold them, would not force them to make a shift like the scorching sun might do. It would comfortably surround and hold their individual shape, just as it is.

I imagine this would feel like an elephant calf being bathed by its mother. I saw this once, under a full moon, on the banks of a meandering river in East Africa. The mother sucked up river water with her trunk, raised it over her baby, then let the water splash down on the moonlit curves of her baby's back. Over and over. Slowly and steadily.

Who might this Super Heroine anoint with comfort? Whose cries might she hear? It is a broad spectrum. Blows to the soul come in all shapes and sizes. Perhaps it is the nine-year-old boy whose mother will not pay for his dance class, the thing that makes him happiest. Or the young girl who wants long hair, but her father insists on cutting it bowl-style every two months to be "practical." It might be the woman who is warned that if she fights for her children in a courtroom she will be portrayed as an "overprotective mother."

There are others: the fifty-year old woman who can no longer repress the memory of her bus driver feeling her up when she was twelve; the boy who watches his inebriated father smash all the dinner dishes after his mother suggests it is the father's turn to wash; the faithful woman who, upon discovering her husband's infidelity, lets out howling sobs until she loses her voice; the nineteen-year-old man who risks his reputation and credibility to testify against the man who molested him ten years before, only to have him found innocent; the pregnant teen whose church forces her to give up the baby because she has "nothing to give her child but love." They would be held, all of them, just as they are. They would feel the roots underneath them, like a hammock of intertwined arms.

Lunar-infused, boundless empathy would not be our heroine's only superpower. She would also have a fire in her belly. She would mostly tend this fire like a hearth, like a source of warmth and comfort, but she could also bring it forth and breathe it out. (She does not have a dragon tattoo; she is the dragon.) Our new and improved Wonder Woman would not be afraid of aggression. If she suppresses her anger, the fire in her belly burns her from the inside. But when she exhales the fire, she has control of it.

What triggers her breath of fire? The killing of an unarmed boy by a cop of a different color. The kidnapping of hundreds of Nigerian school girls. Yazidi women abducted by militants and the ransacked souls of the men left behind. Thousands of Congolese boys forced to fight, kill, and commit heinous acts against their own. The list goes on.

When the flames come forth, this woman would roar. She would bellow like a thousand women, un-drugged and un-plugged, in the final stages of giving birth. She would send a rumble through the ground that would resonate in the feet of every elephant, that would cause whales to breach en masse, shooting for the moon. What hard-breasted, go-go costume could ever elicit this kind of response? What good are super powers unless they sound the call to action?

LOVE? A prayer for us

Carmen Maria Mandley

Let it be us, I say!
Let it be you and I and she and he and them,
The ones we know and
The ones we trade with,
The ones who fill our coffers, fill our coffees fill our bowls fill our
    hearts fill our shit lists fill our short lists fill our long nights fill
    our good nights fill our moons and suns and books and nooks,
    Greek Gods, the critics, the poets, the hot heads, the pot heads,
    the bi-polars, the fur-toting patrons, the broken kids, the token
    troubled ones, the actors, the lovers, the basketball stars that tower
    over the trees, the flyers, the whores with constant bruised knees,
    the moms who don't know why or how, the guys who trim our
    trees, the ones we've loved in our dreams, the ones who've been to
    Rome, the ones waiting for injections off of Martin Luther King,
    fathers who don't know better, sisters who love ferociously, lovers,
    cadavers, workers, bankers, lunatics and all of us in-between.

Let's have this night.
This one night.
Let it be us.

Let's put on our finest array and have cataclysmic food fights on the
    White House lawn.

Let's bring back Burroughs and talk about Fletch.

Let's laugh out loud at funerals to celebrate life.

Let's hover over the freeze-dried nun, tight in starch tread black and
    white trench. Let's fly after the largest group of them we can find
    with 50 kids with 50 wiffle ball bats.

Let's make a church built of crayons that melts whenever anyone talks
   of fire.

Let's fall in love until our heads burst.

Let's kiss strangers only in the darkest of music halls.

Let's kiss strangers only in the darkest of places.

Let's kiss strangers only on the darkest of nights.

Let's run naked through the Bible Belt with Jesse Helm's fresh face
   tattooed on our buttocks,
Screaming Judas was framed!

Let's get a gravesite for Jeff Buckley in the middle of Moore square
   and put Grace on repeat.

Let's buy a thousand hungry cats and set them free in a Peter Max show.

Let's paint ourselves, smash against canvas kissing and sell us for
   thousands on Ebay.

Let's wear dance belts only to the ballet on Thursday.

Let's paint a bar code on the Saturn and take a drive through a Kmart
   check out.

Let's paint Ray Charles on every Bible.

Let's wear boys' clothes to bed, only if we've stolen them.

Let's wear girls' clothes to bed and take only the most tasteless of pictures.

Let's run Ben Nye Blood all over white hands, stand in Abercrombie
   and scream "Out damned spot!" to every passerby.

Let's say I love you to every telemarketer, ask them how they fall in love, ask them what a sigh feels like, and ask them to the show.

Let's do Shakespeare, and do Shakespeare, and do Shakespeare, because he really knows where it's at.

Let's put a velcro wall in every gallery, throw an art merchant up and try to sell him.

Let's name a dog after every beat poet.

Let's name a cat after every rock in Virginia's pocket.

Let's close our eyes at stoplights and let go.

Let's crank call the White House asking for the good Bush.

Let's stop under every streetlight to get a better look at each other's hands.

Let's see every play.

Let's eat every storm.

Let's count every raindrop, believing that each is a planet hitting the earth and every moment is the last we have to kiss.

Let's notice the wind, and the wild, and the words, and the wary.

Let's fall in love with people too young, people too old, people who live, people who fear, people who write, people who know us as shadows, people who die, people who are dead, people who are willow cabins at our gates writing loyal cantons of contemned love and singing them loud even in the dead of night (and Shakespeare wrote that, not me).

Let's drink red on a Wednesday, white on a Sunday

Let's go to the show, sit in the house seats, discover Tilly, Fall into
    Connor, and leave the other band behind

Let's do our acrobatic act in the lobby of the Performing Arts Center,
    just after the Russians

Let's idolize Icarus's blind flight, knowing he plummeted, but wishing
    he would have burned because burning gets him closer to the gods

Let's be Touchstone, and Jaques, and Oliver, and Orlando

Let's be Coriolanus, Marc Antony, Hermione, and Perdita

Let's be Leontes, Dion, Amiens

Let's be those great men of the Globe

Great God, let me be Robert Armin or Will Kemp, just for a day; I
    would sell my soul for it

Let us be all of these

Comrades

Warriors of the night, the day, the hush and hum, the blood and
    bones, the in-between, the solid sun and the moon

Let us ride razor blades and drink whiskey to welcome the new day
    and the day next and the day next and the day next

Let us celebrate Arthur and Ray and William and Hunter

Let us sing unto their bones

of Glory, Glory

Gloriana

Seraphim, Gabriel, Mother, Father, skyward we all will rise as

We guide the spirits of dead men glorious

We are warriors for the waking day

We will with eyes open, mouth open, thighs open, heart open

Eat this whole

Eat it entire, flesh and bone

You, you and I

All of us

We sing a song of glory

cantiamo una canzone

cantiamo

cantiamo

Let it be us I say

Oh Comrades, Moloch Moloch...

Amen.

Goodnight.

PART SIX:

STRONG SHOULDERS

THE LOVES AND LABORS OF WOMEN

The Labor I Never Had

Beverly Pimsleur

B oth of my childbirth experiences were memorable and dramatic, but the one that had the most lasting effect was the labor I didn't have.

In December 1962, I was living with Paul, my French professor boyfriend; we had moved in together six months after our second date. I thought I was safe from an unwanted pregnancy because I wore a diaphragm, the contraception of choice in the 1960's. I kept it in my underwear drawer. Taking it out of its beige plastic case and smearing it with gooey gel before inserting it often delayed the romantic moment — if I hadn't been prepared — but using it gave me a sense of security and control. What I didn't know was that diaphragms were not reliable for women with inverted uteruses like mine.

Paul said my unexpected pregnancy triggered his decision to marry me, assuring me he intended to propose, just not that soon. But his proposal came with a qualifier. He got up from the couch where he had been sitting beside me and paced around the room. Averting my eyes, he said, "I don't think I'm ready for a baby."

I remember how relieved I felt; I had been thinking the same thing. I didn't want to abandon my Master's degree studies or give up my teaching fellowship to start a family. Paul had received government funds to develop a self-instructional language program in Greece. I was as excited as he was, looking forward to going and working with him. Now, we had to re-think everything. We discussed the pros and cons of what to do until late into the night, and agreed: marriage, but no baby.

The upcoming New Year weekend seemed perfect for an elopement. We could be wed, celebrate 1962 as Mr. and Mrs. and be back in time to teach our classes at Ohio State University. The challenge of making this marriage happen was given to me. I dialed "O" for operator; in the pre-Google world telephone operators were a limitless source of information. Within minutes I found that West Virginia was the only nearby state that didn't require a 24-hour waiting period for a marriage license — the helpful operator even furnished me with the name of her uncle, a Justice of the Peace.

The next day, after a three-hour drive through the Appalachia foothills, speckled with snow like leftover confetti, we pulled up in front of the justice's house. He led us into his burgundy wall-papered living room and asked, "Where are your witnesses?" When both Paul and I both gave him a blank look, he called his wife in from the kitchen. Five minutes later we were wed.

It was Saturday night, party time at the inn where we were staying after our unceremonious ceremony. Raucous laughter from the bar under our bedroom was so loud that the floorboards vibrated. Paul had warned me that the accommodations were not going to be fancy. "Think of it as an adventure," he quipped.

I suspected, and hoped, that our whole life together would be an adventure. My new husband thought it would be fun to buy some moonshine from the gap-toothed guys camped out behind the inn. I hung back while he negotiated a price. But when Paul put the package on the bedside table, I began to cry. This was my wedding night, I was supposed to be happy, I was marrying the man I loved, but I didn't want to drink hooch out of a brown paper bag. I was pregnant, feeling queasy and instead of having a honeymoon, I was going to have an abortion.

I couldn't rely on dialing "operator" for this one; abortion was illegal in America. But, of course, women had them. I knew who to call: my friend Lisa, whose sister had terminated an unwanted pregnancy. Lisa gave me a phone number in Canada. She told me to say, "I need a fast way to get from Montreal to Baltimore," the code phrase. It started to feel scary; what the doctors (if they *were* doctors!) and I were doing was punishable by law. A hushed voice gave me the name of a man in Maryland. When I called he told me to be on a specific street corner in downtown Baltimore at 6:00 a.m. with an envelope of $300 in cash.

I took a plane to Baltimore to stay with my best friend and her husband, who was doing a residency at Johns Hopkins Hospital. When I had confided to them the reason for my visit, they were empathetic and supportive. The next day at dawn I went to the designated street corner in a downtown garbage-strewn neighborhood. Cars and trucks clattered by even at that early hour. I scrutinized each one, hoping the next one would be the black Ford station wagon I was waiting for. "What if it doesn't come, then what will I do?" I wondered.

The car arrived only a few minutes late. After verifying my fictitious name the driver took my envelope of cash; he gave me a blindfold and told me to lie down on the floor in the back of the wagon.

I struggled to restrain myself from taking off the uncomfortable mask. The cold January air chilled my scalp, the nubby car rug scratched my leg in the gap between my shoes and my jeans. I tried to roll off my purse's brass clip, which was cutting into my side. We stopped four times, and at each stop someone stumbled in and lay down beside me. Maybe because of not being able to see each other, we didn't exchange a single word. After what seemed like an hour, I heard gravel under wheels; we must have turned off the highway. Were we there? The disembodied voice from the front seat barked, "Don't get up and don't take off your eye cover. Someone will come help you out." I guessed we were somewhere in the backwoods of Maryland.

I heard the squeak of the door handle on the hutch of the station wagon. A hand grabbed my forearm and half-yanked me out of the car. The short walk, crunching pebbles under foot, ended up in a chilly room. No one had said a word and the silence made me more anxious. I tried to remind myself that this was the same doctor who had helped my friend's sister and that it had turned out all right. A few minutes later, I was led into another room, helped onto a bed and my feet put in stirrups. I was relieved to hear, at last, a soothing voice, presumably that of the doctor. He assured me that this was a routine procedure, that I had nothing to fear.

"It won't take long. You'll be home by dinner time."

I felt only mild discomfort during the procedure. I don't know what kind of anesthetic I was given, but it was enough to knock me out. The next thing I remember was a female singsong-y soprano (a nurse? a woman trying to impersonate a nurse?) saying, "I'm leaving a few sanitary napkins for you, and don't be alarmed if your breasts are sore for a few days. You can take off your eye cover as soon as I leave the room."

Even in my foggy state, I noticed she avoided the word "blindfold."

When she left, I saw that I was alone in a dimly lit, tiny space only big enough for the cot I was lying on. It was over. I was limp, but I was fine. After a few hours the arrival process was reversed. On with the blindfolds, into our prone positions in the car. Again, there was no conversation among us. I only remember asking the girl whose body seemed closest to mine if she was all right. Or maybe she was the one who asked me.

Back at my friend Elaine's, I called Paul to let him know that I was okay. He said he had been waiting by the phone all day and was as relieved as I was. When Elaine's husband came home that night, he suggested that he give me some shots, "just in case." I don't know how he got whatever he gave me (penicillin, antibiotics?) or whether he was doing something a resident shouldn't do.

The "nurse voice" had not exaggerated. I had very sore breasts for the next few days, as if my milk was aching to flow. It was only then that I fully realized what I had done. There would be no milk, no baby. I tried to tell myself it had been the right choice; I tried not to have second thoughts. I became obsessed with the idea that I would not be able to have another child. When I miscarried two years later, I was sure something had gone wrong on that table in Baltimore. Friends tried to comfort me, pointing out that women often don't go to term with first pregnancy. Only I knew it wasn't the first.

One year after the miscarriage, I gave birth to our son, and our daughter was born two years later. I was one of the lucky ones; my abortion did not affect my ability to have children. But I knew all women were not as fortunate. I became involved in the then-new movement for women's rights and the fight for legalized abortion because I knew that no woman should have to ride blindfolded in the back of a station wagon. I continued to be an active voice for pro-choice as the movement grew.

In 1990 I went to the Roe vs. Wade march in Washington, DC with my twenty-year-old daughter, Julia. On the train from New

York, she asked me, "Did you ever have an abortion?" I knew it was the right moment to tell her the story.

"I can't believe Dad didn't go with you!"

I remember being surprised by her response. At the time, it had never occurred to me to ask, and he didn't volunteer.

Paul and I never talked about that trip to Baltimore. I am sure we would have discussed it, someday, but the chance never came. He died unexpectedly of a heart attack at forty-eight, just when the work he had begun in Greece was starting to have the success he dreamed of.

When I wake up at 3 in the morning nowadays, I often think of that first pregnancy. Do I ever regret our decision? I don't know how my life would have played out if we had had a child so soon after our marriage; perhaps I would have regretted it, perhaps not. And I wouldn't have had my two children, born when we decided we were ready for a family. What seemed the right decision fifty years ago still seems the right one today, even though it returns to disturb me in the middle of the night, the unknown weighed against a known.

Baptism by Fire

Adrian Dunn

Sitting in Harder Stadium in the afternoon sun under a cloudless sky, I'm alone in a crowd. It's 1970 and these are my people. All are young UC Santa Barbara students and former students, like me, waiting to hear Bill Kunstler speak. All I know about him is that he became famous defending the Chicago 7 after the riots there two years ago. He's on our side.

There must be a couple thousand young people here, all in an upbeat mood, expectant. Just like them, I'm sick of the war, sick of young men I know being drafted, sick of the insane politics in Washington. I can't even visit home without my dad calling me a communist because I'm against the war. He talks to me about falling dominoes, something he read about in *Time* magazine, his main source of information. Meanwhile, every young man I know is struggling to stay out of Vietnam. Nick got a 4F for bad eyesight. Others have 2A student deferments because their parents can afford to keep them in college. Craig plans to leave for Canada if his number comes up. No one I know can get a CO—conscientious objector—because unlike Nixon, they weren't raised Quaker. My mind is churning with the reasons I'm here, when Kunstler appears on the podium.

The crowd roars as he steps up to the mic. He takes off his suit jacket. With his graying, longish hair, sunglasses, white shirt and tie, he's an attractive figure. He starts talking about the rights of Americans to protest their government's actions when they feel those actions are immoral. He gets into details about the protests at the Democratic National Convention in Chicago, then ends by talking about the situation here at UCSB. While he's talking, I'm thinking, "I'm not a pacifist, but is violence ever justified to make change? Isn't this what we're against?"

"I had never thought breaking windows is a good tactic," Kunstler says, referring to the breaking of the Bank of America windows in Isla Vista only last night. "But, on the other hand," he continues, "I cannot bring myself to become bitter and condemn young people who engage in it." The crowd breaks into applause. I clap along with them.

"The real violence occurs in the back rooms of police stations," he says. I know that to be true. Several of my friends were beaten up by police just last month, when they were arrested for protesting the firing of an antiwar professor, Bill Allen. "The shadow of the swastika is on every courthouse, on university campuses, on Government buildings," Kunstler continues. This seems like an exaggeration to me, but the crowd loves it.

By the time Kunstler wraps up his speech, everyone is pumped. The crowd spills out of the stadium like ants going out on patrol. I follow the crowd out of the stadium parking lot and cross El Colegio into Isla Vista, the student community that has been my home the last several years. I smile at the nearest faces, who smile back. We're ready to take action. "Rally in Perfect Park!" someone shouts. "Rally in Perfect Park!" I repeat to those next to me. People are walking in twos and threes, some sprinting ahead as if they don't want to miss anything. The destination: Perfect Park, a grassy lot in the middle of the Embarcadero Loop in the downtown section of Isla Vista.

We walk directly toward the sun, which is beginning to hang low in the sky. I squint against the glare, wishing I had brought my sunglasses. We turn down Embarcadero del Mar, past the two-story frat houses with their Greek letters, past a pink stucco sorority house, then past more dull, boxy apartment buildings. The crowd picks up its pace, so I am trotting to keep up. There's no plan, just motion. A rally at least feels like we're doing something. In another five minutes, we pass a couple of single-story shops—a realty office and a head shop. I smell incense and hear Bob Dylan singing mournfully, two things that make me feel instantly at home.

A eucalyptus tree and a few palm trees mark the edge of the open expanse that is Perfect Park. We are met by hundreds more young people, who came down the other side of the park on Embarcadero del Norte. The crowd looks jubilant. Guys with long hair, young women in jeans and t-shirts, many printed with anti-war slogans. A few "Vietnam Veteran Against the War" shirts. One guy with an American flag sewn across the seat of his jeans. Curiously, I don't see anyone I know here, though it is a big crowd, maybe even a thousand, all milling around, talking to each other in short sentences, waiting.

I step up the curb into the dry grass of the park. "Now what?" No sooner had I asked myself than I see three black and white patrol cars circling the Loop, one after another. The first one in line proceeds a few blocks up the road, then suddenly stops. Two cops in full riot gear jump out and grab a guy walking on the sidewalk. They wear black helmets with plexiglass shields pulled down over their faces. From a distance, I can see one of them repeatedly raising and slamming down his baton, but they're too far away for me to hear anything.

"Shit, what is going on?" I ask a young man next to me. "Did you see that?"

"The cops just busted that guy for nothing," he shouts back. "Looks like they were beating him up." Many of the folks in the park have seen it, too, and start shouting. We watch in disbelief as the cops force the man into their car and speed away.

After that, the crowd is focused and angry. Patrol cars continue to circle the park, several at a time, and the crowd pulls into its center. Several people shout, "Pig, Pig, go home!" I'm scared, but exhilarated, too.

A few people sprint away from the park; they've had enough. But most of the crowd pulls together like an amoeba. One body with no mind. It pushes out extensions and pulls them back in response to each cop car, each angry shout, each perceived threat. I'm nervous, on alert, my feelings interconnected with the crowd. Any stimulus that begins at any point surges through the group like an electric current. The crowd rushes forward toward a cop car. One face contorted in anger shouts, "Down with the Pigs!" He hurls a fist-sized rock at the heavy patrol car. It bounces off bullet-proof windows, doing no damage, but making it's point. Several more guys pick up rocks and hurl them. "Pig, pig!" I stay near the back of the crowd, well away from rocks or cops, but moving with it as it pulses forward and then retreats.

The crowd is a multi-headed monster, at odds with itself. Some young men are ready for battle, wanting a fight. Others hold back, "Come on, man, just cool it!" Some laugh for no reason. No one knows what we're doing here; it's all reaction. Anger spins through the crowd, followed by fear. I hang on the edge, watching and waiting, keeping my options open. Some faces look exultant, like they're at a party. Some look frightened. This is starting to feel out of control. But I can't move. I'm riveted to the scene, which keeps shifting. The charge in the crowd is growing, and I feel stuck in place, electrified but uncertain.

I take a step back, off the curb into the street, and rush up Embarcadero del Norte, to distance myself from the group. The sky is growing a deeper blue. I glance back in the direction of the beach, invisible behind rows of houses, but just two streets over, at the edge of Isla Vista. Knowing the beach is there, its waves predictable, is a comforting thought. "Soon it will be dark; maybe I should leave."

Then I see them, off to my left, across the park, on the edge of the crowd. He is dark, handsome, with the familiar chest and broad smile that I love. Next to him, but not touching, is a laughing woman. Her curling red hair falls in heavy layers over her white blouse, and shifts when she moves her head. She is short, her legs mostly concealed by a blue gathered skirt. She is like no one I've ever seen before, red-gold hair and pale skin. Short-waisted, a girl-woman, she looks just like the original illustrated Alice in Wonderland.

Seeing them together sends a jolt to my solar plexus. They move in a bubble of their own. He is looking at her, not at the crowd. She laughs again, safe next to him. I feel invisible in my jeans and t-shirt. I glance away, but still see them, their image burned into my mind. His wide cheekbones and smiling half-moon eyes. He loved me so well, then left me sometime last year. I thought he'd left town. The pain in my middle swells. I can't breathe. I stare at them harder, the way a tongue seeks the sore tooth and presses it again. Is it to overload the nerve? To find out if I can bear it? To make it different?

A patrol car, packed with cops, glides by just in front of me. Reflexively, I take a step backward, trip on the curb, but manage to regain my balance. A few streaks of orange are beginning to show in the darkening sky. The cops turn on headlights that sweep in broad cones of light around the park. I hear rocks hitting their target, the windshield or the rear lights of the patrol cars. Then the unmistakable high-pitched sound of breaking glass as someone hurls a bottle that shatters in the street. "Why do men always like to fight?"

Suddenly the cars are gone. I gaze across the crowd and see heads in the dark, jackets glinting in the street lamps, arms and legs in jeans moving erratically, hear voices shouting. I notice it all from a remove, nursing my private pain. One group lights a trash dumpster on fire. My old love Paul and his new woman are gone, faded into the night. I'm left standing alone trying to find an anchor within myself once again. "I gotta get out of here."

Just past Borsodi's Coffee Shop-closed early-I turn right down Madrid and find a phone booth. I dial Maeve's number. "Hello," she sounds like she's been in bed. "Maeve, can you or Andy come and get me? I'm in Isla Vista and I have no way to get down there. All hell is breaking loose here." It's only 20 minutes on the freeway to Santa Barbara. "I'll walk back to El Colegio, if one of you can pick me up."

Andy comes in his car just before the cops block all entrances into and out of Isla Vista. On the ride to Santa Barbara, I tell Andy about the crowd and the cops, but I don't mention Paul.

Safe in Maeve's house, I make up a bed on their couch. Snuggled under a clean quilt, I can finally breathe. I open my eyes in the dark and check for damage, my hands holding the center of my chest. I manage a few grim tears. Why did Paul have to come back? When he left a year ago, part of me went missing. A year before that, I told him I wanted a baby with him. That's how I learned how cosmic wishing works: when you send a wish out into the Universe, it will come back to you in some form, though it may not be in the form you are expecting. Cosmic timing isn't necessarily on your schedule. Some wishes take ten years, some just one. Some come back in a very different form than you expect, so be careful what you wish for. Paul had come and gone a few times, when I found out my wish had come true. By then, it was too late to ask him to stay. I couldn't even blame him; he was always so sweet and sincere. Even when he was sincerely leaving me. "He loved me too well." I press my back against the couch pillows, my cheek against the quilt, and fall asleep.

The next morning, Maeve makes breakfast in her robe, oblivious to all the chaos of the night before. Her domestic world is intact. She has her man and a home to take care of. Andy has the radio on. He smiles and says, "Last night they burned the bank down." I know he means the Bank of America, across the street from Borsodi's. He's chuckling, as this amuses him. "The bastards deserve it," he says. Andy does research at the University and is friends with the fired professor. The three of us sit down to eat under a poster of Karl Marx.

The phone rings; Andy answers it in the next room. "Shit," we hear him say. He returns to the kitchen. "Russell was arrested last night. He was beaten up pretty bad." Maeve puts her toast down. "Is he OK?" she asks. "Yeah, nothing broken," Andy says. Russell is their housemate and friend, the oldest and most intellectual of our group of friends. I can't decide whether Russell is a hero or a fool, but I keep that thought to myself.

Governor Reagan calls for a curfew and orders the National Guard into Isla Vista. I'm scared to go back too soon. Mainly, I don't want to see Paul again. I hang out in Santa Barbara, waiting for things to calm down.

A week later, I take the bus to Isla Vista and walk downtown to view the wreckage of the bank. It isn't even cordoned off, and I am able to walk right up to it. It stinks of smoke. The two front brick walls are standing, but the roof is gone. Inside I see blackened steel beams and a tangle of burned wood and wires. A spindly eucalyptus is still alive in front of the ruins, a survivor of the fire. "What a ridiculous waste," I say to no one at all. I thought I might feel like a point had been made or a battle won, but I don't. Standing there, I feel as empty and burned-out as the structure in front of me. I feel no love for the bank, or for the bank's burners, but maybe a little for the sapling struggling to grow in this dry, compromised place.

I stand next to the little tree long enough to imagine a future—one without violence, one with a man who stays and the war over. The next day, I take a Greyhound bus north to find it.

What I Did Not Expect, When I Was Expecting

Suzi Banks Baum

On the day it happened, I gardened.

On the day it happened, I lounged in the hammock noticing dragonflies.

On the day it happened, I swam in a freezing cold ore pit and floated like a seal: fat, round, infinitely buoyant.

On the day it happened, nothing in my instinct dictionary led me to know what was about to occur.

But I did opt out of the morning rehearsal at Tanglewood.

I did not keep my dinner down.

I did hollow into bed early next to my husband, comforted that when it did happen, all of our gear—a freezer full of Ciao Bella sorbet to sustain me for the 17 hours of labor I was sure to endure, my small overnight bag waiting by the door of our tiny apartment in Greenwich Village packed with soft socks, an oversized t-shirt, and 2 tennis balls for back massages—all these things stood ready just a two-and-a-half-hour drive away from where my husband and I rolled around like dice on a betting table in the July heat, uncomfortable on our futon on the floor of our sparsely appointed bedroom in our upstate home. We rolled and sweated and thrashed in the sheets until the pace of my pulse and the discomfort in my hips made him flick on the flashlight and read down the list of "What false labor looks like" comparing our facts to the list next to it: "What real labor looks like."

My contractions were irregular.

I had a general tightening across my belly.

Moving around seemed to ease the discomfort.

No bloody show.

Just a hot summer night one week before I was due.

In that small low-ceilinged room on the second floor of our house on a very dark country road, my mother-in-law slept below us. Our navy blue Toyota Camry sat in the driveway. The fresh corncobs we'd shucked for dinner were feeding a clutch of raccoons out at the compost pile. As Miss Clavel in the *Adventures of Madeleine* would say, "Something was not right."

So we roused my mother-in-law and headed out under the stars at 2 a.m., back to New York City, back from our tiny country house where the day lilies were weeded and the baby crib stood waiting for our eventual return. We headed south to where, false labor or not, we would be where our midwife expected us to be: close to the hospital, in our apartment with the sorbet in the freezer and the overnight bag at the door.

Perhaps it was riding in the back seat of the car, such a commodious seat for my wide body, but as we drove south, winding along the Taconic, those false labor symptoms made me have to pee. We approached the exit where I knew Gas City would be open so I demanded we stop.

By day, Gas City on Highway 54 in New York State is a simple gas station and minimal convenience store. Nothing fancy at all.

By night, Gas City is transformed into a porn shop. Picture me, in all my false labor glory on a hot summer night, careening into the station, opening the glass door to a blast of air-conditioned chill. To my right under the cashier's counter was a temporary rack of magazines covered with over-inflated, lace-wrapped bulging breasts and titles relating to leather, toys and fantasy sex. The cashier blushed and ducked as I maneuvered the door closed. He pointed in the direction of the bathroom that I could reach hardly fast enough to lose my dinner in the not-so-tidy porcelain bowl. If false labor included complete evacuation of my insides, then you could tick that one off the list.

I sat on the toilet, the full bulk of me, feeling my mass of momentum. False labor was a bit dramatic, but now that I'd cleared myself out, I could handle it. I looked forward to the mango sorbet waiting for me in our apartment. I looked forward to our big sturdy bed and the air conditioner. False labor could last for a long time. I expected to ride it out and attend my nursing class the next night.

The rest of the ride was a blur. My mother-in-law fed my husband Sen-Sens from her voluminous purse. She kept a mantra going of all the hospitals she knew as we threaded our way through Dutchess County to Westchester. They were timing my false labor contractions on the digital clock on the dashboard and nothing seemed alarming to them. As we got to Manhattan and drove down to Greenwich Village, I heard my husband seek clearance through the cordons enforcing a curfew that summer. He said to the policeman, "My wife is in labor," and we passed through.

I noticed he did not say "false labor."

After dropping my mother-in-law off at her apartment, we went on to ours. I waddled into the lobby and up the elevator while my husband parked the car. I drew a bath because I knew from the chapter on false labor that a bath could ease the irregular contractions and maybe I could go to sleep.

We thought, us smarty-pants-book-educated-wanna-be-parents, that we would be wise to call our midwife, since it was now 4:15 a.m. and I had had a rather dramatic bout of false labor. Wouldn't it be good to just check in with her? She asked to be on the phone with me as one of those false contractions rode through me in the tub. Then she ever-so-calmly asked to speak to my husband. I could hear the volume of her voice through the receiver. His tone changed. He hauled me out of the tub, stuffed the Ciao Bella sorbet into the picnic cooler and grabbed that overnight bag. I was hardly dry when I was back in the car, weaving through more cordons, then, deposited on the curb in front of St. Vincent's Hospital while he again parked the car.

I held onto a street sign—the metal warm, the sharp edges pressing into my hot palms. I was a figurehead at the prow of a boat, mighty as the waves washed over me, my gaze fixed on the horizon, prepared for the long journey I had in front of me.

Amelia Earhart said, "When a great adventure is offered, you don't refuse it."

What I expected was a long labor.

What happened was that our son was born thirty minutes later, at 5:13 a.m. on Sunday morning, July 17, 1994, just barely arrived in Manhattan.

What happened was this great adventure that has seen me to this day, gaze ever out on the horizon. This labor is nothing but real, nothing but daily, and nothing but a vista that reveals what I am made of with every breath.

Let Him Eat Cake

Camille Tewell

I am carrying a Spiderman cake for thirty people. A broad circle in shape, the cake spills out of the confines of its flimsy cardboard container. It's massive, but I cannot use my stomach or chest to support its weight because this would smash the icing. So I hold it awkwardly, a little out in front of my center of gravity. Hurrying from the car to the picnic shelter, my arms begin to tremble. It's sunny, hot. I left my sunglasses in the car because it was overcast only a few moments ago. I am squinting, sweating, and struggling, walking as fast as I can beneath the burden because there are many more things to bring down from the car and my eldest child cannot occupy the baby forever.

As I'm walking I think to myself, "This is terrible. We are never doing this again." A moment later comes the rebuttal: "Terrible? Terrible is watching your son nearly die from salmonella. Hefting a birthday cake on a hot June day is not terrible. And hey—at least he gets to have a real cake for his birthday just like any other kid!" After this internal dialogue I laugh out loud because even inside my head I sound ridiculous. No one is nearby to hear me and wonder, or feel indifference.

In what seems like moments, parents arrive with hungry kiddies in tow, but our food isn't organized and our hotdogs aren't done yet. Somehow two adults with three kids— including a preschooler and a crawler—cannot unload two cars and set up a birthday cookout in thirty minutes, although I guess I thought we could. So, we're behind. But eventually food is served, candles and cake happen, and now it's off to the rides, except that they shut down almost as soon as the kids reach them. The guy running the mini-planes bends the rules a little and allows each party kid to go once.

"Only one wide? This pawty is not so fun, now!" says my Spiderman. And Jesus, it's hot. I sweat and feel bad for him as well as for the moms, dads, and kids that drove all this way to sweat at an event that boasted not just rides but a train and a historic carousel. Guess I missed some key info when I reserved the shelter and planned it all out.

At some point the guests begin to leave, saying it was a great party and that they had fun anyway. Maybe all is forgiven. At least it's done.

After the dust settles, my husband and I look at one another across the shelter. We have no less than ten trips worth of stuff still on the tables to pack into the cars. All of the adults who held the baby during the party have gone home. It's just the kids and us, until some juvenile delinquents arrive to occupy the table right next to the sign that reads: "Picnic shelter by reservation only." The more vocal delinquent—a tall, teenaged boy with a staring problem—asks if he can have some of our lemonade. The baby starts to cry because it's her bedtime, and Spiderman mutters in the direction of the squatters, "But dis is MY birfday pawty."

•

Spiderman came into this world during a slightly misaligned period of our marriage. I remember my mate during that labor, checking his phone frequently and looking rather vague about the whole event. It spoke to the place we were in, not at all to the place our son would have in our lives. "You phoned it in," I chide him now about this labor. And he really did. When I pushed that 9 lb, 4 oz boy into this world—at the very moment of his birth—I laughed (yes, laughed!) because I was just so glad he was here, and I was just so glad I wasn't pregnant anymore. Thanks to an effective epidural, I was lucid, watchful, and joyful as it all happened, reveling in a feeling of mystery as the ether cracked open and this new soul took up his residence with us. As I swelled with awe and love for my son I looked at my husband and thought to myself, "He's missing it." He was there with me in the room, but he wasn't really there.

Perhaps I started it all with my independence during Spidey's IVF conception. I did my own shots, even the progesterone ones with the fat needle—an inch and a half long—done each day of the first trimester, right into the hip muscle. They hurt like a mother. In slowly, plunge slowly, remove slowly. If you rushed any part of it, the serum would run down your leg. You cannot rush intramuscular injections. You also cannot allow someone squeamish to give them to you, so I did them myself. He was distant during the pregnancy itself, too. When you don't feel the kicks or discomforts firsthand, do you feel as invested? I think for my spouse the answer was no. Suffice it to say, by the time the birth rolled around, maybe he just didn't feel very necessary.

Fast-forward nine months postpartum and our big baby boy isn't so big anymore. They say he's "failing to thrive," with a weight below the third percentile. My husband is paying attention now. We are strung up together on the same buoy, holding onto one another in a sea of worry and confusion because Spiderman doesn't eat properly. He vomits often and makes diarrhea and mucous in his diapers. He sees allergists, GI docs. He gets an endoscopy, which provides us with little information. There are visits to the ER and the blood lab, but these are unremarkable in light of the menace that comes at fourteen months in the form of salmonella. We spend the duration of our beach vacation that year at a strange hospital watching Spiderman battle this invisible foe.

Usually I keep the Salmonella memories submerged. When I have a need to revisit them, they drift in and out of focus as phantom images and feelings: Terror for hours in the ER as he spasms again and again, writhing uncontrollably. Changing his diapers over and over until it seems pointless because as soon as I change one, he makes another dirty. Trying to keep him from rolling off the examination table when the fits take him. Loathing the stupid television playing Dora or god knows what in there, as if anything could possibly distract him from what he's experiencing. Crying and shaking in the bathroom because for some reason it seems safer in there, where normal bodily functions happen. I see the shape of that bathroom with its mirror, sink—the usual things. A quotidian space that speaks to life before whatever nameless horror began torturing our baby. Nameless because for several days no one knows what has made him so ill.

I see myself hiding in this ER bathroom, sickened with fear.

Then later. My baby that cannot be soothed by anyone, not even me. He knows no one now, so tight is he in the grip of the germ. He sees no one, hears no one. He answers only to the spasms. He wakes only to roll and scream when they come. What leaves his body is clear and slightly neon green in color, with a texture like jello, unlike anything that should leave anyone's body. He is so far away now. I feel certain no small body could ever survive what is happening to his.

I keep vigil. I sleep in his room. I touch him and speak softly to him when he screams. I listen carefully to the doctors and ask lots of questions when they visit our cell. These are the only things to do.

CAT scan. Spinal tap. Wrong diagnosis first, then the right one—finally. Rolling down the hallway in a wheelchair, with a limp Spiderman in my arms. Rolling through miles of hallway to the ultrasound place. A woman moans when we roll by her and says, "Oh God, please, no" because no one can bear to see his tiny body and the fluff of sweet red hair that should be blowing in a breeze someplace instead of rolling down endless hallways cold and full of death. I have become a stone. I don't even look at her. I can't.

The ultrasound room is some circle of hell, buried deep in the bowels of the serpentine, sprawling hospital. The tech tells me with some concern that Spidey has particulate matter in his bladder. What the holy mother this can mean is beyond me, but it must be important because the techs don't usually comment when they scan, do they?

Now I'm sitting, waiting in a darkened, empty space for someone to take my superhero and me back to his cell. We are waiting for too long. Too long by far. There is no one nearby to ask why this is. I cannot get up and find someone because of all the tubes and trolley attached to my son so I sit and endure a rising, silent panic. I keep thinking about what the tech said about his bladder and the words "We are not done yet" stamp into my brain. His organs are failing, I think. He is dying, he must be dying.

This waiting space is so low, so dark. This is a space for drowning. Nadir. I hold him and cry.

But he does not die. He leaves the hospital after five days, or maybe six? He weighs a full pound less than before—he for whom every ounce was critical. But at least he's alive.

Of course, Spiderman still cannot eat actual food. This foe waited in the wings during his hospitalization but returns with a vengeance once he's out. He takes two different meds to help with vomiting and digestion. He drinks all of his meals because the only thing that gets him to gain weight is a medical formula with amino acids in place of proteins (16 scoops per 30 ounces of water per daily jug—I will never forget this calculation). We track every ounce he consumes, the dosing of meds, his moods, and his digestion details on endless Excel spreadsheets. We are clerks. We are scientists. If we faithfully record and examine the data, we are sure we can solve this puzzle. It won't be until he is two and a half that Spidey eats solids, and even then he will eat slowly and with the oral motor skills of a one-year-old. When you don't progress on foods like other babies— as my first baby did, as my third baby will do—your mouth and tongue muscles have a lot of catching up to do. It takes two different rounds of feeding therapy, spaced a year apart, to get him up and running in the right direction.

Maybe superheroes face more than their fair share of villains. Even when Spiderman began eating and gaining weight, new devils of language delay, fine motor delay, and sensory processing disorder arrive to hijack our joy. But he's so beautiful with his long, curly red hair that I cannot bear to cut, even if people think he's a girl. He is the darling of every passing stranger and checkout clerk, every evaluator and therapist. I am pretty sure that if I just love him up as much as I can it will fix all that ails him. I'm a pro now at loving him up and advocating on his behalf. We trade doctor visits for IEP meetings and therapies; he goes under anesthesia one more time for the dental work made necessary from years of reflux and formula. We tell him the silver caps mark his big, strong teeth—his superhero teeth. If only he can get his web shooters working, everything will be fine.

By the time he is five, all the therapies and specialist appointments are gone. The only real struggle is beating him at Uno. Seriously. He's just that good. He will trash talk you as he plays, too. There is no "letting him win." You will get spanked while using your best adult skills because of his superpowers, I guess. When I sleep at night, I'm pretty sure he scales the walls.

Hours after his fifth birthday party, feeling kind of drunk with fatigue, I post the perfect picture on Instagram. My red-haired boy leaning over his electric red, webby cake, candles flickering from the stream of air leaving his slightly open lips. The cake is so huge, so decadent—an embarrassment of riches to make up for those years he couldn't eat cake. A cake much too big because I tried to plan the perfect party and would never want to be short a slice. A giant cake, because superheroes require large gestures. It was good cake, even if it was gluten-free. It tasted of love and the triumphs buried within it.

The Dawson College Shooting: A Mother's Reflections

Carolyne Van Der Meer

On September 13, 2006, Kimveer Gill, 25, arrived at the downtown campus of Montreal's Dawson College and opened fire on students outside the Maisonneuve Boulevard entrance to the school. He continued shooting when he entered the building. One victim, Anastasia de Sousa, died at the scene, while 19 others were injured, some critically. After police shot Gill in the arm, he turned his gun on himself and committed suicide. This was the third fatal shooting in Montreal after the École Polytechnique massacre in 1989 and the Concordia University shooting in 1992.

My six-year-old son and I sit down to a quiet supper, the newspaper still strewn around us. I set the pages down to concentrate on our evening meal. I have just read the exclusive interview with Kimveer Gill's mother in *La Presse* and I find myself overwhelmed by her remarks, by her reflections, by her shock. I cannot for a moment imagine what it must be like to be in her shoes, to be facing, as she put it, a double loss: the loss of her son and the loss of innocence in learning that the boy she raised is a murderer. It is almost unbearable even to think about it—and she has to live it.

My little boy is a perceptive child and has no doubt seen the shine of tears in my eyes. He wants to look at the newspaper photos—I am reluctant. At the same time, I have never been one to shy away from questions or lie to him to protect him from the truth. The world is an ugly place—best to prepare him now for the realization that life is not a bed of roses—something that will hit him at puberty anyway. I let him look at the pictures the day after the shooting, and although

I was filled with tension, I wanted him to understand that guns are scary, dangerous things, not to be taken lightly, not even as toys. "I understand now, mommy," he said as he looked at the photos of the victims, their faces filled with terror. And a few days later, he threw his few toy weapons in the garbage, all on his own.

But now, as we sit at the kitchen table, he is curious once more. He wants to see Kimveer Gill's mother. He's trying desperately to understand. I look at him and he's deep in thought, a frown furrowing his small brow.

"What's the matter?" I ask.

"I'm imagining it was me," he answers.

"What do you mean?"

"I'm imagining it was me who died and me who did the shooting."

"Why?" I ask.

"Not because I want to, but because I just am," he says, "and it makes me feel bad."

I put my arms around him. These are complex emotions and concepts—and as always, my little boy is not afraid to take them on.

My mind returns to Gill's mother. I mesh the image I have of her, fresh from the newspaper, with my own experience of being a mother. I think about how close I am to my son, how well I know him, how much he shares with me, how he trusts me implicitly and comes to me when he is trying to make sense of the world around him. And suddenly, I realize that Mrs. Gill's loss must be staggering. It is normal to think of the killer's victims and their families, imagining that they are our children, that we are the grief-stricken parents. But what is it like to be the parent of a child gone wrong, the parent of a murderer?

"Why was he so angry with the world, mommy? Why did he do what he did?"

My son's words crash through my thoughts.

"No one knows," I tell him. "He was obviously very ill."

"Maybe he just gave up, mommy, and said, 'Well, fine then,' and decided to do something not nice. That happens you know, mommy. Some people do that."

His simple words are jolting. This six-year-old's perspective is in some ways wiser, more informed, than my own. Yes, that happens;

yes people do just give up and do bad things. Sometimes, there are no answers—and in his tiny youth, my son seems to understand this. I draw him to me and feel his small arms around me. I want to savor this moment, hold him close, protect him from the world's savagery—for as long as I possibly can.

Machine

Cheryl Anne Latuner

It happens from time to time that I feel like this—not too often, thank God—that I feel wound as tight as a drum, at the end of my rope, frazzled—all those clichéd expressions that try to describe how a person experiences, physically, the stress that acts on her spirit. Roger has been working long hours every day this week. It is Sunday morning and he is once again out on a job. I have spent too many days alone with my baby.

We don't use child care. It was my decision—our decision—that I would stay at home, full-time, with our daughter. I wanted to give her what I had—the security of her mother's always being within arm's reach. Fortunately, we have an "easy" baby. Provided she and I are rested, we can be in each other's company for long stretches without fraying the basically smooth fabric of our existence together. But this week has overstretched my capacity to be the sole attendant of a two-year-old. The patience, resourcefulness, creativity, wisdom one needs to manage the onslaught of a toddler's desires, cravings, testings, and tryings are exhausted in me. Usually Roger relieves me for a while in the evenings. Not this week. I'm worn out. All I want is to be left alone.

Finally, he arrives at home. I have just gotten Lucie down for her nap. I am testy, irritable. I lock myself in the office, work on paying bills.

I look out the window on this drab, drizzly afternoon and I get this idea: I could go out. He is at home now for the rest of the day. I could simply drop all my responsibilities and flee. Though he has just worked a cruelly long week, he could shoulder things for me for a few hours. In the back of my mind I have held the possibility of our going out together this afternoon: at the music school where I take my daughter for a half-hour singing circle each week there will be a fundraising recital at four o'clock. I had thought we three might try it. What if I just go alone'?

I check my watch. Three o'clock. I could leave right after she wakes. I hurry through the bills. Three-thirty. She is still asleep. I am dressed in grubby old gray jeans. All my other clothes are in the room where she's sleeping. I was going to shower, change. Suddenly I realize, just go. If I leave *before* she wakes, I will not have to nurse her.

I grab my purse and run downstairs, apprise Roger of my plan, breeze past his resigned face, and I'm out the door. I can barely believe it.

*

The occasion for the music recital is to celebrate and raise money for the recent renovation of the music school's new home, a big old brick school house just a short walk off the main business district downtown. The renovations are only partly done—upstairs where we have our "class," the room is sheet-rocked and spackled, but as yet not painted. An icky green rug remnant adorns the floor. But here, in the recital hall, to the inexpert eye, the work is complete. Gleaming new whitewashed walls surround a bank of huge double-hung windows that look out the front of the school. The room is bright, airy, peaceful. One end of the room, adjacent to the window, sports a polished hardwood floor that accommodates a piano, and I sit and watch the arrival—with the first musicians—of folding chairs and music stands. I am just on time. I grabbed what looked like the last parking place in the lot behind the school and have found one of the last remaining seats at the back of the room, next to a gentleman who looks as though he, too, has come alone.

As I sit I am acutely aware of my grubby attire. Many people are dressed casually, but others are dressed up, smelling sweetly of fresh shampoo and cologne. I am sure I reek of staleness and half expect to see someone sniff in my direction. But I am out—out of the house—and soon my attention drifts inward, to what I am feeling.

What I find there shocks me. In contrast to this serene whitewashed exterior, I can perceive how revved up I am. The level of tension in my body is so high that it is like a machine. I am churning. My insides are vibrating. Some awful note inside me has been struck and is reverberating uncontrollably through all my cells. I feel unhealthy, almost panicked.

I am shocked at how physical it all is. I had thought of it as mostly mental stress. Now I contemplate the physical side of it and find this: a sense that my daughter has been too much on my body. Her nursing has felt too hard these past few days, too demanding of me physically. I have hardly been able to tolerate her sometimes long nursing sessions—the ones she demands to fall asleep, and to wake up. I have been storing all that physical antagonism inside. It is ready to erupt.

I take these feelings, these sensations, with me into the music program. The first piece is a movement from a work for flute, piano, bass, and drums by Claude Bolling. The movement is called "Baroque and Blue"—baroque for its classical parts and blue for its jazz parts: the piece has both. The shift from one to the other is surprising, and funny. The contrast, the slightly jolting effect, feels like the contrast within me, the tension between calm control and riled-up energy.

After the next number, a ballad sung and played on the piano by a soloist, the singer stands for a performance piece she has written, called "Model Mother." It is fast talking set to music, exclaiming the frenzied life of the perfect mom, all the gyrations of her day, her life. What a crazy coincidence!

The lone gentleman beside me laughs. Not an inward chuckle, but a big, gusty, loud laugh. He seems to love to laugh. It's nice to hear. I'm glad I'm sitting next to him—his laughing can be a release for both of us.

I forget myself for a while. The music is charming and funny. All the musicians and performers are staff members, and they've chosen a selection of pieces that will entertain both old and young. There are many children in the audience, all sitting quietly, seriously attending the music.

Someday my daughter, now just over two years old, will be among them. She loves music now. She sings all day, knows the words to dozens of songs, makes up words of her own. She can already sweetly carry a tune. She is fascinated by instruments, their sounds, their players. Music always gets her attention. I can tell that it strikes deeply at some chord in her. Her music class is designed to encourage all these tendencies. It is for toddlers alone. But before long she will outgrow it, and then there will be other classes for her to take here. Singing classes, playing classes. My daughter will grow up with this building, this program, as part of her life.

It is halfway through the recital now and I realize that the rainy afternoon has been clearing into a bright evening. I gaze toward the white-painted, double-hung windows. There are pots of pink and white and red azaleas on the window sills, splashes of color against the clean, calm whitewash, the late sun glistening off the wet leaves of the tree outside the windows.

An incredible change has come over me. My tight, taut, machine-driven body is suddenly soft. I am soft in the belly, limp in the legs. My breath reaches more deeply into me. I feel tired. But not exhausted. There is some new energy in me, a quiet energy that alters my emotions, my state of mind. I feel peaceful. It feels like a state I've been away from for a long time.

This music is just what I have needed—a lull, a deep rest. I am absorbed by the atmosphere in the room, by the change in the weather outside. My spirit is clearer. I am happy to do nothing but sit and take it all in.

With each piece, the configuration of the audience changes a little. Performers get up from their audience seats to play, other audience members take their place. As I look toward the windows, I now see a woman I know casually. She has just taken seats there with her husband and two daughters. I met her about two years ago now, the first time I attended a La Leche League meeting. She was one of its two leaders that day.

I can't take my eyes off her and her family. They are all dressed up in their Sunday best. The youngest, a large, broad-faced child of about four with porcelain skin and platinum hair, sits in her lap. The women's hair is plaited in numerous longer-than-shoulder-length braids that fall from their temples. All assembled, watching the music against the white-washed windows, the red azaleas, the blue glow of the bright evening, they look like a painting. Clean. Serene. A portrait. A Vermeer.

A pang of longing goes through me for that serenity, that neat picture. Right now my life feels messy. I'm always struggling to impose some order on it, which the baby makes impossible to maintain. Her demands on the household are erratic, whimsical. Her demands on me are constant.

It takes me a few minutes to scratch beneath the surface of that neat picture to get to the reality I know lurks beneath. I think back to the first time I met this woman, that first La Leche League meeting, when Lucie was just a few months old, and her younger daughter was around two. I sat there cradling my itty-bitty baby in my arms. Her two-year-old jumped in her lap and wanted to nurse. I remember that inwardly I was aghast. A large child, she overflowed in her mother's lap, legs and arms flopping past her mother's body, large head with a full head of plaited hair pressed against her mother's breast. I thought, is it possible that could ever be me? I shuddered. But I had an inkling, even then, that children do not always wean by two years old. I think I said a prayer then that my child would stay petite.

How hard we use our bodies for things that better our lives. I look from this woman, whose secret life of physical involvement with her children is not a secret to me, to the musicians playing their long-rehearsed pieces on the stage, and I know this much is true: practice in dance: in playing instruments, in singing, all require a physical discipline, an arduous one. The more serious the career, the more arduous the physical work. We never question the rightness of that, the certainty that hard work pays off. There's my daughter's music teacher up there playing her well-practiced flute—her own children sitting in the audience.

I suddenly wish that I had Lucie sitting in my lap this very minute. The part of me that gives physically and freely wants it, the part that is confident of why I promote this intense physical relationship I have with her—why I nurse, still nurse. It's the part of me that is certain my hard work will pay off—in her sense of security, her own confidence. It's the part of me that desires both to nurture her and to be a model for her as she grows up with this building, this special community in her life—as she learns to use her heart and body in ways that will fulfill her.

*

I leave the recital hall and stroll into town. I have needed this time alone. I savor it a few minutes more. The stores are all closed this Sunday evening. I peek in their windows and am reminded of my past life, when I lived in a big city and window shopping was an everyday affair. That was long ago. This is a different life. I am a different person.

Is it? Am I?

How long will it really be before her life—my daughter's life—eclipses my role in it? Sooner than I can imagine, perhaps, school and her maturity will carry her off, away from me. My old life—at least in part—will return to me. In the long run, it will have been so short a time that I have had the opportunity to devote my body, my self, to her.

Translating Pain Into Colors and Words

Raquel Partnoy

Twenty years ago, when I moved to the United States, I felt that its English language was a kind of shelter which I could use to write about the terror my family and many others had endured during the seven years of dictatorship in Argentina: disappearances, torture, killing at the hands of a terrorist state. This new language gave me the necessary physical and psychological distance to be able to write about what I had experienced during that time. Writing essays, poems, and my book-length narrative poem *City of Red Horizons* made me concentrate more on English grammar than on my feelings.

I have been nourished by three languages and cultures. My mother's Yiddish tongue and the Jewish traditions she brought with her to Argentina awakened my love of reading Jewish writers and learning about her world, as well as understanding more about her sad memories. Argentina was the country her family chose when they escaped the horrors of Czarist Russia. I grew up there and the Spanish language enriched my life through the magnificent authors from Latin American and Spain. I have memories of myself, an already avid reader at fourteen, going to my city's bookstores to buy affordable editions of novels by well-known authors. For years I kept that collection, which I regarded as my treasure. Later in my life, the English language allowed me to read the original works of great poets, and also testimonies of Holocaust survivors. Reading those testimonies, I noticed many similarities between the methodology used during the Holocaust and the one employed by the military dictatorship in Argentina. I decided to unify both subjects and paint a series I called "Surviving Genocide." At the same time, I wrote an essay on the subject.

Early in my career I used to paint landscapes of Bahía Blanca, my hometown in Argentina. Although I often drew large human figures on paper, I had not yet thought about including them in my oil landscapes. It was not by chance that in 1976, small figures began to appear at the doors, windows, and skies of my cityscapes. That was precisely the year Argentina began to experience one of the cruelest chapters of its history: the military coup that was responsible for the disappearance of thirty thousand people, who were massacred by the government.

When my daughter was disappeared and my son fell into a state of depression, I thought that I would need more than a single work to describe what was going on in my country at that time. I began working on series of paintings and essays. Gradually the figures grew larger on my canvases and became the main characters of my work. It took me several years to produce the first series of paintings in which I was able to start expressing my experiences. Later I realized that much had gone unexpressed in those paintings, too, so I began writing poems inspired by each of them. I produced a sort of dialogue between the images I had in front of me and my memory.

The voices of the authors who have experienced injustice, or who have written about it, like Adrianne Rich, Silvia Plath, Allen Ginsberg, Muriel Rukeyser and others, have encouraged me to write and tell the story of my family, which is part of the saddest chapter of my country's history. Lately, I have started to "translate" my poems to Spanish and this is a very different story. It is not the same thing to write "would they leave my daughter safe on the streets?" instead of ¿dejarían ellos libre a mi hija por las calles? "Make them disappear" is different than "hacerlos desaparecer." I feel deeply the weight of the Spanish words; they are heavier and more painful than the English ones. While switching from one language to the other I can feel my Jewish roots, and the experience of my ancestors, coming alive in my writings.

Although I have devoted most of my years to painting, I believe that both painting and writing have always been the engines that gave me the strength to keep on living—to survive.

Catechisms: Three Poems

Mary Kate Jordan

Neither Labor Nor Spin

Consider the lilies, he said.
We bowed our heads and considered.
The others, also seven and
more familiar with dandelions,
heard 'lilies' as a generic.

But I remembered
a living bouquet,
a singular night:
orange striped tigers
on tall strong stems
in uncut grasses
at the pasture's edge,
leaves like green flags
in the rectangle
of light that fell through
the open kitchen door
while I brushed my small
white teeth with baking
soda, and water
flowing from the pipe
hammered deep into

the side of the hill.
Gold fireflies tangoed
under pale white stars
while my grandfather
kept watch beside me.
After he walked me
upstairs to bed, I
slept like a flower.

Mother in Labor

My mom, a Classics major before World War II,
translated twelve life-tasks. She found most worth doing.
 Not as Herakles did them.
As she valued them.

Cleanliness and godliness united in her:
Mom might have mucked the Augean Stables alone.
Disorder was her Hydra.
She might steal weapons
(only to cut off the Hydra's, and Satan's, heads)
but golden apples?
Simply to give them away.

The test she refused? *"Slay the Nemean Lion"*,
a beast for whom she felt real
and fierce compassion.
A lion sculpture in Geneva – marble, carved
into a wall, the beast dying – brought her to tears.

At her own death, she whispered
-a shimmer, an image, a sound inside my mind,
the voice of a lion sinking into the earth -
"Mary, can't you cut this cord? It's too hard for me."

That trapped lion undid me,
finally unraveled our habit tug-o-war.
"You can cut it yourself," I said. Spoke without words,
as she did. Sounded hard. Spoke true. "You can do this."
Each word, a rescue ring tossed out as a lifeline,
floated on her ocean of self-deprecation.
Sank. Bleached the reef called doubt with bold, focused sonar:
Yes, you can yes you can yes you can. Yes. You. Can.

Time out of time later, two minutes? seven? one?
she exulted: "I didn't know I could do that!"
Then, with a sound like the rush of wings, she was gone.
A sky lion now. Carved in stars. Brings me to tears.

Roses

Even the oldest of the trees continues its wonderful labor.
Hummingbird lives in one of them.
~ Mary Oliver, *Someday.*

Valiant. Thorny. White or
rainbow: brilliant red. Pink.
Coral. Maroon. Yellow.
Some cut for corsages,
Others in vases

or broken underfoot.
Some, still on their bushes,
perfume the moving air
or become bright red hips,
roots deep in dark earth.

Women nearing seventy,
upright or downtrodden,
each one of us fragrant,
each one of us a rose
blooming in winter.

Each rose a hummingbird.
Each of us a tree.

Boots

Barbara Newman

I trudge through knee deep mud,
thick, binding, each step
weighted with resistance.

It holds me like a suction cup…
pulling me into the *place of stuck…*
where the fit is snug and "seemingly" just right.

This is the Comfort Zone.
It is filled with cushy down pillows, soft blankets
and a very very hard edge.

It's just a trick.
Comfort Zone doesn't want me to leave…
I am her safety, too.
We have been codependent for so long.

"STAY," she whispers, "You know it here."

"NO," I say, louder.

I realize I need new hiking boots,
strong ones that feel good on my feet,
and work hard to protect them….

When the mud is like a rock wall, it is no time for pretty shoes.

My desire to move forward screams inside of me.
A wail that can no longer stay silent.
Its surround-sound presence—calls me forth.

I breathe. I can't do this without strong legs. And shoulders.
So I straighten my posture, take another breath,
and lean in to the resistance.

It immediately softens.

I am willing.

I am willing to see.

I am willing to see the beauty in this denseness.

I sit with it for a while.

And so I ask…
what is here?

I close my eyes…

There's a forest.
I am venturing in…slowly
on this path of curiosity.

I notice a sprinkling of fallen pine needles under my feet.

What is this, I ask?

A reminder that things get prickly sometimes.
And if I let go, they will soften, and eventually fall away.

I continue to walk…
what do I see?

A curtain.

White, slightly opaque, flirting with the wind.

What is here
what is this space trying to tell me...?

It's some kind of veil
and it's blocking my view...

What does it have to show me?

That I need to open my eyes.
A bit wider.

I move forward.
I like these new boots.
but *this...*
this is hard work.

Digging into the psyche
is no walk in the park.

I lean in again.
breathe into it.
The mud softens a bit more.
The rock wall gets smaller...
and yet,
this forest is vast.

There are walls and walls of curtains.
I swim through them...
like seaweed.

What are they trying to say?

They are flowing.

In constant motion…

"I will not tread water.

I will not stay in one place."

I do the breast stroke…

feet solid on the ground.

The threads of my story open.

These curtains….

they are windows to somewhere.

Wait….is that not guidance?

I stop in my tracks.

What does the looking glass have to say?

Be clear.

Be clear with what?

A crow caws…

It is loud…

and clear.

There it is.

Be clear with my voice.

I soften more.

What else is there?

These curtains…
they lead me…
from one room to another…

It is the house of me.

The sun is sinking.
The Fingers of God have disappeared.

But God has not left.
I am not separate.

*Just because I can't see something
doesn't mean it isn't there.*

I soften.

And wait.

What else does this space have to say.

what is it here to reveal?

I dig deeper.
After all, I am an archeologist of the soul.

I am in labor again.
two children birthed long ago…
and I am back in the delivery *rooms*…

expanding. contracting.
expanding again…

like a dragonfly…
in the deep dark primordial squish
shedding
shedding
shedding
until I emerge…
free…
stained glass wings glistening in the sun…

mud crusted hiking boots, left at the edge of the forest.

Smudges

Linda Kaye-Moses

As maker of things, it is clear to me that waiting behind every piece being made is a secret intention: the creation, in spite of its logical impossibility, of a kind of immortality. There are also smaller and unintended quasi-immortal objects that are made every day, noticeable remnants of ourselves—smudges—that pass for permanence of a sort.

Rising from sleep each night, I shuffle quickly into the bathroom, and as I move past the protruding chimney wall and into the hall, I reach for the corner with my left hand, brushing it slightly to steady myself, my groggy gait not quite stable. Each of these midnight expeditions has left a smudge on the wall, a shadow, that over the years, has become a message to anyone who might notice, a grayed stele of untranslated and disturbed dreams, of grumbling protestations; a smear of transfer from one state of consciousness to another that is by necessity more grounded. This is a sign of my passage, a fragment of this part of my life and, perhaps, a modest though enduring reminder of the breadth and width of an act of creation.

As a maker of jewels, I am aware that the artifacts that are most likely to survive the repeating roll of civilizations are the objects with which we adorn ourselves. These ancient objects were always at my back, pushing me from behind, encouraging me to make my own work, my jewels. These jewels crowd the future with my presence. They are the audacious attempt at immortality that recently has been activating an inordinate profusion of my synapses. These jewels are becoming my smudges on the wider world.

I don't want to write this next part. I don't even want to look at the events that must be described! But that's nothing new...I didn't want to look at them when they were happening. This is not about me, though it is also about me. It's about the spring and summer of 2013, and how I stared into the terrible canyon of the delicate mortality of our son, Adam, and of myself. It's about Adam and about me and about the dog and about the meaning of life. That's an awful lot of what it was and is about, but the truth is that reflecting on it, I am not certain that the meaning of life ever entered into my conscious thoughts or even came close to being defined, while I was experiencing it or even since.

There is an insoluble mystery that accompanied Adam and me that year: the mystery of how, after being confronted with mortality, the meaning of life becomes, well, meaningless. What meaning there is embeds itself in the immediate, specific, and precious moments of each day, and that, though only barely enough, must suffice.

That year, a mass grew on the stem of Adam's brain. This serpentine mass wrapped around that sweet and sensitive man's body, and for the remainder of the most delicious seasons of the year, when everything else was growing lushly, Adam's brain was blasted with enough radiation to burn away the tumor. All the odds say that it's still lurking, in some infinitesimal form, in some remote furrow of his brainstem, waiting for the conditions that encouraged it to call it forth again, but right now it is NOT, not there, not seen, not, not, not.

The month after Adam's tumor appeared, my brain, after seven decades on the planet, chose to announce the presence of a double cerebral aneurysm on my left internal carotid artery, an unknown stalker that had been with me since my mother brought me onto the planet. It finally began to shout, with an impossibly loud voice, that my life on the planet was circumscribed by two miniature balloons in my head, six and five millimeters in cross-section, ready to erupt. Up until the moment of that discovery, I had envisioned the inside of my head as a repository of a compressed and infinite length of neurons and vascular windings, extending into every crevice inside my skull...an unlimited environment of sparkling connections, memories, and intellections. I was forced to revise these imagined geographies to include a detour, a diverted path that, if ignored, would release a flood, destructive to the terrain, and which had the power to bring me to my knees, to redefine the intimate and personal 'me,' and perhaps even to kill me. So I did not ignore these vascular swellings. I found a surgeon who, with brilliance and gentleness, eliminated the threat.

At the outset, however, I was facing the possibility of losing the recognizable personalities of myself and my son, and maybe the lives that supported those personalities, too. I became untethered, awash in wave after wave of grieving, accompanied by excessive and necessary weeping, wailing, and howling. I lost any awareness of alternatives and descended into the darkest of spiritual caves. When I thought it could become no more harrowing, a week after my diagnosis, our gentle dog Misha was diagnosed with a tumor on his lung.

I am godless. That is who I am, that is how I structure the cosmos. It is a demanding position to take, without comfort, without the ease of lying back into the arms of a comforting presence. I admit to the difficulty, and simultaneously hold to the unknowable mystery that is the essential quality of an unconscious universe. During that spring and summer, I wished it were otherwise, and I spent a considerable amount of time begging for healing for myself, Adam and Misha, my view of an implacable and mysterious universe dissolving in my lamentations. Believing, as I do, in the potential of healing 'prayer'—undirected, but powerful nonetheless—I focused on that potential, as I had done in the past, invoking Adam's name, constantly, and I reached out to my dearest friends and asked them to hold Adam in a healing light. I visualized his tumor shrinking. I visualized my aneurysms deflating. I held Misha in my arms and imagined his lungs filling with health-giving air.

I exhausted myself, dispensing my energies as if they were limitless, which they were not. I spent so much time wailing, I looked out at the world through swollen eyelids, able to see only darkness. I was convinced that expressing my distress proved that I was a caring mother and dog owner, and that I was not in denial about my own diagnosis. Without the *sturm und drang*, I subconsciously reasoned, how would I know how much I cared about our son, my dog and myself? I felt guilty if I released myself, even for a moment, from the distress of my grieving. I could not go on in that manner without descending into sleeplessness, depression, and eventual illness. The fear of those consequences finally drove me to ask for help from our daughter, Jude, whose wisdom has always exceeded her age, and from a counselor, both of whom reminded me that screaming into the bleakness was only one path among many, and it was the one path that wasted what precious energy I had available.

I'm a weeper. Give me something sorrowful, I cry. Give me something wonderful, I cry. That's what I've done all my life when touched by passion, joy, sadness, death, terror. Very gradually, that year, I came to realize that not every emotional event requires tears; that tears are not always the appropriate response to intense feelings. Very slowly, my weeping diminished. I began to visualize Adam, Misha, and myself as glowing with healing light, and slowly the shadows detached from my heart and floated away.

Given the realities, there was not much I could actively do to heal any of us. The weeping, no matter how physically vigorous, was a passive, immobilizing activity. I learned to focus on the healing, not on the darkness. Jude reminded me again and again that I did not have to walk on the dark side. I began to exchange the violent passivity of tears for the passionate exercise of creativity. That's what I'm good at...making stuff. And so I began to draw mandalas for Adam, for me, for Jude, for my daughter-in-law, Lisa, my son-in-law, Rob and for my dear partner and husband, Evan.

Adam's mandala included images of the tumor-as-phantasmagorical-caterpillar wrapped around his imagined brainstem, morphing into a magnificent butterfly, becoming healthy in his body, and his music. Lisa's included her love of birds and gardening, plus the same butterfly, safe and protected. Jude's pictured her lifelong involvement in live theater and cinema, plus her love of deep red roses. Rob's showed his academic achievement and his love of tennis and music. Evan's included his investment in photography and the autoharp, and images of moons and stars, because he is my moon and my stars. Mine had jewels, a piano keyboard, lilacs and images of my aneurysms transformed into beautiful, fringed pendants. All of the mandalas were suffused with dense colors, and each of them included a unique image of a sun, flooding all of us in healing light.

These were deliberate *smudges*, persistent images and tools for the future, reminding each of us to focus on healing. They were images that revealed the parts of each of us that sustain us and make us the beings we are or can be. Envisioning and drawing them drove me from the shadows and into a light filled with the colors and forms of healing.

Misha, whose surgery revealed a hematoma, not a tumor, returned to his life as it had been before the procedure, spending more time in our office, curled up in his bed under my desk, with only a few short months of extra intense cuddling, snuggling and quality time left with us. I did not draw a mandala for him, because, of course, he is a dog, and accepts life on *its* terms, without imposing any extraneous *mishegas* or whining on it. He had no need for a mandala, because his focus remained intact: on food, treats, loving hands, cushioned places to sleep, rabbits, cats, mice, voles, and other dogs...anything else was simply not worth his attention.

I learned from Misha to attend to those things that are worthy of notice, although in my case, those things included my family, sunlight on a day of impossibly blue skies, our abundant crop of blueberries, purple New England asters, and my art.

Adam's tumor was blasted away by radiation and also, I believe, by the mightiness of purposeful and loving meditation. He has survived, and he is changed, though not in ways that I had anticipated. He seems more patient, more introspective, with an acknowledgement of the vagaries of the universe. And I learned from him that even though I can be assaulted or ignored by a universe involved in doing its own thing, I can choose to travel my path with purpose and defiance.

As autumn began, in that particular year of crises, it was finally clear to me that during the next decades of my life, I would experience perhaps ten, or maybe fifteen of the most completely *perfect* Fall days—maybe a few more, given the exploits of modern medicine, though the improbable benefits of that promised extension seem remarkably overrated. In light of my presupposed quota of *perfect* days, I have become preoccupied by the need to repeatedly smudge the world, leaving countless traces of my passage, my presence here.

There are many enduring smudges impressed on our world, some huge, like the pyramids of Giza, and some diminutive, like an unknown dog's paw print made in fresh cement, or subtle, like the worn stone stairways of Volterra and Knossos. Some are heartbreaking, like the residuum of Pompeii, and some inspire delight: a breathtaking meadow of abandoned and naturalized lilacs, left to wander on their own, immortalizing some unknown farmer's wife. My smudges—my jewels, my drawings, my writing, our children—all transform the world in ways that I hope will endure. These smudges, even those on my bedroom wall, must suffice as the reward for and legacy of my time on the planet.

On My Way to Rehab

Lee Schwartz

I knew the country was on no one's map,
a place for shattered bones and demented minds,
becoming an old friend far from home,
losing myself along the way, fragile as raw silk,
teary as a popsicle, cracked open to heal,
a boulder with moss growing on its skin,
an ancient cemetery with my name barely
visible, weather eating away my dates,
lakes and ponds with ducks and geese
protecting a prep school of vanity youth,
longhorn, shaggy cattle, brown fences, red barns,
farm tractors poised to work the fields,
all the sky and earth breathing and sweating
while I walk the fine line, all the scenery and stoplights
I never noticed, choking on Mom's Restaurant
and the waters that run below breakfast and dinner,
hungry to take all this with me,
feeling it all slip away like a wedding ring in a dark movie,
trying to wake up to myself, what was and is no longer.

Underground

Susie Kaufman

The thought occurred to Daisy, as it did several times a day, that her life would likely end in an ass-over-teakettle tumble down the basement steps. The steps were dangerously steep, littered with dirty towels and children's underwear midway on the road to the washing machine. They were slick from fifty years of contact with the grime of family life. The light switch at the top of the stairs was fussy, sometimes refusing to illuminate the cellar. And even when it did choose to work, Daisy tried to look straight ahead, not to the left where moldy boxes stacked at precarious angles contained the archaeological record of four generations of Siegels. Some day, Daisy and her brothers would have to get rid of all this junk. There was a time when she envisioned a great festive sorting, Jesse uncovering his warped tennis rackets, David his 8-tracks, but lately she imagined an enormous, mechanized shovel scooping up the rodent-nibbled mountain of Siegel stuff and taking it someplace where it could decay without sentiment.

Daisy passed the basement laundry area and walked into her mother's bedroom without knocking. It was 8:30 in the morning and Charlotte Siegel had moved from her bed to the table to eat her breakfast, leaving several days' worth of balled up tissues around the pillow and trailing along the floor. Daisy found her mother idly turning the pages of *The Chronicle*, chomping on a bagel laden with cream cheese. On the table, the remains of yesterday's breakfast, lunch and dinner decorated old newspapers, bills, and advertising. An array of pill bottles glared at Charlotte while she tried to interest herself in the probability of Hillary Clinton running for president. Charlotte had been born during the first FDR administration and had always taken pride in her political savvy. But now, the various blood pressure and cholesterol medications, as well as pills for her lower back pain, seemed to overwhelm the space, both on the table and in her mind. She refused on principle to take the antidepressants.

Dr. Ling seemed like a decent person, gentle and attentive when Daisy took her mother to Kaiser for her check-ups; but really, what did she know about how Charlotte felt when she woke up yet again in her cave-like, windowless bedroom and contemplated another day. What did she know about this endless running out…running out of milk, running out of Depends, running out of energy and something to say. Daisy wanted to know how she slept. She slept just fine. She slept day and night, in her easy chair, on the couch, in bed. When she slept, she visited with Jack, her husband dead 22 years. They laughed at life and talked about Balzac.

"I want to go to Safeway and the library on Marin."

"Today's not a good day for that, Mom. I'm working on a song and the band's waiting for me so we can figure out the set we're going to do next weekend. I can scoot to the store real fast and get whatever you need. Orange juice, toilet paper?"

Daisy was an aspiring songwriter and part-time weed dealer. She and her two kids lived in Charlotte's North Berkeley house virtually rent-free and she drove her mother's car. Quid pro quo, though her brothers didn't quite see the equity in it. Jesse, in particular, had a way of suggesting that she had the deal of the century.

"You don't know what I need. I don't know what I need till I get to Safeway. I like to look at all the frozen dinners."

Daisy sighed. By the time her mother got dressed and they did the grand tour at the supermarket and the Alameda County library, half the day would be gone and the boys would be racing in the front door, cheerfully combative and ravenous. Charlotte exchanged her grungy pajama bottoms for a pair of stained pants. She turned her back to Daisy for help hooking her bra and bent with difficulty to put on socks and shoes. They looked around for the cane that was always in hiding behind a bookcase and went out the basement side door and up the driveway.

The drought had brought spectacular weather if you weren't a farmer or someone who hoped to be able to afford lemons and tomatoes next year. No more morning fog over the bay. Just a robin's egg sky overhead and spring flowers: spiraea, California poppies and a bush with red blossoms, leptospermum. Daisy turned on to Shattuck and breezed down to the store. There was no point trying to help Charlotte with the shopping. Daisy had to remind herself every time that in the supermarket aisles her mother was a hunter-gatherer, stalking and harvesting. She could not be disturbed and could not be hurried.

Forty minutes later, the trunk of the car overflowing with nasty-smelling cheeses and packages of microwave pork enchiladas, they made their way to the library. Here, after the brief intermission in the car, Charlotte turned up the heat on seek and ye shall find, combing the stacks for books that were worth reading but not too long. Coetzee, Naipaul, William Kennedy. Some part of her mind, which remembered nothing that anyone said to her, nothing about what pills she was supposed to take morning and evening, nothing about what her grandchildren were interested in, still resonated with language, syntax, the great parade of words.

Charlotte had wanted Daisy to be a reader, a thinker, but the clothes didn't fit. She was what they call a people person and this very quality, her gift for empathy, her love for the rough texture of the life around her, made her a songwriter. It made her vibrate with the longing, the regret. It also stuck her with all the caregiving, now that her father Jack was gone, her ex re-married on the other side of the country, and her brothers working full-time.

Back home, Daisy sat at Jack's old baby grand upstairs and listened for the song. That's how she thought of it. The song would tiptoe in and introduce itself when it was good and ready. She needed to be patient. This seemed to be the message she was getting from every direction. Be patient with your kids. Be patient with your mother. Be patient with your songwriting. The first few lines had shown up unannounced over the weekend... "How can the days be so long and so short? Why is the night never coming? When will I get back the life that is mine? La la la la la la lala...." Iambic pentameter, Charlotte called it.

Daisy answered her cell phone, knowing it would be her mother.
"I need to see Dr. Ling."
"We just went to Kaiser last week, Mom. What's going on?"
"I can't walk. Why can't I walk?"
Daisy didn't want to tell her what the doctor had suggested... that Charlotte was forgetting how to walk and would one day forget how to swallow.

"Dr. Ling says you need more exercise. Tomorrow we'll walk up Mariposa and look at the wisteria, ok?"

"OK, Daisy Duck. Tomorrow and tomorrow and tomorrow."

The song wasn't coming. It was stuck in the pipeline. She needed some kind of creative Drano, something that would flush the gunk out of her brain. Daisy decided to go over to visit Jack's tree in Live Oak Park. When her Dad had died, painfully, witheringly, in 1993, the city said Charlotte could plant a Japanese maple in the park in his memory. The tree had survived even though it never rained and no one ever weeded or fed it. It was hardier than Jack, but nowhere near as clever.

Daisy sat on the dry grass and let her mind wander over to her father. There he was in his mustard-colored bathrobe, chain-smoking Pall Malls in the old days, flipping pancakes and downing his fourth cup of sludge. He was a jazz musician pretending to be an academic, her Dad. All that smart patter, that deconstructionist rat-a-tat-tat was really a repurposed saxophone riff. He was 60 when the melanoma caught up with him, but he never seemed to age. Everything was new for him. First life, then death. They all died young anyway, the greats. Mozart, Charlie Parker, Lenny Bruce.

"When will I hear different drumming?" The line came to her randomly.

But Jack never seemed to be waiting for something to happen, never seemed to be expecting anything. He just took each Tuesday as it arrived and squeezed the nectar out of it. He hit that tennis ball. He drank that gin. When he died, the family scattered like so many pool balls at the break, Jesse marrying a girl from Kansas, Daisy falling in love with another woman and following her to LA. David kept one eye on Charlotte, but it wasn't easy to figure her out. She seemed to be running on inarticulate rage, scraping the bottom of the personals barrel, picking out the most awful, incongruous men, just to stick it to Jack's memory, just to let him know what a shit he was to disappear on her when she was only 58.

What would Jack have done if fortune had reversed itself, if he had lived to watch over Charlotte in her decline, to preside over this advancing disorder, inside and out? Daisy knew what he wouldn't have done. He wouldn't have fussed over her. Charlotte hated being fussed over.

"Don't go out without your cane, Mom. You might lose your balance and take a flop. Don't eat too many cashews, Mom. You know how nuts make you constipated. Don't lose your hearing aids, Mom. Those things don't come cheap."

Jack would have concentrated on the party that remained to them. Dim sum, wine, maybe a toke or two. He would have elevated the conversation like the day he died when he wanted to talk about ancient Egyptian art. Jack would have pestered Charlotte to live until the living was done. Daisy knew this message from beyond the grave was meant for her, too. Not that her Dad wanted her to be reckless. He just wanted her to appreciate, for the love of God, the nasturtiums in the garden, the noise of her children. How he would have loved them, her cocoa-colored boys, athletes, jokers.

"Here where the sun does its dance on the bay. Whispering, singing and weeping. Gentle the light at the start of the day. Lifting me out of my sleeping."

Better. More presence. Less yearning. Daisy poured a glass of California Malbec, got in a few deep, satisfying breaths, went in to see her mother. Charlotte was dozing in her favorite chair, her legs up on a hassock, Evelyn Waugh open on her lap. Charlotte was receiving instructions direct from Jack and following them to the letter. She kept telling them to leave her be. Live their own lives, she told her daughter and her two sons. It was just that vigilance and living in the moment didn't mix all that well. Daisy couldn't seem to stay in her life and keep one eye on her mother at the same time. She couldn't wrap her arms around the present without being paralyzed by the fear of the future: Charlotte falling, having a stroke, dying for God's sake. This was not an hallucinogenic nightmare, the product of a fertile imagination. People die. Her father, for one. Blood coming out of his mouth while the family looked on, none of them able to breathe in this sacred moment as if continuing to inhale and exhale were somehow in poor taste when Jack was no longer able to do it. She had been an expert witness, she and Charlotte and Jesse and David. They had all stayed with him until they heard the gate slam closed behind him.

Daisy crumpled the lyrics into a grapefruit-sized ball and tossed it expertly into the trash. Her boys would be impressed by her hook shot. They would be coming home from school soon, demonstrating their soccer footwork, complaining about playground outrages. They didn't spend much time with their grandmother. She was too slow-moving, too hard of hearing. She didn't have their goofy, free-form energy. Daisy was the intermediary, the ambassador. She decided to start on a dinner that they would all enjoy.

She got the chicken parts out of the fridge, pressed a lot of garlic on them and sprinkled the top with lemon juice. She put up some rice and poured another glass of Malbec. There would be plenty of chicken and rice and plenty of wine to share with her mother. But Charlotte, she knew, would not want to climb the stairs to eat with them. She would rather taste Daisy's caring for her from down below in her own silent space, savoring the warm goodness of it underground.

The Yoga of Aging and Dying

Mary Beth Ogulewicz

"Savor this moment," I often urge my yoga students on the mat. Savoring life includes savoring the sweetness and sacredness of death.

What I have learned is there is as much beauty in death and the dying process as there is embracing the culture of youthfulness of the body and life. Much of the exhortation of yoga is focused on an intention to restore vitality, regain liveliness or range of motion in the body. When facing an irreversible diagnosis that deteriorates the body and mind, when dying is looming, that upward trajectory intention is no longer a possibility. Caretaking my father for ten years with Alzheimer's and helping him cross over, my yoga practice took on new meaning, adding depth and presence to the process of dying, and expanded life to include embracing frailty, loss, and permanent physical separation as part of the natural cycle of life.

In western culture, we are infrequently intimate with the process of dying. Saying yes to dying and embracing it as a sacred and meaningful transition of life transformed what had been an unpleasant experience with the passing of my mother to a beautiful sacred journey with my father. Informed by my practice, early on I set an intention to not take death personally this time. To simply allow it to unfold with ease, to greet it with an open heart, even welcome it and what it had to teach me and him. To remain open in my heart no matter what feelings arose. Certainly, there were waves of overwhelming grief and times my body racked with sobs, but rather than resisting the feelings or grasping at the straws of medical intervention, I remained fully present, experiencing it all, eyes wide open as we faced uncertainty and walked this path together.

Yoga is called a practice for good reason. Until I met great challenge, I had no idea how the tapas I cultivated would reveal a cocoon of strength and support. Until then, I was unaware that my years of training were preparing me for this very moment; escorting, dancing with and celebrating death. Shepherding death, I was taken aback by how effortlessly my practice of pranayama, meditation and yoga came to the fore and buoyed us. Faced with rolling his failing large frame, I filled with confidence. I looked at his body and realized I know the body. I knew exactly what to do from restorative yoga training—how to prop, how to protect and support. No bone on bone, pillow between the knees, support any bony areas that protrude and rest on the ground.

I witnessed and received the ripple effect of my practice when my 16-year-old daughter observing me overwhelmed, and frequently reminded me take in three deep full letting go breaths and exhale completely, as I had done so often with her. Or when my 14-year-old son tweeted to his school friends "I will not be emotionally available today." Healing chants filled the room, as did the gentle reminder of so many of my teachers, "Can you be fully present, here, in this moment, without wanting another experience? Not resisting. Not grasping. Just be fully present here." I was grateful for Jonathan Foust's sharing just months earlier how he had aided his father's passing. As I loved my father out of this world, I did the same for weeks, placing my hand over his heart, sharing tender moments of his steady warmth in my life.

Though my father could no longer move, I was able to give him the gift of travel, a last savoring of the visceral joys of life taking him hiking up the foothills of Mount Tom where he grew up and swimming in the Connecticut River, using my yoga nidra training. Though he was bedbound, he felt, touched, smelled, and moved freely, satiated with the sensory experience of life one more time. The experience of hiking in the forest and swimming in the cold currents of the Connecticut River were stored in his memory untouched by Alzheimer's. Watching his body relax and peacefulness settle into his bones as he traveled using guided meditation, I had that moment, that confluence of events, past and present, when my years of practicing fully met the moment of challenge and I thought, yes, I was born to do this.

Stephen Cope writes about dharma and suggests we all have a duty, a thing we must do in this lifetime that if we bow away, shirk from, we will feel the incongruence of self betrayal. That for me was the responsibility of taking care of my father. There were times it was annoying, unpleasant and irritating. Times I felt angry for having to bear all the burden by myself. But I found in that bedroom the support of the teachings and my sangha to ride the biggest wave of all. I was never alone. Burden dissolved and gave way to the beauty and intimacy of guiding my father's soul in love and faith to the other side.

In his final moments, I lovingly cradled his head in my hands as I had done so many times for my students in savasana. This time would be a last holding. I lengthened the back of his neck and massaged his occiput. Unable to speak, he clapped his hands to display his pleasure and appreciation. I assured him he was deeply loved. Told him he had been a great father. Assured him he completed the work that he had been sent here to do. Shared his faith that God was present with us in that very room, and all he needed to do was take one step. I would not leave him. He would never be alone. I was with him here, and my mother just on the other side, waiting. He raised his eyebrows, took in a deep breath and left.

A home ideally roots you and frees you. Over the years, yoga excavated my heart, allowed me to rediscover my indomitable spirit and deepened my faith, opening me to the wonder and mystery of life. I am grateful for the tools for healthy living which include using those same tools to fully live death, the one inevitability we must all face. Concepts like Aparigraha, Ishvara and Pranidahna have blossomed in meaning in the wake.

With this experience, I learned I could powerfully and intimately embrace death and be a loving peaceful presence for my father at a time when the urge to blink or wince is so strong, and the fear of the permanence of transition paralyzing. For my father, a man who had worked so hard his entire life and asked for so little, being able to use my yoga teacher training to provide physical ease, peace for his heart and spirit, and flood him with love was a small return for a lifetime of boundless generosity and love.

"Serve with a full heart. By making others happy, you make yourself happy. The key to your heart lies hidden in the heart of another" (Swami Kripalu).

Four Poems

Elizabeth O'Rourke

Remembering Raferty
Irish poet 1779-1835, author of "Cill Aodain"

The last light in the upstairs bedroom was the best thing,
and the first few nights we slept readily
with the dog's head resting in the soft dip
between rib and hip.
We did things we never had:
counted five hoots lined up at the window at three in the morning,
gave each other long quiet kisses in the backyard.
I liked to watch the steam lift from my tea mug while the last of
   the night
combed the dark out of her hair.

There, we were an abundance:
of arms pushing paint rollers and hard bristled brushes,
of knees on tiles.
Hope draped us in deep hued vestments.
After working, we broke the bread and baked the pasta,
poured out in verbs our plans, dimensions, and blueprints.

The house, we called Cill Aodain, and it was true--
everything grew there.

I will look again every summer for the cornstalks, for the mint
    underfoot.
There is a patience in the seasons and a calm in the wait.

Deothas

The nurse took you for cleaning and measuring and I called,
"May I have her back now?" again, then again, because
at once the waters we had lived in were gone, now lands and hands
    between us
and I wanted everything touching.

There were twelve hours of the scythe to your path and the teary
    crippling.
I could not listen to songs with words.
My legs were shifted by others.
I forgot names of things: blanket, glass, screen.
I opened every rib to find a breath.

The morning pushed back the sheets and peeked through the
    window corners
and it was the day you were born: alive and crying.
"Deothas," Irish: the calf's longing for its mother.
My longing for you, Hope, now yours.

We are stone-written: the way the rain always stops,
the way the beach becomes wide again,
the webs, rewoven in the dew.

Longer Days

This is why we work all day:
so we can come home.
For me to pull on your shirt
for my skirt to be off
or at least up.
This is love, for us, in spring:
for you to walk in the door
to put that bag down, for the last time today
and take a beer from the fridge
to give me the first sip.

I let the long days make me touch you more.
I close my eyes and hope I look like you do in soft late light.

A Poem in April When I'm Looking for a Trowel in the Shed

Is it time, again
to tear everything apart?

My Edible Muse

Judith Berg

It's mid-July in that stretch of New York State that lies between the Hudson River and the Massachusetts border on the East, and the heat is already bearing down at nine in the morning. There is a giant factory running at full capacity, the factory known as Nature. Lawns demand to be mowed, beans to be picked, weeds to be pulled. My inner nature chimes in with the reminder that there are words to be written. All told, there's plenty of work to be done. And my body, having known seventy some Julys, wants none of it. I can see the clean, cool, glistening pool at the other end of the vegetable garden, far away from my laptop, and follow the body's bidding.

My walk to the pool takes me right past the garden. Peering in, I can see the plump pout of the sweet peas and the silent mockery of the green beans now at their peak. Those that are overripe admonish me from their starchy interior bulge: do not dally long in the cool pool. The steamy heat blanketing the garden threatens to push the beans to ruination in a matter of hours. So, after a quick dip, and a wistful glance at my book waiting on the sleek orange chaise in the shade of the green canvas umbrella, I dry off, don my ratty garden clothes and head off with baskets in hand. As for the words, they'll just have to wait. This morning, the food factory rules.

Those of us who grew up with enough to eat surely remember being told: "Clean up your plate, there are starving children in China, Africa, India"... always somewhere else, never close to home. Now, two developments combine to make us excruciatingly conscious of our food supply. First, the slow food movement of the well-fed tells us to spend more time growing, preparing and eating our food. Those of us sporting the optimal blend of food lust and guilt over our nice lives actually sign on. We labor at our day jobs to earn what is aptly described as disposable income to buy the essential seeds, and then spend our treasured leisure hours ordering and planting the seeds. Talk about slow. I've spent days obsessing over the right balance of edible pod pea to the old-fashioned shucking kind, nights pondering the optimal choice of five basil varieties out of the available eight. Does anyone in her right mind need more than five kinds of basil?

Once the seeds are safely tucked into the soil, our seduction is ensured. We race like expectant parents to the birthing place each day, looking for that promising, even adorable, emerald green dot or blade bravely poking through the earth. Fortunately, the little buggers are cute enough to yoke us into submitting ourselves to the painstaking task of cultivating our progeny to just the right stage of growth before voraciously cannibalizing them.

Not so fast: first, we weed. This filthy, endless, hot test of endurance is also one of the most satisfying activities I know. Where else do you get to simply pluck a bully out of existence? I sit my fanny in the dirt, wearing holey clothes devoted to this sacred service. If the crop is in infancy, every tiny green growing thing must be eyeballed to determine if it be weed or wanted. I am guided by the dictum that a weed is just a plant growing where you don't want it to be. This can save a lot of deliberative time because June's pea shoots can show up where you've planted July's lettuce. Anyone for pea shoots in your salad?

The green bean is my muse. When the shape is slim, yet rounded, and the color deep green, I pick, trim, and wash, then settle on just the right heat to bring them to that wanted blend of succulence and crunch. Then, I must decide how to dress them up for their debut at July's table. Ah, how we love our beans! Will they be accompanied by some fine fellow of a fish, a fabulous fowl, or that brute, red meat? And how will I accessorize my bean for the food fete that used to be known as plain old supper: a pinch of dill, marjoram, or the reliably classic summer savory? Walnut oil, roasted peanut, or olive? And if olive is the winner, we must have solid knowledge of its provenance. Did those olives grow up in Greece, Italy, France or California? No sub-par bath for our bean.

While savoring my morning fair trade coffee and organic apricot semolina muffin along with the daily news, I read of the rapidly burgeoning food awareness and consequent demands in the developing world. Imagine, they want to eat just as well as we do. This same paper speaks of the new foodie trend here at home. We, who have journeyed from fast to slow have now spawned a splinter group. These guiltless wonders are paying *others* to plant, tend and harvest in their own backyards. Imagine, they come home from their day jobs to a basket full of clean and glowing, freshly harvested tomatoes, beans, cukes and peppers, ready to be gussied up after a quick steam bath or sauté. Is there no end to the shame and perversity of the guilt-free? Ah, what must it be like?

Truthfully, I am of mixed mind. The satisfaction and, yes, thrill of producing one's own food is mixed with a sense of enslavement and its spawned twins, dread and a furious loathing. The latter doesn't kick in until about the third of twenty or so prolific plants has yielded a bonanza of beans so mind-boggling, that my fingers are overwhelmed and don't know where to aim first. Why are there so many of them? Don't they have any sense of proportion? Still, here I sit in the dirt, my hands lost in the jungle of plenty. I feel, I look, I assess. The beans demand my presence in the 90-degree garden, engulfed in the dirt and the heat. But, I rule their fate. Those bulging with starchy interiors get thrown over my shoulder onto the ground. Those that are deep green and lean earn a spot in my basket.

My guarded secret is that I feel for, and yes, identify with these beans. Sometimes I take a nibble of the aging bean in my aging mouth. As my teeth bite into the center of the bulge, which yields its starchy pith, I grieve for the bean, doomed to be spat out to its final resting place on the ground, discarded for its advanced age, because I took too long with my book by the pool. Will I get the full treatment before I turn to starch? Too much time with beans and slow, slow, food means less time to weed and pick my words. In this day, this hour, do I pick beans or write? Silly question! These beans, all of them, young, old, starchy and sleek, they feed my words.

Laundry

Sharon Coleman

I love hanging laundry on the clothesline. I start doing it as soon as possible after the frost departs. Recently, I reflected on this practice of mine. I was just back from Naples, Italy, where I was delighted to see a colorful bazaar of clotheslines strung from many apartment windows, waving in the wind like so many Tibetan prayer flags. People even hang their clothes at ground level, on streets, right next to sidewalks and parked cars. The number and variety of these displays (seen at times even in high rent neighborhoods) gives an intimate peek into the fabric of their lives. I think that these Italians regard laundry as just part of the community, like letting their children run and play in the piazza.

In our American culture, there are those who regard laundry drying on a clothesline as an eyesore. I wonder if this is because it carries haunting associations with poverty. In the little hamlet where I live, I was surprised to learn of a road that has rules against homeowners hanging their clothes out-of-doors.

Before I knew of this, I had placed a clothesline at an optimal location on my property, a location that happens to be partially visible from my road. Thus, my neighbors could glimpse the color of my sheets if they chose to do so when driving by. Fortunately, no one on my road has complained about my practice and some even do the same.

I choose to hang the laundry outside even though I have a clothes dryer. Why? Well, my sheets and pillow covers become infused with nature's scent. Towels acquire the texture of loofahs, allowing me to feel even cleaner after I bathe. For my mother there was no choice. She just didn't have a clothes dryer. I remember that when I was six or seven years old, she used a wringer washing machine in the basement. When she was doing the laundry and I was upstairs, I sometimes heard her singing or calling to the cat because she was afraid of seeing a mouse scamper across the floor. Our basement was a dank affair, more like a cellar, where our coal-fired furnace and the coal bin also lived. Sometimes I watched my mother at the washing machine. Her hands, red and chapped from housework, turned the crank and guided the clothes through the wringer. Thinking back, I wonder if she ever longed to be a winning contestant on "Queen for a Day," a quiz show that we saw on our black-and-white television. It would have been nice if she could have been the housewife who was wrapped in a royal robe, crowned with a tiara and awarded a new Maytag automatic washer and dryer. Maybe she would have cried like some of the housewives did when they won.

Instead, she trudged the basket of wet clothes up the cellar stairs and out into the light of day. I can still picture her fleshy arms extended as she secured the wooden clothespins to a pillowcase, my father's shirt, my brother's socks. I remember her humming or sometimes whistling, as if to provide background music for her own movements or to accompany the fluttering of the family laundry in the fresh breeze. When I heard her then, it filled me with a sense of well-being, as I imagined that she was feeling happy. Maybe it was the warmth of the sun on her skin, or the buzzing of the first insects with the approach of summer that pleased her. Or maybe it was the repetitive motion of lifting an item from the basket and pinning it to the line that felt somehow comforting to her.

I enjoy this memory of my mother seeming contented because she was usually a "glass-half-empty" type of person whose habit was to worry and complain—about money, paying bills, her husband, and her kids. Growing up, I heard random stories about her family's life when my aunts and uncles reminisced in their usual clamorous style while dipping artichoke leaves into sauce at Grandma's Christmas Eve dinner table. Surrounded by the aromas of garlic and fish and by the sound of my grandma's urgings to take another massive helping of baked ziti, I listened. I guess I wanted to understand my mother, to be closer to her. I learned about my mother's life from the yelling and laughter of my family.

My mother and her parents had immigrated to America from Italy when she was just three years old. She had to quit high school at the age of fourteen because her father, an older man, dropped dead of a failed heart. There were neither pensions, nor insurance policies;

there was just a dire need for money. I guess the responsibility fell to my mother because she was the oldest of the three girls who made up her family. She took the best job available for an immigrant child at that time, working on an assembly line in a factory that produced a high-quality brand of women's shoes called Enna Jetticks. I'm not sure my mother missed being at school anyway. As an Italian immigrant kid, she was teased for her "funny" name and for parents who spoke no English. She was probably afflicted with shame about being an outsider; I know she tried to become American as quickly as possible. Even though she was intelligent and capable, she never finished her high school education. Instead, she married my father, a tall, handsome, red-headed man whom she met at the shoe factory. Together, they produced five children.

When I think about these things I feel grateful to both my mother and father for the thousands of sacrifices they made without hesitation. I remember the evenings they sat at our green Formica-topped kitchen table, snakes of smoke coiling up from the cigarettes in their ashtrays. They were attempting to relax for the night while they regarded the ocean of paper that was our monthly bills: mortgage, gas and electric, orthodontist, telephone, car payment and more. They haggled over which bill had to be paid first.

I think my mother's life history fueled her habit of goading and encouraging her kids: "Do well in school." "Get a good education so you can get a good job." "Save your money." Looking back on all this, I think I have fulfilled her dreams, but in my own way, of course. Besides having my own automatic washer and dryer, I have the education she taught me to prize and I enjoy work that's rich with meaning. Even my mother's unhappiness taught me something: it ignited in me a desire to live each moment with appreciation, knowing its precious, fleeting quality.

Right now, I'm recalling a scene from my travels in less-developed countries: I'm standing in a large stream with other women. We are washing the clothes and belongings we use every day, finding things to laugh about with each other as a welcome respite from a hard life, telling stories and giving advice, as we lay our wet clothes out on large rocks to bake dry under the sun. This image comes to me sometimes as I step outside to hang my laundry on the clothesline.

I know that tossing my things in the dryer would be faster, but I choose to indulge in what is to me a privileged activity. When I am out there pinning things on the line, I begin to feel my mother standing next to me. Sometimes the urge to hum overtakes me. I feel part of an ageless female rite, a sacred ritual of the earth, of labor, of glory in the humble fragrance of cleanliness and care.

Working It Out:

23 Women Writers, Artists, Scientists and Scholars Talk about Their Lives and Work

Hilde Weisert

A poem for Sara (Sally) Ruddick,
Feminist philosopher, 1935 – 2011

Twenty-three faces look out from the book's cover,
young, earnest, marked with intelligence and hope.
Twenty-three women struggling with a simple thing:
To sit down at a desk, stand at an easel,
lean over a laboratory table, and surrender
to their own, original thought –
To the work.

Why was it so hard? Didn't they have it all –
education, babies, husbands willing to "help" --
And still so hard to close the door, for an hour
or a day, close out the willing husbands,
the babies following with alert, expectant eyes,
the kind, bemused professors that had called them "bright"
but not quite known what to do with them.

And even more, why so hard, once the door closed,
once every obstacle was lifted, to lay claim
to the empty page, blank canvas, forbidden realms
of their teeming minds? Why the deep, inexplicable
paralysis, this "acute pain of worklessness"?

One by one, each of them worked through
that pain in these pages. Read them
and you will see a generation
coming to life in its work, coming to serious,
womanly work embedded in their lives,
work and pleasure not enemies,
but joined.

Sally ends her essay ("A Work of One's Own")
saying simply, elegantly, *"I turned,*
as I had learned to do,
to other women.
We put together this book."

**

So this was how: twenty-three women facing the pain
with courage and fear, and making the claim together.

Thirty-seven years, Sally, Pamela, Adrienne, Evelyn,
Virginia, Alice, Catherine, Naomi, and the rest,
and we still need your book,
still need to hear those voices, still need
to see you *working it out*
for us, at any age,
and for the work still before us.

Warning: Contains graphic and disturbing images.

Magnolia Justice

Jana Laiz

I remember the Winter long ago, the one that lingered like regret. And the Spring that waited…But I's jumpin' ahead of myself. I'll start from my beginnin'. First thing I want to tell you is, I have consciousness. That's right. I feel. I see, I hear, I smell, and I dream. Thing is, I do it slower. I do everything slower.

I started out small, like we all do, tryin' to reach up and feel the sun's warmth like a blind child reachin' out to find her mama. I managed, hard as it was. So many of us tryin' to find our way. But it was quiet then, easier. Birds and rain and wind. Those were the sounds of my smallness. And they were the sounds of my middlin' too. 'Cept for the steady hum of the blood runnin' and the loud movement of the underground. Most folk think it's quiet under there, but it ain't. Them worms makin' a path through the Earth ain't easy and we feel it and hear it, too. Maybe how y'all hear a bulldozer nowadays. But then, we's connected in ways you ain't and never will be. And I don't mean that figuratively. We's really connected, gotta be, or we'd just fall. So my lullaby was the stars singin' their high-pitched song. The soft wind ticklin' my body. Even the gentle rain pourin' down on me, findin' its way into the ground around me, beneath me. All those things were my lullaby, my early melodies. But all that changed.

Now I cain't forget. But never you mind. I'll get to that later.

My first season, my first buddin', I was young and small, but oh, I was fragrant! My blossoms were the sweetest in the county. I heard them say it. "Ain't that Magnolia the sweetest in the county?" And I was. I could smell my own self, and I smelt real good and heady. And I stood straight, though still small.

That first season, things were quiet around me. I stood out in a field of flowers and fruit trees and pecan trees, all of us quiet, hardly speakin' to one another. Weren't much to say at that time. Nothin' much happenin', 'cept for the critters comin' to steal the fruit from my neighbors' branches, the folk comin' and admirin', but not much else.

We saw the folk from the big house and them that worked in the fields, but no one paid us no mind, 'cept, like I said, admirin'.

The light folk walked by at twilight, commentin' on this, that or the other, arm in arm. Once when I was still small a man took a knife to my trunk and carved something there. I never did know what he wrote, but the girl he was with was sure happy, so I knew it couldn't be bad. Hurt mighty, though. I cried out, but of course none but my own kind heard, and there weren't much they could do, 'cept sympathize.

The dark folk, the ones that worked in the fields nearby me, they never said much, but they sang loudly. I liked their singin', though times were, made me feel sad. But I swayed to their melancholy tunes. Them days, I didn't understand why their songs always sounded sad. That was before. Now I knows. Wish I didn't.

Sometimes, when I was more spread out, wider and taller, they'd come out from the fields and sit down by my side and lean against me, breathin' hard and smellin' like cotton and sweat. They never stayed for long, someone always hollered for them to get back out to the fields. And they'd get up, tired like, defeated, and trudge back out to the cotton. Sometimes they patted my woody hide, sayin' "Thankee for the shade." I liked their company, though their smell was strong, but I didn't mind. They never carved into me. Once in a while one of 'em might pluck a flower from my bough and give it to another, but I didn't mind that, neither. I wish I could've talked to them, or rather, I wish they could've understood what I said to them when they sat there, restin' in my shade, tryin' to feel like people.

As I grew, my blossoms were fat and pink and perfumed. I was the prettiest out there in my field. The pecans were attractive, the great Spanish oak around the big white house with all their moss decoratin' up the place, they was pretty too, but none held a candle to me. I never lorded it over no one, that's not my way. But I knew.

Later years, they planted more Magnolias, lining a path on either side, but I was the first one. Now they calls me the old one. I's still standin', all these years later, not quite so straight anymore, not quite so fragrant. But back in those days, Lordy, I outshone them all.

The light and dark children often climbed upon me, sometimes together, sometimes separate, and I told them the old stories as they sat on my limbs, breathin' deeply of my perfume. Whether they understood me or not is anyone's guess, but I's always hopeful. Seemed funny to me that the children could play together, but not the big folk. No, from where I stood, it didn't take me long to learn their story. The light ones stayed in the big house and told the dark ones what was what. Those dark folk hopped to it, too; I seen the consequences if'n they didn't. But like I said, the children played together, but the light ones always had their way, always told the dark ones how to move, what to say. I didn't like it much, but that's the way it was.

I watched them children grow into big folk, and then there was no more playin' together, no more laughin' at each other's silly antics. No, the light ones followed their mamas and daddies and got demandin' and the dark ones put down their heads and their dark eyes and said, "yes'm" or "no sir," and the like. Made me sad to see, but ain't no one listenin' to the thoughts nor opinions of a tree anyhow, so I just kept real quiet.

There was one time I shudder to recall, one big dark feller he fell down in the fields. Must have been sick or something. Done fainted right there in the cotton. Overseer tell him to get up! Hot, fiery words that made me tremble. The dark man couldn't get up. Sick he was, but that overseer didn't care one whit. He dragged that man up on his staggering feet, and what he do?! He done brought him over to me. I trembled and shook, but weren't nothin' I could do. That overseer leaned the sick man against me and took a whip to his naked back. I really don't think the man even felt it, he was already half gone. He lay there by my underside for hours. I felt his blood seep into the soil at my roots. Late that night, a dark woman came out of a little shack, silent, stealthy, and stooped beside him, cryin', ministerin' to him with cloths of cool water and unguents. He groaned some, and finally got hisself up off the ground beneath me and leanin' on her, made his way back to his sleepin' place. I felt sick with relief when he left, though I had tried to comfort him. I sang to him, whispered words, but I'm sure he didn't hear. He was heavy with sickness and sorrow and it made me sick and sad, too.

There were some happy times, I do admit. The light folk from the big house had big tables brought out and placed all around me. Sweet smelling, steaming vittles were placed upon them tables and scores of fancy folk would come over and eat and sit on chairs around me, admirin' me, talkin', gossipin'. Music was played by some fellers. The gentlemen and ladies danced some. I swayed to the rhythms. Gentlemen smoked cigars, ladies fanned themselves and fancy light children held hands and danced around me. One even tried to climb me, but was hollered at, somethin' about Sunday best and such.

Some of the dark folk were dressed fancy, too, but they weren't eatin'. They was only servin' the food. I saw the dark children hidin' and spyin', their mouths salivatin'. When them parties was over and done, the dogs and pigs got the scraps. Not one crumb went to them dark, hungry little ones. No sir, not a one.

Years passed, the fullness of the moon came and went in unending tradition. I grew taller and broader. Things didn't change much from where I stood for some time, but then everything got a little faster. The birds woke me at strange times during the new moon, when everything was dark and warm and the night lay heavy with sweat. I sees from every angle, you know, and I saw shadows in the darkness, movin' shadows, following other movin' shadows away and away. And I understood. I never said nothin' to a soul. But every time, next day at sunup, the dogs would be a-barkin' and light folk were a-hollerin', runnin' around with guns. Sometimes the shadows came back in shackles. Mostly them shadows got away. I hoped they made it to the land of the Maple and the Fir.

This is how it started. Dark folk and some light ones trying to change things as they were. For my kind, we change some, but mostly, things change around us. And we stand and watch, sometimes with pleasure, sometimes with grief. We weren't sure what to make of these changes, but I thought they was good. And that's when the folk with guns came. Scores of 'em, sleepin' in the fields, wavin' flags, shootin'. It were no pleasant time, you can be sure of that. Them guns were loud and everything smelled liked blood. Not the sweet blood of my kind, but the hot, slick, spicy blood of folks.

I noticed something strange though. Blood of the light ones and blood of the dark ones, well sir, they was the same. Couldn't tell them apart by color nor of smell. If them red pools lay there in the field, you wouldn't know one from another. They mingled together out there, seepin' into the earth.

Them harsh folk with their clothing all the same and their guns, well, they couldn't see it. Couldn't see what we saw. To us, folk were folk. Big, small, light, dark. Same blood, same bones. Didn't matter the color of the hide. We saw the way the water fell from their eyes when they was sad, light ones or dark. We saw their crinkly faces and the lightness of their step when they was glad. But it didn't matter to them harsh folk that they was the same. They saw somethin' else. Difference. They thought they was better and they was fightin' to keep it that way. And them dark folk weren't treated right. No sir. Trees ain't the judgin' type, but I saw what I saw and I knows what I know. They wasn't treated right. And it got worse. A lot worse.

The fightin' raged on and on, from buddin' time to flowerin' and back again. It got so I was used to the smell of it and the loudness of it. But it rankled me and mine. We could only talk of it in the stillness of the night, when there was respite from the beatin' of the drums, the shootin' of the guns. I was one of the lucky ones, never havin' a bullet pass through my flank. I know others that weren't so lucky. Bullets don't make us fall, but they do their damage just the same.

We shook ourselves and wondered when it would end, when we'd be able to hear the birds and the wind again. For myself I can only say it went on too long. By the time it was over I felt stiff in my limbs. My blossoms felt grimy. My kind, well, we hear things, we's connected through roots and earth and the seasons and we communicate in ways unlike folks and I learnt the truth. Them dark folk were free. Free to live like people and the light folk in the big house couldn't order them around no more. I watched the dark ones, confused lookin' and mighty scared, wanderin', wonderin' where to go, what to do. Some of 'em stayed on, havin' been birthed and grow'd up on the place. But I watched and listened carefully to the light ones. There was a difference in their tone and manner toward the dark ones. I'm thinkin' t'was fear. I never heard it comin' from them before, but I was sure that was what it was. I, for one, thought they had it comin'. But from where I stood, things didn't change so much, 'cept the dark ones tryin' to get along, almost more fearful than before. At least before, they knew their lot. They had their sleepin' places, their meager food. Now, they weren't sure what was what. Some went away, to colder climes, I heard. But them that stayed, well, bein' freed didn't make the light ones any better towards 'em. Different maybe, like I said, scared and even angrier than before, but no better. It was worse for some time, neither of them knowin' how to act. The dark ones had to ask the light ones for work to make the coins and papers to buy their bread. And it seemed to me, though the light ones now paid the dark ones, they knew who was still master.

Times went on like this and gradually, it became quiet again and my kind could fall asleep to the stars' lullaby and the wind could rock us again. But it never felt as clean nor comfortin'. I, for one, tried to put the past from my mind and stood straight as I could in my advancin' age. And still I watched. Things were changin' again. The dark ones were beginnin' to rise up a bit, tryin' anyways. The light ones didn't like it none. That's when the nights got all blazed up. That's when the ghosts appeared with their burnin' sticks and their fiery talk. They torched the little sleepin' places where the dark ones lived. I seen the dark ones runnin' and screamin', grabbin' their young 'uns. Sometimes there was no escapin' and I smelt their burnin' flesh and I felt sick. I wished I coulda run, but I ain't got that option. And here is where I've been leadin' up to this whole time.

The winter came, not cold, never cold, but cool. Mostly the summer nights were when the ghost men came out, hollerin' their wrathful words. Maybe the heat made them angrier, heated them up. And maybe that's why what happened next happened at all. 'Cause this day was different. It was unnatural warm.

Dark folk was workin' in the fields, preparin' the earth for the Spring plantin'. The day was near done and they's all sweatin' and commentin' on the unusual weather. I's surprised when one dark feller pass me by, makin' his way to the big house, before he's told he can leave the fields. He goes to the back door and calls for his boss to please come out; he's got somethin' to say. The big light one comes out on the back porch askin' what he's doin' there before the day's work is done. I sees the dark one tip his hat and 'pologize. He asks for some money owed him and for the day off next day to see his girl, the one he's to marry. He smiles and tells the boss that he's plannin' a weddin'. The light one, arms folded cross his chest, tells him to get back out to the fields and not to bother him no more. He'll get his money when everyone else does and not a minute before and he'd better be out in them fields next day like usual. Them words are spoke harsh, and the dark man goes away. I see his pain as he passes me by. I tell him to pay no mind, but of course, he cain't hear me.

Next day, he's pullin' stones out the ground for the missus' garden and the boss comes out a-tellin' him never step upon his porch again. The dark one stops his diggin' and I see he's got a big rock in his grasp. He tries to apologize once more, but the light one, he points a pistol at the dark feller, movin' toward him, threatenin' and yellin'. I begin to tremble and I hear my own dry leaves rustle. The dark man is taken by surprise and I see him fling the rock toward his attacker, like he's tryin' to protect hisself. I see the light one fall to the ground, his red blood pourin' out his head.

I don't wants to look no more. I've seen too much and this ain't too different from what I seen before. But what happens next is what I need to tell y'all, what I want out of myself and gone. But I know it never will be, not 'til I'm earth itself and my glorious blossoms are merely a legend.

That dark feller, he look'd at what he done and he groan loud and look as terrified as any folk could look. And he run. Far and fast, he run, but I knew it wouldn't be long before he couldn't go no further. What I didn't know and still shudders to recall, is how evil folk can be to one another.

That night my sleep is restless, cause I feel somethin's comin'. There be whispers in the night from my own kind and it don't feel right. Whispers about a dark man killin' his boss in cold blood, rapin' his wife as he lay dyin' and I know this ain't the truth. But y'all already knows, I cain't testify. Light folk are combin' the countryside for him. And I know they's gonna find him. I can feel it, like I can feel a storm comin'. What I don't expect is what they's gonna do to him once they have him.

Next day, when the sun is high and the coolness of the winter night has gone and the day is heated up this unusual heat, I sees the man being dragged by some light folk. He's not puttin' up a struggle as they got him in chains. He falls once and they kick him and tells him to get up. There be scores of light folk followin'. Women and children, but mostly men with angry faces.

I've waited this long to tell this grisly tale, and I ain't even sure I can come out with it now, but seein' as I've gone this far, guess I better finish. They unchain the man and he drops to the ground. They's right near me now. I sees some little boys throw pebbles at him. They laugh and their mamas laugh with them. Big light men drag him to standin' and then they bring him to me. I starts to tremble and shake and I wish I could run. I tells 'em to get away, but they come closer and they throw a rope over one of my branches and they pulls it taut around me. It's real tight, but that ain't what's troublin' me. No, alls I feel is fear. And not for myself neither, but for the dark feller. I've heard the whisperings from my kind, unspeakable things I didn't wants to believe but I now knows is true.

They put the dark man on a wooden box and then they put the rope round his neck, but they don't make it tight nor kick the box away just yet. They's got their heinous work to do first. One big, light feller smiles at the crowd that has gathered around me, folk standin' on toes, pushin' and shovin', children on parent's shoulders to get a better look. His smile is evil. I can see it when he turns round. He pulls out a big, shiny knife and it glints in the sunlight as he holds it up. Someone throws him a tomato and showy like, splits it with the knife real smooth. Everyone cheers. I knows I's quiverin' now and I don't wants to look, but I cain't help myself.

The dark man is shiverin' and cryin' softly now. Maybe I's the only one can hear him or maybe it's that I can feel his fear, him bein' connected to me and all. That light man, he comes up to the dark one and puts the knife to his throat and then with a swift movement, peels off one ear, then the other. The dark man screams out, but I cain't hardly hear him through the cheers of the crowd. Folk be putting out their hands, beggin' for the ears. The big light one gives one to a little boy and he takes it like it's candy. The other goes to a woman with angry glee on her face. She holds it up and hollers somethin' I cain't understand. By now I am sick, but I, like the dark feller is a prisoner. I cain't escape my own self. And I's mad, because I ain't never wanted to escape myself before, but I do now, 'cause of them.

As I said before, things get worse. Other folk want their turn with the knife and more parts are cut off and handed out like Christmas toys. By now the dark man is cryin' out for Jesus, but he cain't be heard through the crowd, that grows louder with each part of him that falls. He screams loudest when they take his manhood and it seems to be the most coveted prize of all, light hands a-reachin' and a-grabbin'. Blood everywhere. Then they pour liquid over him and that's when they tighten his rope and kick the box from under him. And quick as a wink he starts to burn.

I wish he died then, but he don't. He swings and burns and screams and as the flames are lickin' him, they's lickin' me too. I guess I's lucky 'cause them light folk tied him to my weakest branch, so what I do next saves my own sorry life. I's angry now, somethin' I ain't never felt before, and it courses through me like the hot fire that's consumin' him. I sways hard and hard again and he swings crazily and my branch breaks off from my trunk. I screams out as he falls to the ground, my broken branch fallin' on top of him. There he lay at my roots, writhin' and burnin' as folk back up some to watch him blaze. And I cain't look away, though believe you me, I wants to. Fact is, I wants to die along with him.

When alls that's left is soot and sorrow, men and women folk, even little ones, scoop up the coolin' ashes to carry home in their pockets. Souvenirs. And I's left all alone. It's quiet then and I hear my own kind asking me in whispers, but I cain't answer no one no more. I cain't speak. I got nothin' left to say.

Years pass me by and no one seems to want to know me no more. Ain't no folk comin' nor admirin'. No one a-restin' against me. Even the birds ain't landin' on my branches. I feels tainted and dismal and I mostly just sleep, tryin' to remember days when I was the prettiest tree in the field. Rememberin' when I heard the birds singin' and the wind whisperin' its lullabies. But mostly, I tries to forget. But of course, I cain't forget, and the memory clings to me like chokin' vine.

I wakes up now and again and one time I knows I's dreamin' for I think I sees dark ones and light ones holdin' signs together, headin' in the same direction, walkin' like they's equals. But that cain't be and I don't ask no questions then, I still got nothin' to say.

Until now. Now, when these thoughts cain't stay inside me another minute. Now, when my days are nearly done. Now, when I's become a monument to the tragedy of that day. Well, that's one good thing. They put a plaque on me. I don't know what it says, but I think it says 'sorry.' I surely hope so.

I's old now. My blossoms, the ones that do come, are more cloying than sweet. Sometimes as I look out toward the fields and watch the sun settin' in its way, I sees the beauty and I tries to be grateful. The memories have faded some, but truth be told, forgettin's not the hardest part. The hardest part is the forgivin' part. And I knows I better do it 'fore I die. Truth is, I don't knows that I want to. I've been holdin' on to this hurtin' for a long time. Feels familiar.

But y'all know that's why I'm a-tellin' this tale. To let go my pain. Like my fallen branch that I wrenched from by body to save myself, I knows I got to free this hurt and sorrow, or I'm-a get too bitter to behold.

You know, the heart of a tree is deep and wild and still. We live quietly, standin' and watchin', slowly livin' out our lives, givin' to others of our fruit or fragrance or shade. Sometimes others take what they oughtn't, leavin' hurt behind. That's what happened to me.

My heart's likely deeper than some and maybe that's why I feel as I do. But I's ready now. I've had my say. I done told my story. I give it to y'all.

So now, as I get ready to return to the earth that holds me up, I look 'round me real wide and long and hard. I ain't wanted to look at nothin' since that day. I look at what is, not what was and I's surprised by what I see. I sees light ones and dark ones laughin', workin', even schoolin' together, hurt gone…mostly. And I wonder, maybe if'n they can forgive, I can too. And as I do, I feels lighter than I felt in a long time. When I return from where I come from, I don't wants to be bitter. I don't wants to poison the ground with my anger. No sir, I want the earth sweet, like my blossoms in their glory. Them ghosts need to be free.

So I will mix with the bitter ashes and sweeten them with forgiveness so that whatever comes after me, rising up out of his ashes and mine, will give sweet fruit or fragrance or shade.

About the Editors

Jennifer Browdy grew up in Manhattan and spent weekends in the Berkshires as a child. After earning her B.A. in English and Journalism from Bard College at Simon's Rock, she worked as a professional journalist for several years in the Berkshires and New York City before returning to academia to earn her M.A. and Ph.D. in Comparative Literature from New York University in 1994. An Associate Professor of Comparative Literature, Gender Studies and Media Studies at Bard College at Simon's Rock, Jennifer engages students in issues of global social and environmental justice through writing, literature and digital media. Since 2002, Jennifer has hosted an annual conference in observance of International Women's Day and in 2011 she founded the Berkshire Festival of Women Writers to cultivate the voices and visions of women writers of all ages and many walks of life in the Berkshire region. Jennifer has published widely on women's world literature, and is the editor of two other anthologies of women's writing, *Women Writing Resistance in Latin America and the Caribbean* (Beacon Press, 2017) and *African Women Writing Resistance* (University of Wisconsin Press, 2011). She has published widely in academic compilations and journals, as well as *The Berkshire Edge, Berkshire Magazine* and *Yes! Magazine*. Her memoir, *What I Forgot....and Why I Remembered: A Journey to Environmental Awareness and Activism Through Purposeful Memoir*, was published in 2017, along with a writer's guide for memoirists, *The Elemental Journey of Purposeful Memoir: A Writer's Companion*. She has presented papers and given lectures and workshops at numerous conferences at colleges, universities and other venues nationwide. Her blog, *Transition Times*, dedicated to exploring issues of social and environmental justice from a personal perspective, has received more than 130,000 visitors from all over the world in its first five years. She offers workshops, author coaching and editing services for memoirists at every stage of their writing journey.

Jana Laiz grew up in White Plains, NY and spent weekends in the Berkshires as a teenager. She earned a Bachelor's degree from New York University in Chinese Language and Anthropology, an advanced degree in Chinese from Middlebury College and a Master's in Education from Westfield State College. She served as a refugee resettlement counselor for the International Rescue Committee until 1986, when she moved to the Berkshires and began to take her passion for writing seriously. She is the author of the triple award-winning novel, *Weeping Under This Same Moon* (Moonbeam Silver Medal Winner and ForeWord Reviews Book of The Year Award nominee); *The Twelfth Stone; Elephants of the Tsunami; Thomas & Autumn*; and the co-author of *A Free Woman On God's Earth, The True Story of Elizabeth "Mumbet" Freeman, The Slave Who Won Her Freedom*, optioned to be a feature film, *Simon Says; Tails Told By The Red Lion Inn Ambassador*. In 2007, Jana formed Crow Flies Press and published these and other award winning titles. She has produced audio books with Audible.com and is currently working with Alison Larkin Presents and the Jane Austen Literary Foundation to produce the audiobook for *Weeping Under This Same Moon*. She is the very first Writer-In-Residence at Herman Melville's beloved Arrowhead. Jana is currently working on the sequel to *The Twelfth Stone*, a new novel about teaching ESL and the immigrant experience as well as a juvenile biography of Herman Melville; *Billy Budd In The Breadbox*. Her picture book, *Blanket of Stars* will be out soon. She is passionate about our beautiful planet and endeavors to make a difference in the world through her writing and to work with others who feel the same. Jana continues to teach English locally and writing everywhere. She lives in a 200-year-old farmhouse in the Berkshire Hills of Massachusetts.

Sahra Bateson Brubeck earned her B.A. from Bard College at Simon's Rock in 2014, majoring in Creative Writing with a minor in African American Studies. Her most recent creative work focuses mainly on the tradition of retelling and rewriting ancient myths. She strives to shed light on the convoluted histories and stories of ancient Greek Goddesses, often rearranging and repositioning the interpersonal dynamics that originally comprised the ancient myths, in an effort to add depth to the stories' notions of power and femininity.

Contributors' Biographies

Barbara Barack is a retired psychologist now residing in Great Barrington, a town she has loved since childhood. Her mother, who lived a full, sophisticated New York City life until the age of ninety-eight, nevertheless encountered many hardships throughout her life, which she handled like a lady. Writing a poem about her mother, with whom she shared a wonderful closeness, has helped Barbara with her feelings of loss.

Suzi Banks Baum makes community wherever she goes. Her writing, artistic life and social media consulting are fueled by the discovery of her creative voice, which she found while raising her children. LaundryLineDivine.com, the hub for her own writing, features more than 50 women's voices in the Out of the Mouths of Babes blog series on mothering and creativity. The blog generated Suzi's edited collection, *An Anthology of Babes: 36 Women Give Motherhood a Voice*, published in 2013. Suzi creates artist books, teaches the Powder Keg Sessions writing workshops, and lives with her family in Great Barrington, MA.

Martha Beattie lives in Clarksburg, MA and has worked in early education for the past 25 years. She has a BA in Literature from Massachusetts College of Liberal Arts and a Masters in Language and Literacy from Simmons College.
She still owns the land.

Mary-Ellen Beattie received a B.F.A. from Dickinson College in 2012 and was Dickinson's post-baccalaureate fellow in 2013. Mary-Ellen works as a sculptor and installation artist in North Adams, MA where she continues to write.

Jayne Benjulian is the recipient of a Fulbright Fellowship in Lyon, France and a Teaching Fellowship at Emory University. Her poems have appeared in various journals, including *Barrow Street*, *The Seattle Review*, *The Delaware Poetry Review*, *Women's Review of Books* and *Poet Lore*. Her essays are published in *HowlRound* and *The California Journal of Women Writers*. She holds an M.F.A. from the Warren Wilson MFA Program for Writers.

Judith Berg grew up in Michigan in the 1950's. She raised two biracial children in New York City, practicing as a clinical psychologist in Manhattan. Now, as a 74-year-old grandmother, she is needing to voice the contours and substance of those years. She has been writing fiction and non-fiction with intent for about ten years, honing her voice in classes, workshops, and in a group with other writers.

Ellen Bliss has had many adventures in her life. She has lived in Pennsylvania, California, England, and Massachusetts. Her jobs have included: Nanny, Cake Decorator, Publications Designer, and Technical Editor Coordinator. She has worked in "The City," has "walked across that bridge" and even "had coffee in that café." Ellen is a lucky "Jersey Girl" who looks forward to many more adventures.

Amber Chand, a transformational coach and successful entrepreneur, brings a wealth of experience into her work. She has stepped fully into her new story and is now the creator and performer of her successful one-woman show, "Searching For The Moon: Tales of Love, Despair, Faith and Forgiveness" which is being produced by acclaimed actor, Jayne Atkinson. Amber's entrepreneurial global work has been recognized in various media: her Rwanda Journals were published in *Marie Claire Magazine*, she was voted "entrepreneur of the month" by *Inc. Magazine*, and was invited to be part of the "Wise Woman Circle" at the World Bank. She lives happily in Great Barrington and devotes her life to supporting women and girls in navigating through these uncertain times.

Eden Chubb is a lifelong feminist and rabbit enthusiast from New Orleans. She currently lives in her hometown (with a rabbit) and spends most days locked in her studio procrastinating, drawing, avoiding social interaction, and drinking many cups of tea.

Sharon Coleman came to the Berkshires as a refugee from New York City. Previously, she worked as a management consultant to corporations specializing in Leadership, Team and Career development. A psychologist who offered psychotherapy for many years, she now offers coaching and retreats. Sharon is a writer, a world traveler and a dedicated yogini. She serves on the Leadership Council of Women of Spirit in the Berkshires and meditates with and leads sessions for the Berkshire Mountain Laurel Sangha, a Buddhist practice community.

Anni Crofut is a dancer and jewelry designer who runs the jewelry company *Anni Maliki* with her husband, Mel Maliki. Anni and Mel and their two sons make their home in the Berkshires, but also travel frequently to Mel's homeland, Indonesia. Writing, photography, fashion, gardening, entertaining and home décor are among Anni's many talents and interests.

Barbara Dean is a singer/songwriter, performer, writer and folk DJ who grew up in Queens, NY, and moved to the Berkshires with her husband Graham in 1982. They have four children and two grandchildren. She has written many poems about her life, and she and Graham write songs and perform together; their songs are often about social justice.

Pauline Dongala is originally from Congo-Brazzaville, where she worked for 14 years at the American Embassy in Brazzaville. She moved to the United States in 1999 after a series of civil wars took the lives of many of her family members. She is the founder of a women's empowerment project in Congo and has shared her perspectives on African women's human rights with many audiences, both internationally and domestically. She is the co-editor of the anthology *African Women Writing Resistance: Contemporary Voices* (University of Wisconsin Press, 2010).

Adrian Dunn is a second-generation Californian, transplanted several decades ago to the Northeast. She earned a B.A. in Anthropology, with a Women's Studies minor. Her short essays about preserving the wild have appeared in the *Greylock Independent*. In addition to memoir writing, Adrian wants to use her writing to high-light our common connection with the natural world.

Lisken Van Pelt Dus is a poet, teacher, and martial artist raised inter-nationally and now living in Pittsfield, Massachusetts. She arrived in the Berkshires in 1980 when she came from London to Williams College, where she earned a B.A. in Religion. Subsequently, she earned a Masters from the University of Massachusetts at Amherst in Comparative Literature. She now teaches writing and languages at Monument Mountain Regional High School in Great Barrington, and is co-owner and co-chief instructor, with her husband Bob, of Elm Street Martial Arts in Pittsfield, where she teaches classical Okinawan karate and kobudo (weapons).

Janet Reich Elsbach thinks and writes about the food she feeds her family of five, who live on a small and ludicrous farm with dogs and chickens and sheep (in order of increasing population). She writes a blog, A Raisin & A Porpoise, edits other people's writing when she can, and teaches writing wherever she can, currently at Community Access to the Arts, where she has been involved for over 20 years.

Joan Embree is a mother and grandmother living in the Berkshires with three dogs and one cat. Formerly the owner of Embree's Restaurant, she works as a caterer, private cook and yoga teacher. A passionate reader all her life, she has been writing fiction for many years, having been encouraged early on by the gifted poets Michael and Peter Gizzi. In 2013 and 2014, she won writing contests as part of the Berkshire Festival of Women Writers; in the 2014 and 2015 Festivals, she presented writing workshops with Susie Kaufman.

Carolyn Fabricant grew up in Stockbridge and earned her B.A. at Swarthmore and her M.A. at Hunter College. Her professional work in New York circled around teaching, cooking and the arts, with 10 years as a teacher of English and 5 years in administration at CCNY, as well as many writing, editing, research and public relations proj-ects. She cooked in four New York City restaurants and for Gould

Farm and *Orion Magazine* in the Berkshires. Other area freelance work includes assisting local caterers, interviews and food articles for the *Berkshire Eagle*, projects at The Mount, volunteering at the Berkshire Festival of Women Writers, and conducting a government survey throughout the county.

Hope Fitzgerald has been a dedicated seeker of truth, healing and wisdom since her spiritual awakening at the Findhorn Foundation in 1976. For nearly 20 years, her expertise in Intuitive Dowsing has helped people transform their lives. In 2010, she was directed through channeling to launch a series of workshops introducing an energetic called the *Infinity Wave*; in 2011, Hope launched the Wave Energy Center for Conscious Evolution with Jan Seward, and is dedicated to the positive, expansive development of the individual, the community and the earth. Hope also guides groups on sacred travel to various locations around the globe and has a private practice as a certified Neurofeedback Practitioner, an Intuitive Dowser and a Life Coach, while also incorporating sound, Reiki and energy healing into her work.

Emma Flowers was born and raised in the suburbs of Boston. She knew she was a writer from a young age, but the role of writing in her life continues to grow and evolve. Reading, writing, and listening to poetry has been incredibly formative for Emma. In 2013, she was a semi-finalist for the Helen Creeley Student Poetry Prize. She also spent time writing and researching for Jewish Family Services of Metro West, a social work agency. A New Englander at heart, she continues to learn about the craft of writing at Bennington College in Vermont. During Bennington's annual winter term internship period in 2015, Emma interned at Green Fire Press.

Suzanne Fowle, a wildlife biologist, has worked in a range of habitats in the U.S. and beyond. She enjoys finding the connections between them. She has a M.S. from the University of Montana and a B.A. from Brown University. Although Suzanne's research has included work with turtles, salamanders, mountain goats, giraffes, and native plant communities, child-rearing has become one of her most beloved and challenging science projects. She lives in the Berkshires with her two children.

Carole Fults has been a writer most of her life, but most especially in recent years. A graduate of Nazareth College, she is an artist and photographer with many projects on tap. She enjoys writing about people, places and things that she loves, and is also a gardener, a hiker, blogger and lover of adventure. She lives across the road from her neighbors the cows, who offer her new perspectives daily.

Michele Gara has just returned to work after a long stint as the full-time mother of four children. She has always enjoyed expressing herself through writing, and has long aimed at becoming a published writer. She would like to impact others through words, a dream she hopes to realize through her participation in the Berkshire Festival of Women Writers.

Teresa Gentile is a mother, daughter, sister and friend to a passel of amazing women. Her writing unrolls from the red carpet of life, holes and all.

Jan Krause Greene is the author of *I Call Myself Earth Girl*, a novel that explores how a middle-aged woman opens herself to mystic wisdom when she discovers she is pregnant and is convinced that she conceived the baby in a dream. Krause Greene also helps individuals embrace their unique and authentic voices through her *Finding YOUR Voice* workshops.

Casey Hall is a high school sophomore attending Woodstock Day School. She has been published in the school's bi-annual literary journal, *The Battering Ram*. In addition to her writing, Casey has worked as a children's sailing instructor on the Hudson River since 2013. She is currently involved in a collaborative project with artist Rachel Reimer, creating a webcomic inspired by H.P. Lovecraft's *The Call of Cthulhu*. A long-time film enthusiast, Casey has been a co-producer of several short films, one of which was accepted and shown at the 2014 Woodstock Film Festival.

Anne Harrison retired from a long career in Juvenile Justice and moved from Michigan to the Berkshires in order to be near her young grandchildren. A lot of her writing focuses on her love of the Michigan Great Lakes and skies. After settling in the Berkshires, she was able to spend more time on her interest in women's issues, literature and art history, as well as finally work seriously on her writing.

Sally-Jane Heit, born in Brooklyn, was one of eight children. She didn't want to be one of eight children. She wanted to be adopted. From the womb, she sang, danced, acted, creating agita for her mother and her siblings. Lacking the courage of her convictions, she "went along" with a traditional script. As her marriage faded and the children grew, she escaped. On Broadway, Off Broadway, movies, television…she was another late bloomer. She is still blooming. Today Sally-Jane tours the country giving back to causes close to her heart by donating performances to theaters, universities, conferences and community organizations. Her ambition is to inspire and support others to take center stage in their own lives. She makes her home in Great Barrington, MA and Sanibel, FL.

Jennifer J. Holey is the author of the memoir *Cinderella, The Church, and a Crazy Lady*. She is an Army Veteran, a Trauma/Emergency Room Nurse, a Nurse Practitioner, and a Nurse Anesthetist. An active writer, runner, storyteller and mother, she lives with her husband and son in Williamstown. Her goal as a writer is to empower women.

Jan Hutchinson has studied and written poetry for half a century. For the last eleven years she has scribbled at least one poem every morning. Critics could call her poetic output overly prolific and under-perfected, but she says imagination and laughter help her stay sane and age with a modicum of grace. Jan has published two collections: *Poems of Prayer and Heresy* in 2008 and *Raggedy Prayers and Crooked Ladders* in 2013. Both books feature whimsical drawings by Chet Kalm. Jan has been on the Berkshire Festival of Women Writers organizing committee for several years, serving as the Program Coordinator for the 2014 Festival.

Mary Kate Jordan grew up steeped in Greco-Roman and other world mythologies. She started college as an English major but eventually took her BFA in sculpture. Her book, *The Bridge Called Grief*, called "a trustworthy companion for those suffering loss," unites her words with her black and white photos. She lives in Monterey, MA, where she runs The Jordan Center.

Audrey Kalman has been a passionate storyteller and avid listener for more than 35 years. Her novel *Dance of Souls* was published in 2011; her short fiction has appeared in various literary journals. Her contribution to *Writing Fire* is excerpted from her novel *In the House of Tomorrow*, forthcoming from Sand Hill Review Press.

Maggie Dillon Katz holds in her heart the poignancy of partings and how they can connect or destroy us. She is a contributing author in the Amazon bestseller *Breakthrough! Inspirational Strategies for an Audaciously Authentic Life*. A storyteller and speaker, she is energized by the sea and inspired by walks in the Appalachian woods with Babu, her Alaskan malamute.

Susie Kaufman is a retired Hospice chaplain. She is an active participant in the Berkshire Festival of Women Writers, and appears regularly at IWOW, an open mic in Housatonic MA. Her spiritual writing has appeared in *Lilith*, *America* and *Presence* magazines.

Diane Kavanaugh-Black is a writer, Kripalu-trained yoga teacher, passionate hiker, photographer and instructor in healthy cooking, all wrapped lovingly into her business, *Of-the-Essence Holistic Wellness*. She is currently collaborating on a book about mindfulness and creative practice, in the form of essays in dialogue.

Linda Kaye-Moses is a studio jeweler whose writing has appeared in *Lapidary Journal*; *Art Jewelry*; *The Crafts Report*; *Discovery, Fifty Years of Craft Experience at Haystack Mountain School of Crafts*; and many other publications. She is the author of *Pure Silver Metal Clay Beads and Roots, Stems, and Branches: A Recollection*.

Lorrin Krouss, a former senior legal assistant working in the law department of a major publishing firm, changed her workaholic lifestyle when she moved full-time to the beautiful Berkshires. While pondering what to do with the rest of her life, she was inspired to write fiction and memoir after attending the 2012 Berkshire Festival of Women Writers and she has never looked back! She now serves as Festival Coordinator and Director of Business Development for the BFWW and shares her writing at Festival events throughout the year.

Jenny Laird was a long-time Chicago Playwright and Arts Educator before settling in the Berkshires. In collaboration with her husband, Randy Courts, Jenny is currently writing a series of musicals based on *The Magic Tree House* books for Music Theatre International's Broadway Junior Collection.

Cheryl Anne Latuner is the author of *Baby at My Breast—Reflections of a Nursing Mother*, from which "Machine" is taken. Her work has appeared in *Literary Mama* as well as in a variety of literary journals and periodicals. She lives in Florence, Massachusetts, and teaches English and French at a Waldorf high school.

Donna Lefkowitz was born and raised in Michigan and Wisconsin, but has lived in Lenox for the past fifty years. After graduating from the University of Texas in Austin, she initially worked as a mathematician. After raising three children, she worked in the field of vocational rehabilitation as a counselor, and did substitute teaching. She has had a lifelong interest in work and women's issues. In the 1970's she co-led career development workshops for Berkshire Women under the auspices of Women's Services (now the Elizabeth Freeman Center) of which she was one of the five founders. She began writing after her mother's death which revived many childhood memories. She is now 85 and has long been retired.

Lydia Littlefield is a graduate student of Historic Preservation, a color and lighting consultant for clients with fine and quirky old houses, and a writer seeking to foment hope in the face of predominantly grim news. Lydia and her family have lived in the Berkshires for 25 years, joining ancestors who settled here in the eighteenth century.

Marie-Elizabeth Mali holds an MFA in Poetry from Sarah Lawrence and a B.A. in East Asian Studies from Oberlin College. She is the author of Steady, My Gaze (Tebot Bach, 2011). A poet and underwater photographer, she is a co-curator of louderARTS: the Reading Series and Page Meets Stage, both in New York City. Her work has appeared in *Calyx*, *Poet Lore*, and *RATTLE*, among other literary journals.

Carmen-Maria Mandley is an educator, artist and actor, currently working as Education and Literary Manager at Portland Stage in Portland, ME. She is the founder and artistic director of the Nickel Shakespeare Girls, Founding Artistic Director of Bare Theatre, and a produced playwright and poet. Carmen attended National-Louis University in Chicago, Illinois and continued her training at Shake-speare and Company in Lenox, where she worked as an actor and educator for many years, and at the Dell' Arte International School of Physical Theatre. She has been actively directing, teaching and performing Shakespeare for 20 years and has performed spoken word poetry in Chicago, Orlando, Louisville, and Raleigh, garner-ing many awards.

Deirdre McKenna's imperative in writing is to achieve clarity and healing, and to further elucidate her ideas for her visual art. Some poems simply demand to be written. Through writing she strives to be more visible, more powerful, more creative, and to complete, as Gloria Steinem puts it, her own "circle of uniqueness."

Heather C. Meehan graduated summa cum laude from Bard College at Simon's Rock in 2014, with a concentration in Creative Writing. Her B.A. thesis, "(Em)bodying (E)motion: An Active Exploration of the Poetics of Embodied Language" used poetry and personal essay as a means of excavating and expressing mind-body connection. She has been an active member of the Berkshire Festival of Women Writers organizing committee since 2012 and Festival intern during the 2014 season.

Ellen Meeropol is the author of two novels, *House Arrest* (2011) and *On Hurricane Island* (2015). Her short stories and essays have appeared in *Bridges, The Writers Chronicle, Pedestal, Rumpus, Portland Magazine* and *Women's Times*, among others. She is a founding board member of the Rosenberg Fund for Children, and the author of their dramatic program, "Carry it Forward," most recently produced in New York City in 2013. Ellen lives in western Massachusetts, where she serves as the Program Committee chair for the Straw Dog Writers Guild.

Judith Nardacci is a retired teacher and a human rights activist, especially on behalf of women and girls and the LGBTQAI community. She and her husband live in Lee and have two grown children. She loves books, gardening (especially the digging-up-weeds-and-rocks part), chocolate, cooking for friends, and being part of the Berkshire Festival of Women Writers Planning Committee!

Barbara Newman enjoyed a storied career as a Creative Director in New York City where she built iconic global brands. From perfume to peanut butter, her award-winning campaigns are known the world over, and have left an indelible mark on brand culture. As a content developer across multiple media platforms, Barbara shifted her focus to longer format pieces and now, in a new chapter of her life, she writes essays, poetry and short stories. Inspired by their bold spirit, Barbara is currently developing a feature-length documentary on American cowgirls.

Mary Beth Ogulewicz had the privilege of helping her father pass through Alzheimer's with grace and ease. Formerly a lawyer, now a Kripalu yoga teacher, she found meaning in caretaking, infusing her time with her father with presence and a tender practice of reverence and acceptance.

Elizabeth O'Rourke's poetry has been featured by Krista Tippett's "On Being" blog. She studied at Boston College and received an MFA from Sarah Lawrence College. Born outside of Boston to an Irish Catholic family, much of her writing focuses on the sacredness and mysticism of her daily encounters with the world and what it asks of her. Elizabeth reads and writes at home in Mamaroneck, NY and Great Barrington, MA while caring for her young daughter Hope and testing recipes on her husband Seamus.

Raquel Partnoy was born and raised in Argentina and moved to Washington, DC in 1994. Her essay "Silent Witness" was published in *Women Writing Resistance, Essays on Latin American and the Caribbean,* ed. Jennifer Browdy de Hernandez (South End Press, 2004); as well as in *Surviving Genocide in The Jewish Diaspora in Latin American and the Caribbean: Fragments of Memory,* ed. Kristin Ruggiero (Sussex Academic Press, UK). *Ciudad de rojos horizontes,* her first solo book of poetry, was published by Hemisferio Derecho Ediciones, Argentina in 2013.

Joan Peronto lives and writes poetry in Pittsfield, MA. She is a transplanted mid-westerner, having spent the first 22 years life in central Illinois. After graduating from the University of Wisconsin, Madison, she worked in the reference department of the Berkshire Athenaeum for 34 years and, with her husband, raised seven children. Her poetry has appeared in *Crossing Paths, The Berkshire Review, The Berkshire Sampler, Hummingbird, The P.E.O.Record,* and *The Rockford Review.* She has also written children's poetry, which has appeared in *Ladybug* and *Spider* magazines.

Beverly Pimsleur worked with her late husband, Paul Pimsleur, creator of the Pimsleur Language Programs. She taught Comparative Literature at Ohio State University, co-authored a foreign language series "C'est La Vie," authored "Counterparts" and was a language consultant for her daughter's company, Little Pim. She is writing a memoir, *A Loosely Assembled Life.*

Brianna Pope is a college student studying Public Policy at Georgetown University in Spring 2015, though her home institution is Bard College at Simon's Rock, from which she expects to earn a B.A. degree in 2016. She loves to write.

Wendy A. Rabinowitz was born and raised in Chicago and came to the Berkshires in the 1970s and again in the 1980s with her family, where she founded the Living Threads Judaica Studio. Her love of weaving began 35 ago after seeing a loom at the Chicago Historical Society and it quickly evolved into a professional path. Her artwork has been exhibited at the United Nations in New York City, the University of Judaism in Los Angeles; the Wang Center, Boston; the White House, Washington, DC; the Chicago Public Library; and the Jewish Women's Research Center at Brandeis University, Waltham, MA; the Haifa Center, Haifa, Israel, and in many other galleries, synagogues, cultural settings, and private collections.

Grace Rossman is a senior at Bard College at Simon's Rock. "Activated" by an activism class she took with Jennifer Browdy during the fall of 2013, Grace developed *The Belly Monologues*, a multimedia project focused on body image, relationships, identity, eating behavior, and the many intersections thereof. Following the example of audacious author-activists like Eve Ensler (author of *The Vagina Monologues*), Grace hopes to spark conversation and shift paradigms by honestly and unabashedly acknowledging the world as it is. Currently working on a book of short essays and poetry entitled *Insatiable*, she is ready and eager to sink her teeth into a cornucopia of meaty subjects revolving around desire, consumption, and nourishment.

Heidi Rothberg has been primary caregiver for her husband since his stroke in 2006, and briefly for her mother until her death in 2010. She works at Bard College at Simon's Rock and lives in the woods in Sheffield, Massachusetts, with one husband, one dog, two cats, and six chickens.

Nancy Salz is the author of many profiles and musical theater reviews for Berkshire County newspapers and online arts magazines. *Nanny: A Memoir of Love and Secrets* is her first narrative book. She lives in New York and Massachusetts.

Ruth Irupé Sanabria earned her MFA in Poetry from New York University. Her first full-length collection of poems, *The Strange*

House Testifies (Bilingual Press), won 2nd place for poetry in the 2010 Annual Latino Book Awards. Her second full-length collection of poems is the 2014 recipient of the Letras Latinas/Red Hen Press Awards and will be published in 2017. Her poems have appeared in anthologies such as *Women Writing Resistance, Poets Against the War*, and *U.S. Latino Literature Today*. She has read her poetry in libraries, prisons, schools, parks, bars, and universities across the USA, Mexico, and Peru. Born in Argentina, raised in Washington D.C., she now works as a high school English teacher and lives with her husband and three children in Perth Amboy, N.J.

Signe Eklund Schaefer is the author of *Why on Earth? - Biography and the Practice of Human Becoming* (SteinerBooks, 2013). She is also co-author of *Ariadne's Awakening* and co-editor of *More Lifeways*. She is the founding director of the Center for Biography and Social Art and a longtime adult educator. Human development has been a lifelong interest, now re-enlivened through her observations and experiences of growing older.

Lee Schwartz is a poet based in New York and the Berkshires. Her latest work appears in *Trans Bodies, Trans Selves* (Oxford University Press, 2014). Her collection *Poetry Saved My Life* is published by Trigger Point Press, and her poetry appears in the *Minerva Rising Journal*. Schwartz is a two-time winner of the Allen Ginsberg Paterson Literary Review Prize. She has served as an Artist in Residence at the 92nd St Y in New York City, and is an active participant in the Berkshire Festival of Women Writers.

Yvette "Jamuna" Sirker's award-winning plays include *When the Sky Falls*, from which her Writing Fire contribution is adapted. *When the Sky Falls* won first prize in the MultiStages Theater Company's New Works Contest and Epic Theater Center's Sunshine Series. Her play *Speakeasy* was awarded a Louisiana Division of the Arts Fellowship in Playwriting; *Troubled Waters* won the Gambit Weekly Big Easy Award, and *Pink Collar Crime*, featured on American Public Radio, was awarded an NEA development grant. A member of the Dramatists Guild of America, the Actors Equity Association and the

Screen Actors Guild, she is currently Writing and Media Specialist for Reid Middle School in Pittsfield and Adjunct Faculty of Communications at Berkshire Community College.

A.M. Sommers is about to publish her first novel, *Social Work*. A new transplant to the Berkshires, her New York City career included speech writing and public relations. Ms. Sommers is boning up on early American history in order to write a fictional journal of the neglected wife of one of our most famous and accomplished founding fathers.

JoAnne Spies is a singer songwriter who collaborates with her audience in rhythm and sound explorations. Recent works include *Karaoke Confession* and *Trust* at the Norman Rockwell Museum and *Survivor Tree*, sung at Ground Zero, New York City, with Jane Goodall officiating. Spies heads the Art Cart program at Community Access to the Arts, ATA, co-creating songs with elders and people with Alzheimer's. Her CD's include *2x3*, *Me & Melville*, and *North Avenue Honey*.

Rosemary Starace's poetry appears in *Orion, Blueline, Lake*, and other journals, and in her book, *Requitements* (Revised Edition, Elephant Tree House, 2015). She's co-editor, with Moira Richards and Lesley Wheeler, of the international poetry anthology, *Letters to the World* (Red Hen Press, 2008), and a longtime teacher/mentor for writers and artists. See more of her work on her website, www.rosemarystarace.com. "Kind Thoughts" originally appeared in *Letters to the World* (Red Hen Press 2008) and "I Found I Had Neglected Thirst" in the journal *Poemeleon*, Fall 2011.

Leigh Strimbeck is an actor, director, writer and acting teacher. She began teaching in New York City more than 30 years ago at the Actors and Directors Lab, and served as Ensemble Director at the Bloomsburg Theatre Ensemble in Bloomsburg, PA for 12 years. Currently, Leigh is artist-in-residence at Russell Sage College in Troy. She has directed at Actors Collaborative and Stageworks in Albany, and appeared onstage at WAM Theatre, Capital Repertory Theatre,

Theater Voices and Theatre Institute at Sage and in many films including *UnCivil Liberties*, *Fighting for Freedom*, and *Little Bi Peep*. She is the co-founder of WAM Theatre (Women's Action Movement Theatre and head communications coach for the New York State Defender's Institute Basic Trial Skills Program.

Camille Tewell is a museum educator, amateur photographer, former lab rat, occasional blogger and mother. She completed her M.A. and Ph.D. coursework in art history at the University of North Carolina at Chapel Hill, where she also earned a biology degree. She observes and integrates her life experiences at her blog, Little Chickens.

Lara Tupper is the author of *A Thousand and One Nights* (Harcourt and Untreed Reads), a novel about singers at sea, and *Off Island*, a fictional account of Paul Gauguin's messy marriage. Her work has appeared in *Six-Word Memoirs on Love and Heartbreak* (Harper Perennial), *The Believer*, *fivechapters* and other literary magazines. She taught writing at Rutgers University for nine years and now presents workshops throughout western Massachusetts. A jazz/pop singer, she remains a proud member of the BMIFC (Barry Manilow International Fan Club).

Carolyne Van Der Meer lives and writes in Montreal, Canada. Her first book, *Motherlode: A Mosaic of Dutch Wartime Experience*, was published by Wilfrid Laurier University Press in 2014. Following many appearances in poetry journals internationally, a collection of poetry entitled *Journeywoman* will be published by Inanna Publications in 2017.

Hester Velmans is a children's book author and award-winning translator of literary fiction. Born in Amsterdam, the Netherlands, she had a nomadic childhood, moving from Holland to Paris, Geneva, London and New York. After a rewarding but stressful career in the TV news business, she moved to the Berkshires and began to write and translate full time. Hester's first book for middle readers, *Isabel of the Whales*, was a surprise national bestseller. At the urging of her young fans she wrote a follow-up, *Jessaloup's Song*.

She is a winner of the Vondel Prize for Translation and a 2014 NEA Translation Fellow.

Hilde Weisert lives part-time in Sandisfield, MA and part-time in Chapel Hill, NC. Her poems have appeared in *Prairie Schooner, Cincinnati Review, Cortland Review, Ms.*, and other magazines. "The Pity of It" won second prize in the Berkshire Festival of Women Writers 2014 Contest and "Finding Wilfred Owen Again" won the 2008 Lois Cranston Poetry Prize. She held a New Jersey State Council on the Arts fellowship, was a 2009 Virginia Center for the Creative Arts fellow, and is a longtime Geraldine Dodge Poet. She is co-editor of the anthology, *Animal Companions, Animal Doctors, Animal People* published in 2012 by Ontario Veterinary College. In 2015, her poetry collection, *The Scheme of Things*, will be published by David Robert Press.

Susan Wozniak was born in Detroit to a blue-collar family but always knew she wanted to write. Thanks to a college scholarship and endurance, she became a journalist and now teaches writing. She is working on a one-woman theatre piece and hopes there will be a novel in her future.

Kuukua Dzigbordi Yomekpe, a native of Ghana, characterizes herself as a transdisciplinary artist. She choreographs West African dance forms; cooks a fusion of Ghanaian dishes; and pens memoirs, essays, and social commentaries. Her scholarly and writing interests lie at the intersection of race and skin color, African culture, Black women's bodies, expression of voice, and nonconformance and performativity. All her work is influenced by her education and socialization in womanist, feminist, and Africanist theories. She is the author of several essays and prose poems. Some of her essays have been anthologized in: *African Women Writing Resistance* (University of Wisconsin Press), *Becoming Bi: Bisexual Voices from Around the World* (BRC), and *Inside Your Ear* (Oakland Public Library Press). Her essay "The Audacity to Remain Single: Single Black Women in the Black Church" is anthologized in *Queer Religion II* (Praeger Publishers).

Robin W. Zeamer was born and raised in New York City, where she attended the Rudolf Steiner School. She came from a family of writers, but it wasn't until she moved to the Berkshires in 2009 that she slowly began to discover her writer's voice. Since then she has been writing memoir, fiction and poetry. Professionally, Robin has a background first in Special Education and later in such diverse areas as marketing, publicity, bookkeeping, fund raising, events management, communications and graphic design. She is currently serving as Program Coordinator for the Berkshire Women Writer's Festival.

Sondra Zeidenstein is the author of three books of poetry: *A Detail in that Story*, *Resistance*, and *Contraries*. She is editor of *A Wider Giving: Women Writing after a Long Silence*; *Family Reunion: Poems about Parenting Grown Children*; and *Speaking for my Self: Twelve Women Poets in their Seventies and Eighties*. She is publisher of Chicory Blue Press.

Acknowledgments

The Editors would like to thank Anna Myers Sabatini, Emma Flowers and Sean Vernon for their tireless and cheerful contribution to making our vision for this anthology a reality.

Jennifer Browdy: I would like to thank my sister editors Jana and Sahra, who made this project such a collaborative pleasure. Thanks to all the contributors of the Anthology, and to the wider circle of Berkshire Festival of Women Writers presenters, friends and supporters: we are doing important work of holding a warm, encouraging space for women's voices to kindle, mingle and strengthen. Together we can and will change the world! On a personal note, I thank my parents, Joe and Sue Browdy, bright, creative and loving spirits who have given me such a strong foundation from which to spread my wings. I thank my sons, Nico and Eric, for their patience and kindness towards a very busy mom. And thanks to the many students who have accompanied me on the journey of listening and learning from women writers from all over the world, exploring how together we can carry their voices and visions forward into a better future for us all.

Jana Laiz: I would like to thank Jennifer Browdy for creating a festival that supports a woman's right to write! By encouraging women to express themselves and write from their hearts, Jennifer has opened up a new world of writers, many featured here in this anthology. I want to thank Sahra Bateson Brubeck for her sparkle, making the work of editing a joy. I feel so incredibly honored to be editing partners with Jennifer and Sahra. And thanks to my parents, Joy & Paul Bergins and my children, Sam & Zoë for their continuous support and encouragement of my writing and all my literary endeavors.

Sahra Bateson Brubeck: I would like to thank Jennifer Browdy for providing me with the opportunity to work on this incredible project. Her enthusiastic approach and dedication to the Berkshire Festival of Women Writers is inspirational on many levels. I would also like to thank my co-editor, Jana Laiz, for the creative energy and positivity that she poured into *Writing Fire*. It has been such an honor to bond with these two women over the powerful stories and experiences that are shared in the anthology. Many thanks as well to my partner Cary, who has always supported my love of writing.

Green Fire Press

About Green Fire Press

Green Fire Press is an independent publishing company dedicated to supporting authors in producing and distributing high-quality books, fiction or non-fiction, poetry or prose. When you publish with Green Fire Press, you join a collaborative community of writers, editors and publishing professionals dedicated to helping you communicate your vision as powerfully as possible.

Green Fire Press offers writing classes, retreats and writing journeys through **Green Fire Writers' Workshops,** based in the beautiful Berkshire hills of Massachusetts. We also publish an online magazine, *Fired Up! Creative Expression for Challenging Times*, for which contributions are always welcome.

Find out more at **Greenfirewriters.com**.

Writing Fire...
Perfect for Your Book Club!

Writing Fire is the perfect collection to share with your women's Book Club. These honest, moving stories will elicit thoughtful conversations about every stage of a woman's life journey; from girlhood, relationships, marriage, divorce, illness and grieving, work, play and love.

You'll find so many creative sparks within these pages—we hope you'll be moved to grab your own pens and consider creating your own anthology!

The seeds for many of these stories were planted in events and workshops offered by the **Berkshire Festival of Women Writers** and **Green Fire Writers' Workshops**.

We warmly welcome you to contact us at **Greenfirewriters.com** for information on author visits, writing workshops or publishing opportunities.

9 780986 198076